macmillan education

2

InstaEnglish

Emma Heyderman Fiona Mauchline
Patrick Howarth Patricia Reilly Olivia Johnston

#InstaEnglish Walkthrough

STUDENT'S BOOK

Your book is made up of a Starter unit, 8 regular units, plus Review and Life Skills activities. Each unit is divided into the sections introduced here. Check out how your book is structured so you can make the most of it!

Starter

This two-page unit provides strategic language for you to kick off your studies!

Opening

All units open with a visual treat that will trigger your first thoughts on the main subject. What pops into your head as soon as you look at it?

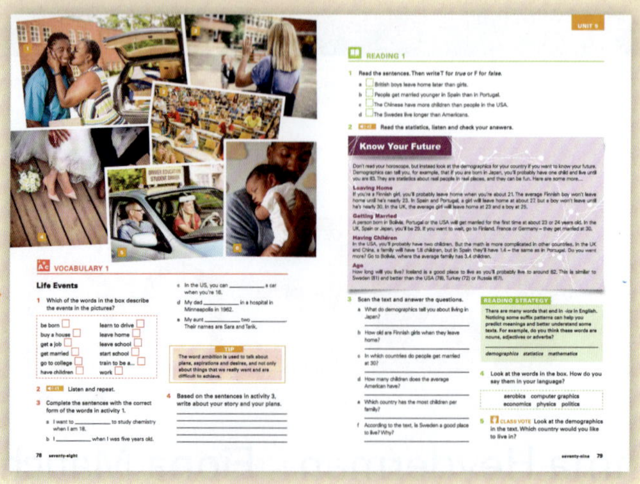

Vocabulary 1

Here you will read, listen to and look at pictures of words or phrases to begin exploring the unit topic. **Tip** boxes give you some advice to help make your learning easier.

Reading 1

Different text genres provide interesting content to practice your reading skills and introduce relevant language to be explored throughout the unit. The **Reading Strategy** box gives you tips on how to improve your reading.

Grammar 1

Grammar topics that were introduced in the reading text are systematically explored so you can easily work out all the rules and patterns.
Pronunciation boxes help you master the tongue to speak more naturally.

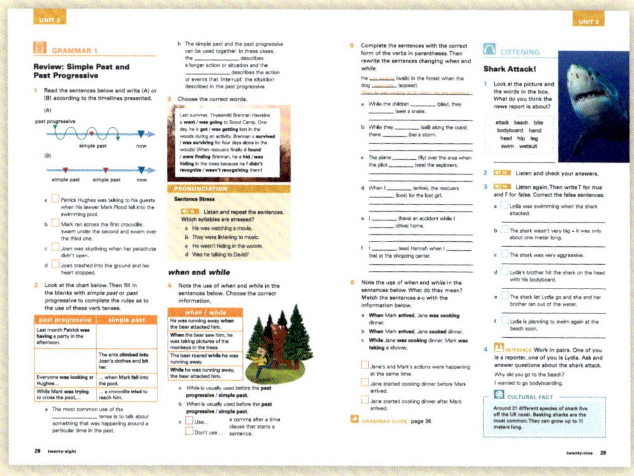

Listening

Learn and practice oral comprehension through engaging and contextualized oral texts. **Cultural Fact** boxes add little bits of cultural info to expand the topic.

Speaking

A clearly guided activity will help you practice your speaking skills using functional language in everyday situations.

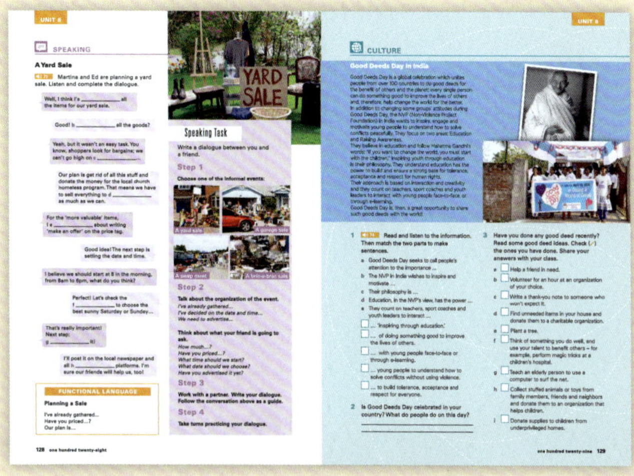

Culture

Discover cultural aspects of everyday life in countries around the world!

Vocabulary 2

The second vocabulary set provides more words and phrases to allow you to go further into the unit topic.

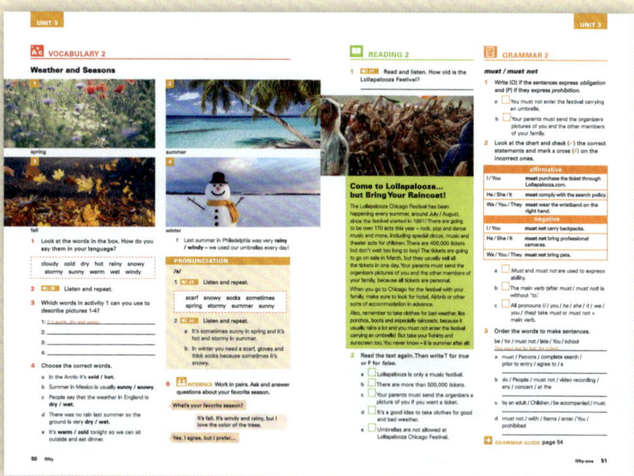

Grammar 2

This section introduces a new grammar topic in the same contextualized and systematized way that Grammar 1 does.

Reading 2

The second reading text digs further into the main topic and provides more language to be explored.

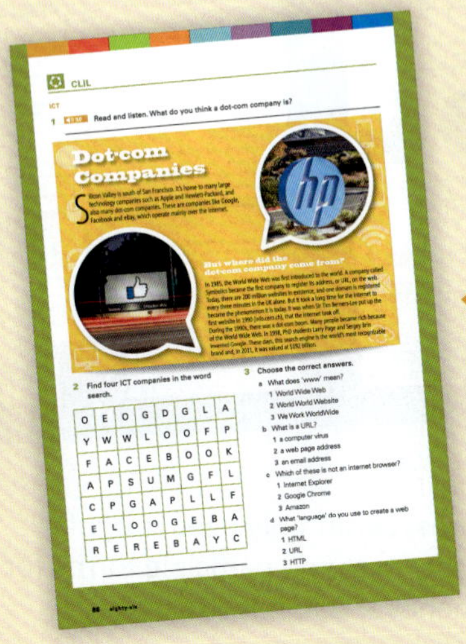

CLIL

Integrate your learning of the English language with other school subjects through fun texts and activities in every odd-numbered unit.

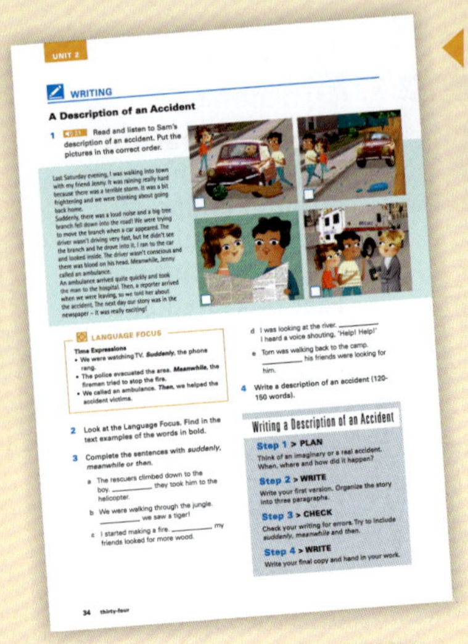

Writing

This section provides a model for the different text types you will get to practice in even-numbered units. The **Language Focus** box highlights useful language for written communication.

Vocabulary in Pictures

Have fun reviewing all the words and phrases learned in the **Vocabulary** sections, all richly illustrated!

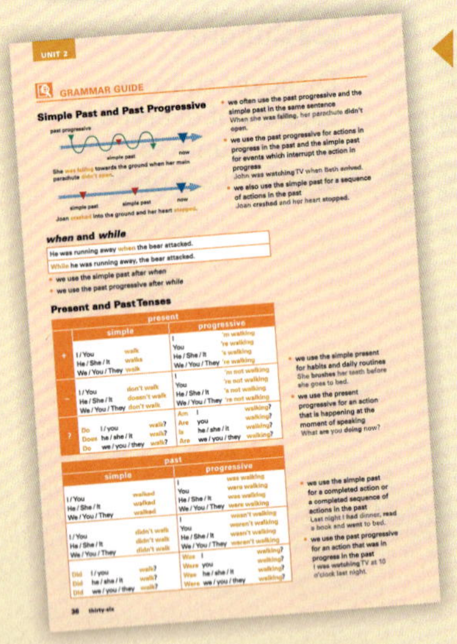

Grammar Guide

This is a reference section for all the grammar topics explored in the unit.

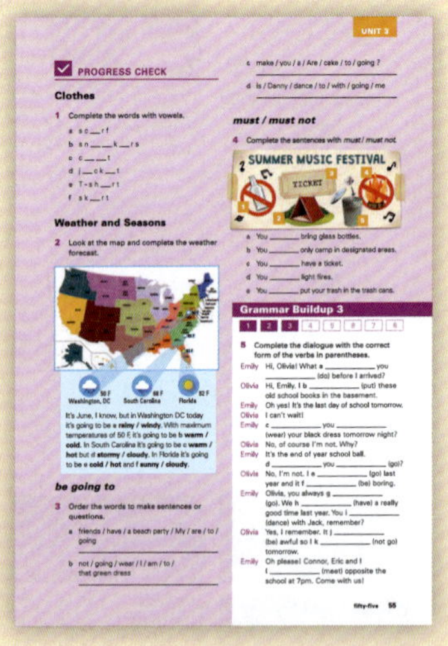

Progress Check

These activities help you revise core language and check your overall progress.

Reviews

Review the vocabulary and grammar from the previous two units starting with a game!

Life Skills

Learn skills to boost your talents, be a world citizen and deal effectively with the challenges of everyday life.

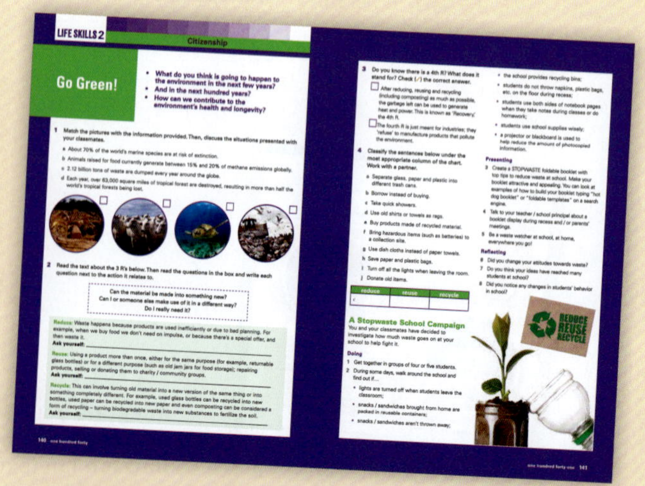

Irregular Verbs

A list with the most commonly used irregular verbs in their base, past and participle forms for you to check whenever you need them!

WORKBOOK

The workbook offers target-language practice and additional study material (consolidation and extension). It can be used as homework, independent study or extra classroom practice. Some of the sections correspond to sections in the Student's book:

Vocabulary 1

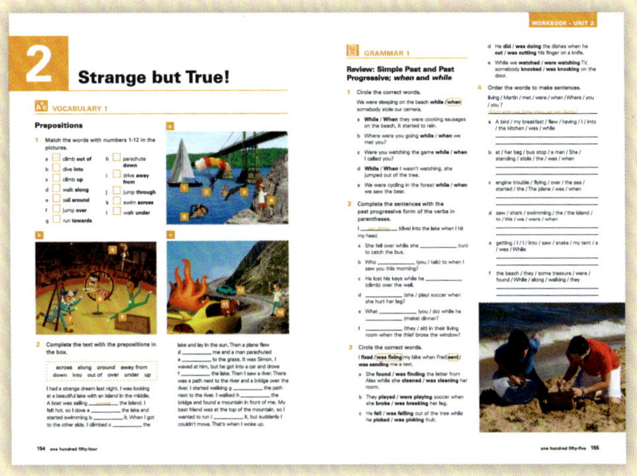

Grammar 1

Vocabulary 2

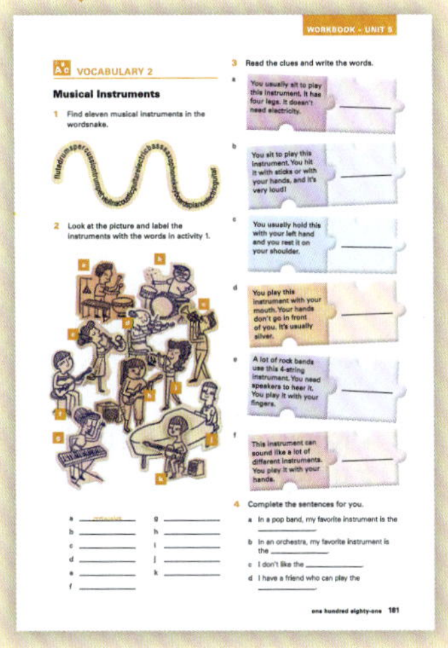

Grammar 2

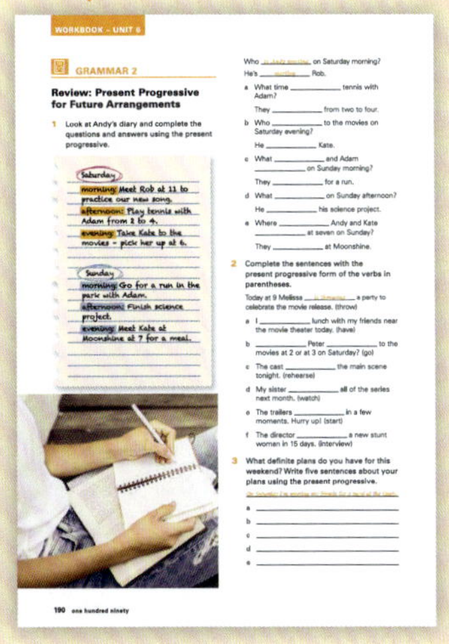

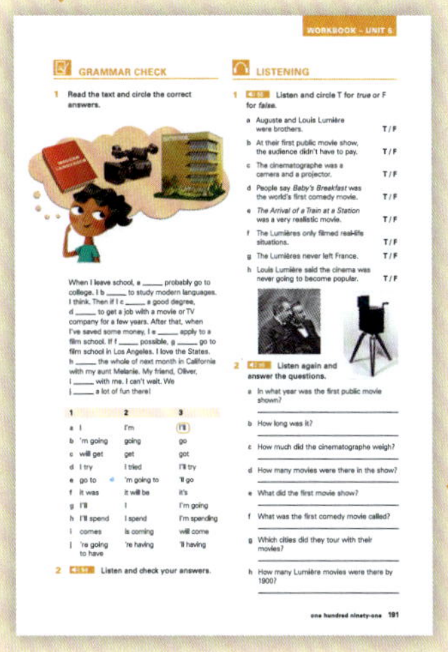

Grammar Check
A text with interesting, curious facts helps you check your reading and language skills.

Listening

Extension
This engaging section offers an extra challenge on grammar and vocabulary items.

Vocabulary Plus
Learn more words related to the unit topic in a fun way! All words are illustrated.

Wordlist

An alphabetical list of the key vocabulary in the **Student's Book** and from the **Vocabulary Plus** sections. It includes phonetic transcriptions and audio recordings.

DIGITAL STUDENT'S BOOK

This is the digital version of your **Student's Book** and **Workbook**, and you can easily access them everywhere! You will be able to read all the texts while having easy access to embedded audio tracks. Beside that, we also offer extra activities that can be monitored by your teacher so you can get the most out of your course!

CONTENTS

Starter

Free-time Activities

1 🔊 2 Listen to Megan, Dan and Rita talking about their hobbies and underline their favorite free-time activities.

- **a** Hi, I'm Megan. My hobbies are playing **the guitar** / **video games** and making models. This is my friend Dan.
- **b** Hello. I'm Dan. I like doing **volunteer work** / **karate** and going to the **gym** / **movies**.
- **c** Hi. I'm Rita. I love going **to the gym** / **out for a meal**. Luckily, I like going **to the gym** / **out for a meal**, too!
- **d** We all love **hanging out** / **relaxing** / **going to a youth group**. We always have a great time together.

Character Adjectives and Formation of Adverbs

2 Match adjectives a-h with their opposites.

a cautious	unsociable
b talkative	funny
c friendly	adventurous
d generous	lazy
e energetic	dishonest
f serious	confident
g shy	quiet
h honest	selfish

3 Complete the sentences with the adverb form of the adjectives in bold.

- **a** **Quiet**, please. Enter the library ___________.
- **b** Jennifer is a very **good** singer. She can sing really ___________.
- **c** Be **careful** with the dishes. Carry them ___________.
- **d** '**Fast** finishers' are students who finish their tasks ___________.

Rooms, Furniture and Gadgets

4 Cross the odd one out. Then add one more word to each group.

- **a** sofa, table, desk, camera, ___________.
- **b** dishwasher, fridge, lamp, stove, ___________.
- **c** toilet, electric toothbrush, microwave, mirror, ___________.
- **d** armchair, sofa, chair, wardrobe, ___________.
- **e** telephone, washing machine, laptop, TV, ___________.
- **f** cabinet, bathroom, bedroom, kitchen, ___________.
- **g** mouse, printer, speakers, bookcase, ___________.

Places to Visit

5 Find in the word spiral the name of twenty places to visit.

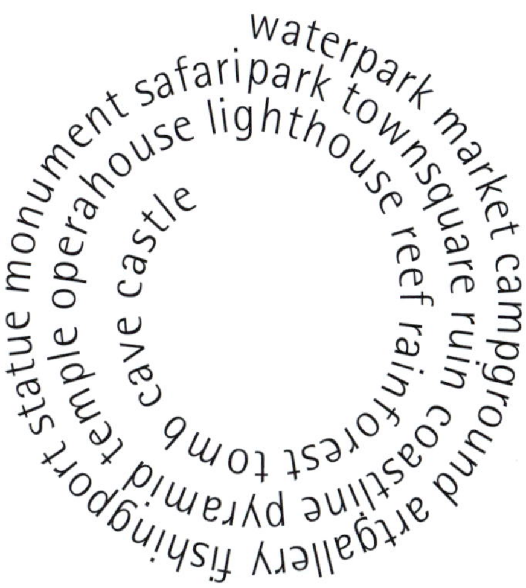

6 🔊 3 Listen, repeat and check your answers.

Comparatives and Superlatives

7 Choose the correct words.

- **a** Bikes are **better** / **the best** for the environment than cars.
- **b** What was **more interesting** / **the most interesting** book you read last year?
- **c** My brothers and sisters are **older** / **the oldest** than me.
- **d** That is **taller** / **the tallest** building in my town.

Simple Present and Present Progressive

8 Match questions a-d with the correct answers.

a	Do you have any questions?	No, he doesn't.
b	Are you having any difficulty with the task?	Yes, he is.
c	Does he usually write answers in pencil?	No, we're not.
d	Is he writing the answers in pen?	Yes, we do.

9 🔊 4 Listen and check your answers.

Simple Past and Past Progressive

10 Write questions.

- **a** have / Did / you / any / night / dreams / last ?
  ____
  ____
- **b** class / before / What / you / doing / this / were ?
  ____
  ____
- **c** yesterday / raining / Was / it?
  ____
  ____
- **d** last week / any / you / visit / Did / relatives ?
  ____
  ____

11 **INTERFACE** Work in pairs. Ask and answer the questions in activity 10.

Was it raining yesterday?

No, it wasn't.

1

Technology

VOCABULARY 1

IT Activities

1 Look at the picture. Can you name the equipment?

1 *games console*
2 ______
3 ______
4 ______
5 ______
6 ______
7 ______
8 ______
9 ______
10 ______

2 5 Check your answers and repeat.

3 What equipment do you use to do each of these things?

[*6, 7*] take a digital picture
a [ ] play a video game
b [ ] make a phone call
c [ ] scan a picture
d [ ] send an email
e [ ] store data
f [ ] go online
g [ ] print a document
h [ ] charge a cell phone/e-reader
i [ ] post a comment
j [ ] download / upload a song
k [ ] read an e-book
l [ ] plug in a memory stick

READING 1

1 Look at the text below. What genre does it illustrate?

a a blog post **b** a newspaper feature

A High-tech Bedroom

We took a peek inside a typical teenager's bedroom and what did we find? Well, we didn't find many books, but there were a lot of electronic gadgets. Student Ashley Judd, 13, tells us about the electronic stuff in her room.

SMART TV

'When I passed my exams my parents gave me a 21-inch smart TV for my bedroom. It's right in front of my bed so I can watch my favorite movies while I'm in bed.'

COMPUTERS

'I got my first desktop computer for my 10th birthday. It's quite old now, but I use it for school work. I also have a laptop where I store all my school work. I use a flash drive to save everything I need to take to school. And I have a portable hard drive which I use to transfer heavier files from one computer to another, as well as to save all my pictures.'

PRINTER

'My parents bought a new printer and they gave me their old one. The printing quality is garbage and the paper often gets stuck. But it has a scanner so I can scan my friend's school notes because they are much better than mine!'

GAMES

'I played a lot of video games on a console when I was younger and I keep them and my old PlayStation on my bookshelf. I don't buy many now, but sometimes I download games to play on the computer if the graphics aren't too heavy.'

PHONE

'I didn't have a cell phone until I was 12. It was a birthday present. Now I have a new one. I bought it with the money I earned from a summer job. I don't usually connect to the internet when I'm out because it's too expensive, but I use it for making calls, listening to offline music, playing games and taking pictures.'

GUITAR AND AMP

'I saved US$300 and bought a second-hand electric guitar and an amplifier last year. Some friends and I formed a band. We wrote some songs and uploaded them on the internet. We're planning to perform live at school next month.'

DIGITAL CAMERA

'I lost my digital camera last month. It had about 600 pictures on it. But a friend gave me his old one which I use whenever I want to take better pictures.'

2 Read the introduction. What is the text about?

a a favorite electronic gadget
b the electronic equipment in a bedroom
c the best electronic equipment

3 🔊 6 Read and listen. How many pieces of electronic equipment does Ashley have in her room?

____

4 Write T for *true* or F for *false*. Then correct the false sentences.

a ☐ Ashley never watches TV in bed.
____

b ☐ Ashley's laptop is newer than her desktop.
____

c ☐ Ashley doesn't play games now.
____

d ☐ She doesn't use the camera on her phone.
____

e ☐ She plays the drums in a band.
____

f ☐ She uses her friend's digital camera.
____

5 Find the words in the text and match them with their definitions.

a peek	☐ obstructed
b stuff	☐ computer pictures
c garbage	☐ things
d stuck	☐ bad quality
e graphics	☐ have a quick look

GRAMMAR 1

Review: Simple Past

1 Read the sentences below. Circle the irregular verbs and underline the regular verbs.

a When I passed my exams, my parents gave me a 21-inch smart TV.

b I played a lot of video games when I was younger. They were addictive!

c I didn't have a cell phone until I was twelve.

d Did your parents give you anything special on your birthday? Was it nice?

2 Look at the charts below. Then complete the sentences that follow it.

	was* / *were **(Simple Past of *be*)**
+	I / He / She / It **was** great! We / You / They **were** twelve.
–	I / He / She / It **wasn't** popular. We / You / They **weren't** young.
?	**Was** I / he / she / it nice? **Were** we / you / they young?

	Simple Past	
	regular verbs	**irregular verbs**
+	I **passed** my exams.	They **gave** me a smart TV.
–	He **didn't play** computer games.	She **didn't have** a cell phone.
?	**Did** you **save** any money?	**Did** you **get** anything special on your birthday?

a The past forms of the verb *be* are ________ for I / he / she / it and ________ for we / you / they.

b *Was* / *wasn't* and *were* / *weren't* are used in affirmative, ________ and ________ sentences.

c *-ed* or *-d* are usually added to the base form of regular verbs in the ________ form.

d In questions and negative sentences, the auxiliary ________ is used to form the simple past tense.

3 Complete these questions with the simple past tense of the verbs in parentheses.

a What ________ (be) early cell phones like?

b What ________ Martin Cooper ________ (invent)?

c ________ the portable phone ________ (need) to be powered through a car?

d How long ________ it ________ (take) for it to be available to the public?

e What ________ Motorola ________ (do)?

f When ________ Apple ________ its first iPhone? (release)

4 Match the answers below with the questions in activity 3 and find out about the history of cell phones.

☐ He invented a portable hand-held phone.

☐ No, it didn't.

☐ It took ten years.

☐ In 2007.

☐ They were 'car phones' – two-way radios used by taxi drivers and emergency services.

☐ Motorola introduced the first public cell phone.

5 Complete the text with the simple past form of the verbs in parentheses.

The Worldwide Web

Thirty years ago, there a ________ (not be) a World Wide Web and there b ________ (not be) any social networking sites. By 1994, there c ________ (be) about a hundred important websites – today there are millions! The web d ________ (develop) when search engines such as Google e ________ (become) available and more people f ________ (get) high-speed broadband in their homes. Today, it is hard to imagine life without the web.

CULTURAL FACT

Top 3 countries with highest number of internet users:
1st - China (772,000,000)
2nd - India (462,124,989)
3rd - United States (312,322,257)

6 Ashley made a list of things to do yesterday. Look at the list and write sentences about what she did / didn't do.

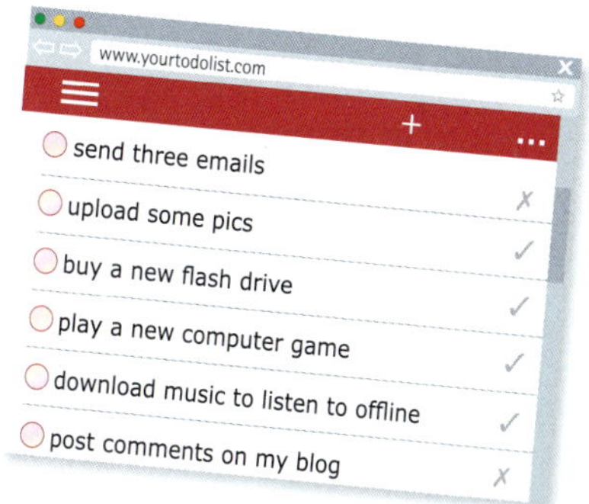

She didn't send three emails. ______________________ ______________________

______________________ ______________________

______________________ ______________________

7 Read the spelling rules for the simple past of regular verbs. Complete the chart with the simple past of the verbs in the box.

download introduce play plug print scan store try

For most verbs, add *-ed*	______________________
For verbs that end in *e*, add *-d*:	______________________
For verbs that end in a consonant + *y*, preceded by a consonant, omit the *y* and add *-ied*:	______________________
For verbs that end in a vowel + *y*, just add *-ed*:	______________________
For verbs that end in a stressed vowel + a consonant (except *w*, *x* or *y*), double the final consonant and add *-ed*:	______________________

8 INTERFACE Work in pairs. Ask and answer questions about last weekend. Use the ideas in the box or your own ideas.

download a song go online print a document send an email surf the web take a digital picture upload a series use Instagram

Did you download a song last Saturday?

GRAMMAR GUIDE page 22

LISTENING

A Social Network

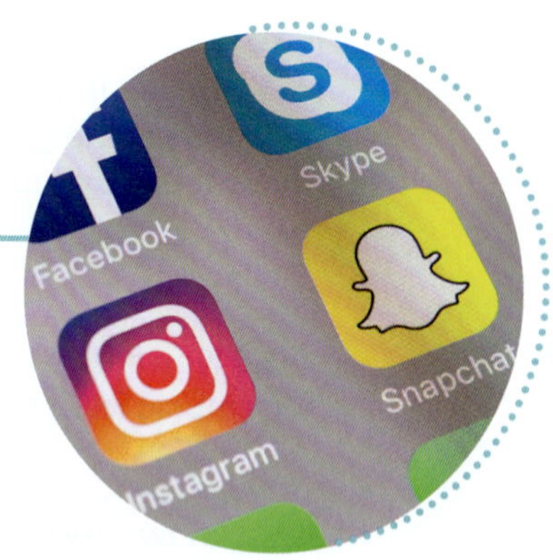

1 Read the sentences in activity 2 and check the meaning of any unknown words. Can you guess any of the answers?

2 🔊 7 Listen to an interview about social networking sites and choose the correct answers.

a ... computer science students started Facebook.
 1 Two 2 Three 3 Four

b Facebook became available to anyone over 13 years old in...
 1 2004. 2 2005. 3 2006.

c Facebook is not permitted in...
 1 schools.
 2 some countries.
 3 all offices.

d Facebook is ... MySpace.
 1 more popular than
 2 not as popular as
 3 as popular as

e The new verb 'unfriend' means...
 1 to argue with a friend online.
 2 to delete a friend from your friend list.
 3 to find friends using your friends' list of friends.

SPEAKING

Online Tech

8 Rob and his dad Doug are surfing the net for Rob's birthday present. Listen and complete the dialogue.

Gee! Look at these **a** __________, dad! They look cool, don't they?

They really do.

Look, dad, wireless, great noise-cancelling tech and top-notch battery life!

I see, but they are expensive!!! So different from the ones sold when I was your age, in the 1980s.

What **b** __________ they like, dad?

Well, the 80s **c** __________ the Walkman era, so we **d** __________ small, portable and usually cheap headphones.

Walkman??? What was that?

It **e** __________ a small cassette player that **f** __________ in your pocket, but it was cool because people **g** __________ their own music tapes by mixing together songs that they **h** __________ off different albums.

So old! Nowadays we can download all our music from the internet!

Yeah, I know... well, let's get back to this new era, then. Which headphones do you want?

FUNCTIONAL LANGUAGE

Talking about Tech Gadgets

Look at this / these... They're cool!

What was it / were they like...?

Nowadays it is / they are...

Speaking Task

Write a dialogue between you and a family member (mom / dad / grandma / granddad).

Step 1

Decide which tech gadget you are going to talk about. Choose from the ones below or use your own ideas.

camera

cell phone

smartwatch

Step 2

Think about specific characteristics of the new gadget compared to a similar one from the past. If necessary, Google search some information about the old gadget.

Step 3

Work with your partner. Write your dialogue. Follow the conversation above as a guide.

Step 4

Take turns practicing your dialogue.

CULTURE

Singapore: Planning to Be the Next Tech Hub

Singapore, a city-state, is a multi-racial and multi-cultural island country with ethnic Indians, Chinese and Malays who are working hard to become Asia's next economic model. Under the leadership of its founder and 'Minister Mentor' Lee Kuan Yew, 45 year-old Singapore continues to be an icon of economic growth and political stability.

Singapore is identifying key sectors where it can join technology with the great market opportunities of Asia: biomedicine, clean-tech and digital media.

As to biomedicine, what Singapore has in mind is to focus on nano-medicine to try to detect cancer at its early stages, to offer computerized medical devices to help the recovery of stroke patients and provide the sustainable manufacturing of synthesized drugs. Singaporeans have an outstanding health service and the result is the lowest infant-mortality rate in the world and high life expectancy: 80 years of age for males and 85 for females.

Clean technology is also a target: water desalination, electric vehicles and hybrid buses are part of the project.

Artificial intelligence is also receiving investment.

Singapore is totally connected, globally aware and ready for more. Singaporeans are not afraid of taking strategic risks to reinvent their economy. The growth rate in this tiny city reached 18% – the highest in the world – making Singapore's dream come true.

1 9 **Read and listen. Then correct the sentences below.**

a Singapore used to be Asia's economic model, but it is not anymore.

____

____

b Singapore identified two strategic sectors where it can join technology with market opportunities in Asia.

____

____

c In biomedicine, Singaporeans just want to focus on nano-medicine to try to detect cancer at its early stages.

____

____

____

____

____

d Singaporeans have the highest infant-mortality rate in the world.

____

____

e Water desalination, electric vehicles and hybrid buses are part of the artificial intelligence project.

____

____

f Singaporeans don't like to take risks to reinvent their economy.

____

____

2 **Can you list positive and negative impacts of technology on society?**

____

____

3 **Has technology influenced any sector in your country? Which sector(s)? How?**

____

____

VOCABULARY 2

Jobs

1 10 Match pictures 1-6 with some of the jobs in the box. Then listen and repeat.

artist ☐ construction worker ☐
doctor ☐ fireman ☐ inspector ☐
journalist ☐ lawyer ☐
policewoman ☐ politician ☐
mailman ☐ researcher ☐
scientist ☐ technician ☐

1 

2 

3 

4 

5 

6 

2 Complete the sentences with jobs in activity 1.

a A __________ is someone who treats people who are ill.

b A __________ uses special equipment or machines.

c A __________ collects and delivers letters and packages.

d Picasso was an __________. He painted many pictures.

e A __________ collects information and does studies.

f A __________ has a job in politics.

3 Put the jobs in activity 1 into five groups. Add one or two more jobs to each group.

-man	-er
fireman	*lawyer*
______	______
______	______

-ist	-ian
journalist	*politician*
______	______
______	______

-or
doctor
______
______

READING 2

11 Read and listen to the article below. Answer the questions.

a What part of Martin's body did doctors implant in his eye? __________

b Do scientists think they can use the technology with other blind people? __________

A Miracle – Thanks to Technology

When most people think about new technology they think about a VR glass or a new cell phone – not Martin Jones. Martin was working as a construction worker when he had a terrible accident. Martin became blind because of the accident and for 12 years he couldn't see at all. Then doctors told him about a revolutionary new technology with a special optical lens that helps people see again. At first, scientists couldn't use the technology – they thought the patient's immune system might reject the plastic lens.

Then researchers discovered they could use the lens by implanting it in a different part of the body – in a tooth! Martin decided to try. Doctors took out one of his teeth, put the optical lens in it and implanted it into part of his eye.

Martin was blind when he met his wife, Gill. When he opened his eyes after the operation she was standing by his bed – she was the first person he saw. 'She's wonderful. It was unbelievable to see her for the first time,' said Martin. Now, he laughs about his 'science-fiction eye' and he's happy he isn't blind.

Scientists say the new technology can help more people in the future. They are already planning more operations.

GRAMMAR 2

Review: Past Progressive

1 Read the sentences. Underline the verbs in the past progressive and write (A) if the sentence is affirmative, (N) if it is negative or (Q) if it is a question.

a ☐ Martin was working as a construction worker.

b ☐ Martin's wife wasn't sitting by his side.

c ☐ Was Martin feeling good after the surgery?

d ☐ The doctors were developing a new technology.

e ☐ Were you reading anything about it?

2 Look at the chart. Then choose the best answer for the questions below.

affirmative	negative	interrogative
I / He / She / It **was working**.	He **wasn't working** when he fell off.	**Was** Martin **sleeping** when his wife arrived at the hospital?
We / You / They **were reading** about that new experiment.	They **weren't learning** about new technology.	**Were** you **surfing** the net when the lights went off?

a The past progressive is used:

☐ to talk about an action in progress.

☐ to talk about a completed action in the past.

b The past progressive is formed:

☐ with the main verb + *-d* (or *-ed*)

☐ with *was* for I / he / she / it and *were* for we / you / they + main verb *-ing* form

c The negative sentence is formed:

☐ by adding *not* to *was* or *were* (*was not – wasn't* / *were not – weren't*)

☐ by adding *didn't* before the main verb

d The question is formed:

☐ by adding *did* before the subject

☐ by placing *was* or *were* before the subject

3 What was happening when Beth got home? Complete the sentences with the past progressive form of the verbs in parentheses.

When Beth got home...

a her brother Mike ____________ (not write) an email, he ____________ (watch) TV.

b her parents ____________ (look) at a vacation website, they ____________ (not prepare) the meal.

c her sister Lisa ____________ (not listen) to music on Spotify, she ____________ (chat) online.

d her friend Jed ____________ (wait) for her, he ____________ (not use) the computer.

e the cats Sammy and Fifi ____________ (sleep), they ____________ (not eating).

4 Complete the text with the past progressive or simple past form of the verbs in parentheses.

Internet Helps Fight Crime!

Two weeks ago a robber took Dave Reed's laptop when he *was sleeping* (sleep). Dave's a writer and he **a** ____________ (write) a book at the time – it was all on the computer. Two days later, when Dave **b** ____________ (try) to find another computer on the internet he saw a laptop similar to his old one. Dave went to the seller's house to buy it. When he **c** ____________ (look) at the laptop, he realized it was his old one! When the man **d** ____________ (not look), Dave sent a message to the police. When the police arrived, Dave **e** ____________ (talk) to the man, but he **f** ____________ (not buy) the computer. The police found more of Dave's things when they **g** ____________ (search) the house. Dave got everything back – thanks to the internet!

5 INTERFACE Work in pairs. Ask and answer the question.

What were you doing at 8pm last night?

I was watching a Netflix movie.

GRAMMAR GUIDE page 22

CLIL

SCIENCE

Microwaves

Waves are vibrations that transfer energy from one place to another. Imagine a crowd doing the wave in a sports stadium. The people sit down, until it is their turn to stand up with their arms in the air, and then sit down again.
Like other electromagnetic waves, microwaves travel at the speed of light. Microwave ovens have a magnetron which produces these microwaves at a specific frequency.
The microwaves travel through the food in the oven, and the water molecules in the food start to vibrate. This vibration or movement of the molecules creates heat, which then heats the other molecules in the food.

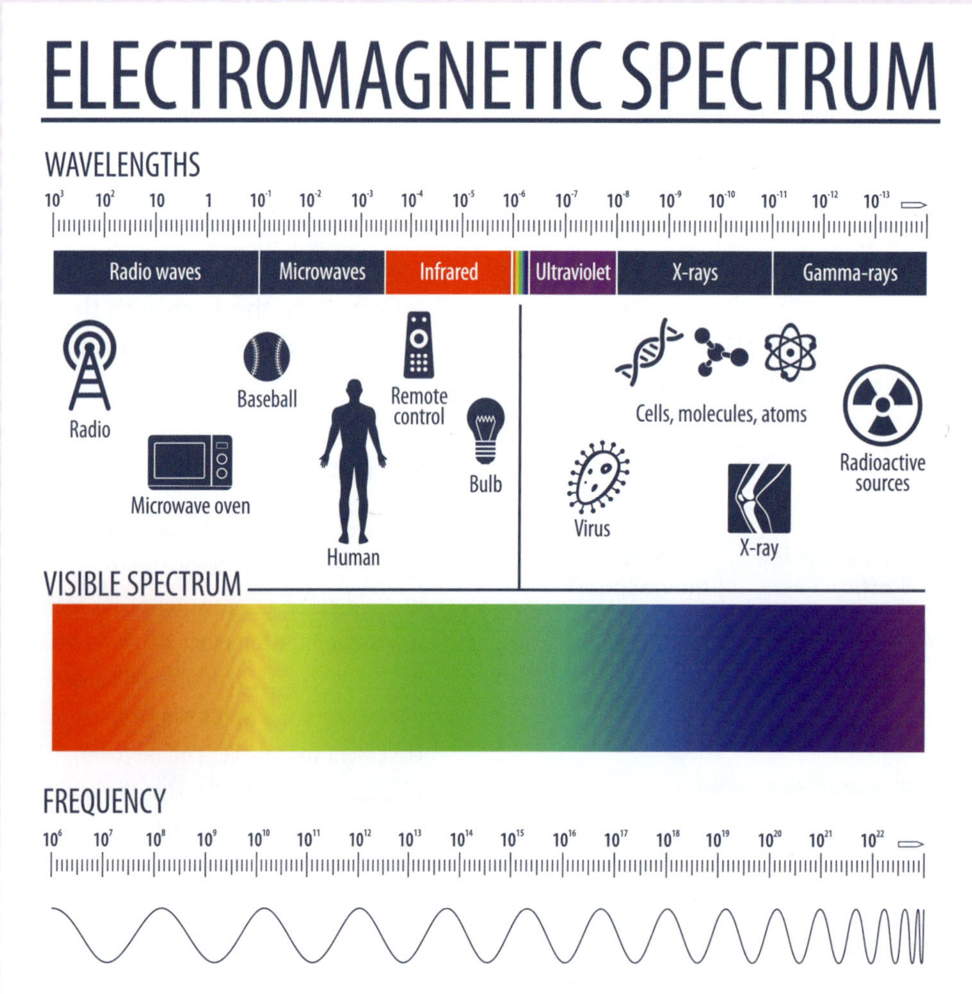

1 🔊 12 **Read and listen. Answer the question.**

Is it possible to cook dry food like rice or pasta in a microwave oven?

____

____

2 **Match the instructions to the labels on the diagram.**

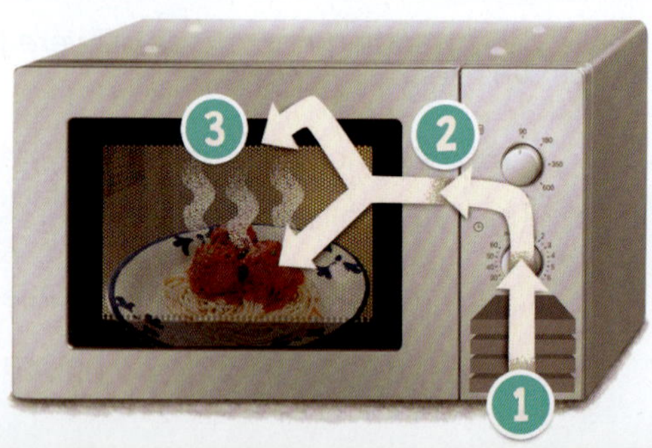

a ☐ Microwaves make the water molecules vibrate.
b ☐ Microwaves travel through the wave guide to the food.
c ☐ A magnetron generates microwaves.

VOCABULARY IN PICTURES

IT Activities

Jobs

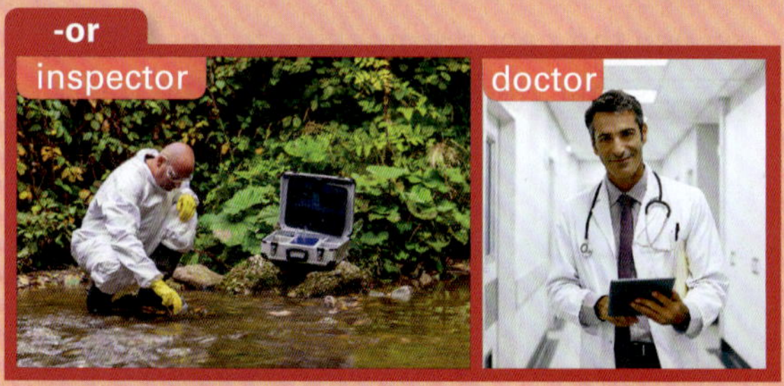

GRAMMAR GUIDE

was / were

+	I	was	famous.
	You	were	
	He / She / It	was	
	We / You / They	were	

–	I	wasn't	famous.
	You	weren't	
	He / She / It	wasn't	
	We / You / They	weren't	

?	Was he / she / it famous? Yes, he was. No, he wasn't.
	Were we / you / they famous? Yes, we were. No, we weren't.

Spelling: Simple Past Regular Verbs

- for most verbs add *-ed*
  invent → invent*ed*
- for verbs that end in *e*, add *-d*
  arrive → arrive*d*
- for verbs that end in a consonant + *y*, omit the *y* and add *-ied*
  study → stud*ied*
- for verbs that end in stressed vowel + consonant, double the consonant
  scan → scan*ned* **refer → refer*red***

Spelling: Simple Past Irregular Verbs

- for the irregular verbs list, see page 142.

Simple Past

+	I / You / He / She / It We / You / They	scanned a photo.
–	I / You / He / She / It We / You / They	didn't scan a photo.

?	Did I / you / he / she / it scan a photo? Yes, I did. / No, I didn't.
	Did we / you / they scan a photo? Yes, we did. / No, we didn't.

- we use the simple past to talk about events in a definite time in the past

Past Progressive

+	I	was working.
	You	were working.
	He / She / It	was working.
	We / You / They	were working.

–	I	wasn't working.
	You	weren't working.
	He / She / It	wasn't working.
	We / You / They	weren't working.

?	Was he / she / it working? Yes, he was. No, he wasn't.
	Were we / you / they working? Yes, we were. No, we weren't.

- we use the past progressive to describe actions that were in progress in the past

PROGRESS CHECK

IT Activities

1 Complete the phrases with vowels.

- **a** PL __ Y __ V __ D __ __ G __ M __
- **b** P __ ST __ C __ M M __ NT
- **c** C H __ R G __ __ C __ L L P H __ N __
- **d** G __ __ N L __ N __

Jobs

2 Complete the sentences with the correct jobs.

- **a** Kathy is a ________. She's investigating new technology at the moment.
- **b** Joe works in construction. He's a ________.
- **c** Sarah is a ________, she works in a laboratory.
- **d** Dalí is a famous ________. I like his paintings.

Simple Past

3 Complete the sentences with the correct form of *be*.

- **a** At 11pm last night Mark ______ in bed.
- **b** Where ______ you at 7pm yesterday?
- **c** They ______ at school yesterday because it ______ Sunday.
- **d** I ______ at home last night because I ______ at my grandma's house. It ______ her birthday.
- **e** ______ Kevin at the party last Saturday?
- **f** No, he ______.

4 Look at Rita's list of things to do yesterday. Write questions.

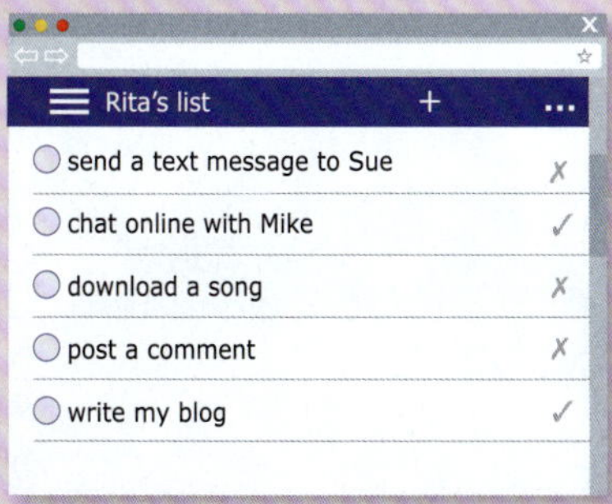

Did Rita send a text message to Sue?

- **a** ________________
- **b** ________________
- **c** ________________
- **d** ________________

5 Look at the list in activity 4 again and write answers to your questions.

No, she didn't.

- **a** ________ **c** ________
- **b** ________ **d** ________

Past Progressive

6 Write questions using the past progressive. Then answer the questions so they are true for you.

- **a** what / you / do / at 10pm last night?
  ____
  ____
- **b** what / your parents / do / at 3pm on Sunday?
  ____
  ____
- **c** you and your friend / watch a movie / at 9pm yesterday?
  ____
  ____

Grammar Buildup 1

1 | 2 | 3 | 4 | 5 | 6 | 7 | 8

7 Choose the correct words.

Cell phones are a relatively new invention. Before them, there a **was / were** two-way radios in taxis, police cars and ambulances, but users b **can't / couldn't** connect to the phone network. In 1910, Lars Ericsson c **installed / was installing** a phone in his car. He d **stopped / was stopping** at different places while he e **traveled / was traveling** across the country. Then he f **connected / was connecting** his phone to the national telephone network with long wires. The first real 'mobile' phone system g **started / was starting** in 1956 in Sweden. Today, people h **use / are using** cell phones every day.

2 Strange but True!

VOCABULARY 1

Prepositions

1 13 Listen and repeat the prepositions.

across	along	around	away from
down	into	out of	over
through	towards	under	up

2 Which prepositions are opposites? Write them in pairs.

under *over*

a towards ________ c up ________

b into ________ d across ________

3 Choose the correct words.

James Bond is always very active in his movies. He often jumps **a out of** / **towards** planes and parachutes **b over** / **down** to the ground, and then he runs **c up** / **under** mountains to the top, dives **d into** / **out of** rivers and then swims **e under** / **over** water to the other side. He jumps **f into** / **over** obstacles and moves **g towards** / **over** his objective. After that, he drives **h into** / **away from** his enemies in his Aston Martin car!

TIP

We can combine action verbs with different prepositions to indicate the direction of movement, e.g. *swim across, swim over, swim under.*

READING 1

1 Look at the words below. Do they relate to text A or B?

millionaire hospital ant dive

A ________ B ________

2 14 Read and listen to the following anecdotes in the blog posts. Check your answers.

A

Strange Stories February 13, 2019

Crocodiles in the Pool

Patrick Hughes is a millionaire. Last month, he was having a party and he took his guests on a tour of his mansion. In the garden he had an enormous swimming pool with four crocodiles.
'I don't know who to give my money to,' Hughes said. 'I want to give it to a brave person. Can anyone dive into the water, swim across the pool and climb out the other side? I'll give that person anything they want – my money, my house, anything!'
Everyone was looking at Hughes when suddenly there was a loud noise – somebody was in the pool! It was Hughes' lawyer, Mark Flood, an unpopular man. Everyone ran along the side of the pool as they watched Flood. He ran across the first crocodile, swam under the second and swam over the third one. He was desperately swimming away from the crocodiles. Finally, he climbed out of the pool just before the fourth crocodile could reach him.
'You are incredible!' said Hughes. 'Tell me, what do you want?'
'I want to know who pushed me into the pool!'

B

Strange Stories February 15, 2019

A Lucky Accident

Joan Murray loves adventure and she often goes skydiving. She doesn't normally have any problems, but one day disaster struck as Joan jumped out of the plane.
She was falling towards the ground at a speed of about 200 km per hour, when her main parachute didn't open.
At the last moment, her emergency parachute opened just 210 meters from the ground. Joan crashed into a field and her heart stopped. Luckily, she fell onto a mound of fire ants. The ants climbed into her clothes and bit her. Doctors believe the bites from the ants started her heart again. Joan was in the hospital for two weeks, but then she recovered completely. The accident didn't stop Joan – she started skydiving again a year later.

3 Read text A again. Then write T for *true* or F for *false*.

a ☐ Patrick Hughes told his lawyer to swim across the pool.
b ☐ The crocodiles didn't eat Mark Flood.
c ☐ Mark Flood chose to swim across the pool.

4 Read text B again and order the events.

a ☐ Joan's heart stopped.
b 1 Joan went skydiving.
c ☐ Joan went to the hospital and recovered.
d ☐ The fire ants bit Joan.
e ☐ Joan's parachute didn't open.
f ☐ Joan started skydiving again.
g ☐ Joan fell onto a mound of ants.

5 Find words a-d in the texts and then match them with definitions 1-4.

a ☐	struck	1	was able to touch
b ☐	crashed into	2	hit very hard
c ☐	recovered	3	occurred
d ☐	reached	4	got better after an accident or illness

6  CLASS VOTE Which story do you think is stranger? Which story is true?

GRAMMAR 1

Review: Simple Past and Past Progressive

1 Read the sentences below and write (A) or (B) according to the timelines presented.

(A)

past progressive

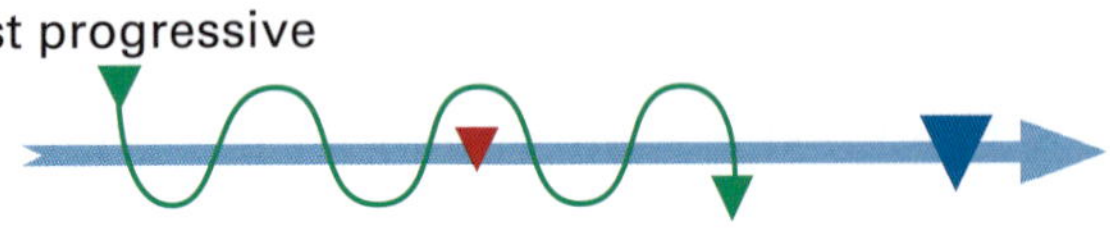

simple past now

(B)

simple past simple past now

a ☐ Patrick Hughes was talking to his guests when his lawyer Mark Flood fell into the swimming pool.

b ☐ Mark ran across the first crocodile, swam under the second and swam over the third one.

c ☐ Joan was skydiving when her parachute didn't open.

d ☐ Joan crashed into the ground and her heart stopped.

2 Look at the chart below. Then fill in the blanks with *simple past* or *past progressive* to complete the rules as to the use of these verb tenses.

past progressive	simple past
Last month Patrick **was having** a party in the afternoon.	
	The ants **climbed into** Joan's clothes and **bit** her.
Everyone **was looking** at Hughes...	... when Mark **fell** into the pool.
While Mark **was trying** to cross the pool,...	... a crocodile **tried** to reach him.

a The most common use of the ________________ tense is to talk about something that was happening around a particular time in the past.

b The simple past and the past progressive can be used together. In these cases, the ________________ describes a longer action or situation and the ________________ describes the action or events that 'interrupt' the situation described in the past progressive.

3 Choose the correct words.

Last summer, 11-year-old Brennan Hawkins **a went** / **was going** to Scout Camp. One day, he **b got** / **was getting** lost in the woods during an activity. Brennan **c survived** / **was surviving** for four days alone in the woods! When rescuers finally **d found** / **were finding** Brennan, he **e hid** / **was hiding** in the trees because he **f didn't recognize** / **wasn't recognizing** them!

PRONUNCIATION

Sentence Stress

🔊 15 Listen and repeat the sentences. Which syllables are stressed?

a He was watching a movie.

b They were listening to music.

c He wasn't hiding in the woods.

d Was he talking to David?

when and *while*

4 Note the use of *when* and *while* in the sentences below. Choose the correct information.

when / while
He was running away **when** the bear attacked him.
When the bear saw him, he was taking pictures of the monkeys in the trees.
The bear roared **while** he was running away.
While he was running away, the bear attacked him.

a *While* is usually used before the **past progressive** / **simple past**.

b *When* is usually used before the **past progressive** / **simple past**.

c ☐ Use... ☐ Don't use... a comma after a time clause that starts a sentence.

5 Complete the sentences with the correct form of the verbs in parentheses. Then rewrite the sentences changing *when* and *while*.

He *was walking* (walk) in the forest when the dog *appeared* (appear).
While he was walking in the forest, the dog appeared.

a While the children ________ (play), they ________ (see) a snake.
____

b While they ________ (sail) along the coast, there ________ (be) a storm.
____
____

c The plane ________ (fly) over the area when the pilot ________ (see) the explorers.
____
____

d When I ________ (arrive), the rescuers ________ (look) for the lost girl.
____
____

e I ________ (have) an accident while I ________ (drive) home.
____
____

f I ________ (see) Hannah when I ________ (be) at the shopping center.
____
____

6 Note the use of *when* and *while* in the sentences below. What do they mean? Match the sentences a-c with the information below.

a **When** Mark **arrived**, Jane **was cooking** dinner.

b **When** Mark **arrived**, Jane **cooked** dinner.

c **While** Jane **was cooking** dinner, Mark **was taking** a shower.

☐ Jane's and Mark's actions were happening at the same time.

☐ Jane started cooking dinner before Mark arrived.

☐ Jane started cooking dinner after Mark arrived.

GRAMMAR GUIDE page 36

LISTENING

Shark Attack!

1 Look at the picture and the words in the box. What do you think the news report is about?

attack beach bite bodyboard hand head hip leg swim wetsuit

____

2 16 Listen and check your answers.

3 16 Listen again. Then write T for *true* and F for *false*. Correct the false sentences.

a ☐ Lydia was swimming when the shark attacked.
____

b ☐ The shark wasn't very big – it was only about one meter long.
____

c ☐ The shark was very aggressive.
____

d ☐ Lydia's brother hit the shark on the head with his bodyboard.
____

e ☐ The shark let Lydia go and she and her brother ran out of the water.
____

f ☐ Lydia is planning to swim again at the beach soon.
____

4 INTERFACE Work in pairs. One of you is a reporter, one of you is Lydia. Ask and answer questions about the shark attack.

Why did you go to the beach?

I wanted to go bodyboarding.

CULTURAL FACT

Around 21 different species of shark live off the UK coast. Basking sharks are the most common. They can grow up to 11 meters long.

SPEAKING

Zoo Story

17 Josh is talking to Mark about an event at a zoo near Chicago. Listen and complete the dialogue.

Mark, **a** __________ I **b** __________ you what I saw at the zoo last Saturday?

No. What happened?

Binti, the gorilla, **c** __________ a hero! She **d** __________ a little boy who fell into Binti's enclosure.

I don't believe it! You know, when animals feel they are in danger, they attack!

You bet! But, in this case, Binti **e** __________ the boy up gently and carried him to the door where paramedics **f** __________. I couldn't believe my eyes!

Really? How come?

In fact, when the boy fell he was unconscious. The keeper said she **g** __________ Binti to carry a doll and bring it to her, so Binti **h** __________ maternal instincts and probably **i** __________ the boy was the doll!

Lucky boy!

Yeah, but Binti's keeper insisted that Binti **j** __________ the boy; she was in no immediate danger and the other gorillas weren't around.

Fortunately, things **k** __________ out alright!

FUNCTIONAL LANGUAGE

Telling an Anecdote

Did I tell you...?
What happened?
Really? How come?

TIP

An anecdote is a short interesting or amusing story about a real incident or a person.

Speaking Task

Step 1

Think of an anecdote. Use the ideas below or your own ideas.

Step 2

Think about the specific details of the anecdote and how to tell it.

Did I tell you about...?
It was so frightening / interesting...
I was so embarrassed / bored...

Think about your friend's questions and reactions.

Really? How come?
What happened?
Where were you?
You were lucky / stupid / brave...

Step 3

Work with a partner. Write an anecdote. Follow the conversation above as a guide.

Step 4

Take turns practicing your dialogue.

CULTURE

Holy Animals of India

It may sound strange to Western civilization, but in India animals are considered sacred. This secular country strongly believes in the divinity of animals, especially those referred to in Indian mythology and ancient Indian culture.

The Cow

The cow is the holiest animal in India. It is treated as a god who has taken the form of an animal, a gift of the gods to the people. For that reason, slaughtering is banned all over the country. However, studies have shown that ancient Indians ate beef in ancient times. It was a myth, composed between 300 BC and AD 300, that led to the transition to not eating cows.

The Monkey

The monkey is considered to be a form of Hanuman – the god of power and strength. The biggest monkey, called Langur or Hanuman Langur, is the most sacred in India.

The Snake

Several old cultures worship serpents. The Indian Cobra is the most sacred snake in India and is revered by Hindus. Snake charmers are followers of Lord Shiva, the Hindu god who wears a king cobra around his neck.

The Elephant

The elephant in India is part of Hindu culture. It is the god (divinity) of success and education. In the past it was used as an instrument of war. Nowadays, during festival seasons it is decorated and worshiped.

The Royal Bengal Tiger

The Royal Bengal tiger, in all its strength and glory, is not only a sacred animal, but also the national symbol of India. Indians also worship the tiger because they are afraid of it.

1 18 **Read and listen to the text. Then write the animal the information below refers to.**

The Royal Bengal Tiger : It is the national symbol of India.

a ________________: Its meat cannot be eaten.
b ________________: It is revered by Hindus and the Hindu god, Lord Shiva, wears one around his neck.
c ________________: It is the god of success and education.
d ________________: It is the god of power and strength.
e ________________: It was used as an instrument of war.
f ________________: Indian people ate its meat in ancient times.

2 **Different animals mean different things in countries all over the world. Are any animals worshiped in your country?**

____

3 **How are animals (wild / farm / pets) treated in your country?**

____

____

VOCABULARY 2

-ed / *-ing* Adjectives

1 Look at the pictures and choose the correct word.

a The **couple** / **mountains** are frighten**ed**.

b The **couple** / **mountains** are frighten**ing**.

2 Complete the rules with *-ed* or *-ing*.

a We use ______ adjectives to describe how we feel.

b We use ______ adjectives to describe the thing or person that causes the feeling.

3 Complete the chart with the verbs in the box.

annoy bore excite frighten interest surprise tire worry

verb	*-ing* form	*-ed* form
______	______	______
______	______	______
______	______	______
frighten	*frightening*	*frightened*
______	______	______
______	______	______
______	______	______
______	______	______

4 Choose the correct words.

a John is **bored** / **boring** because the movie is **bored** / **boring**.

b The results of the experiments are very **surprised** / **surprising**. The scientists are **worried** / **worrying**.

c I'm **annoyed** / **annoying** because my friend is late – again! It's very **annoyed** / **annoying** when people are always late.

d We're **tired** / **tiring** because it's very late, but the documentary is really **interested** / **interesting**.

e They are **frightened** / **frightening** of spiders. They think spiders are **frightened** / **frightening**.

5 19 Listen, check and repeat.

READING 2

1 Look at the pictures above and answer the questions.

a How do you think the people felt in the situation?

______

b What do you think happened?

______

2 Match words and phrases a-e with the definitions.

a get stuck ☐ care for

b look after ☐ come back

c return ☐ become trapped

d work ☐ be able to do something

e manage ☐ function

3 20 Read and listen to the news report. Answer the questions.

a What happened on the way home?

______

b Why didn't they use their phones?

______

c Who did they think about while they were trying to move the car?

______

d Who did they call on the way home?

______

e Are they planning to go again next year?

______

Mountain Couple Get Home Safely

Keith and Jennifer Lee live in Oregon, United States. Every year they go to the mountains. They don't usually have any problems, but last year things were different. They drove up to the mountains as usual, but as they were driving home they suddenly got stuck in the snow. Unfortunately, their phones weren't working so high up. It was a worrying situation. While they were trying to move the car, they thought about their four children, aged 8 to 18. A friend, Sophie Smith, was looking after the children. When the Lees didn't return, Sophie became worried. She called the police and a search began. Two days later Keith finally managed to move the car. They were driving home when they heard about the search for them on the radio. They were surprised! They called the police and then called Sophie. 'They're safe. They're coming home!' Sophie shouted when she heard the news. Everyone was delighted.
Keith is planning to go back to the mountains again next year, but Jennifer doesn't want to go. It was a frightening experience for her – she thinks they should stay in town!

GRAMMAR 2

Present and Past Tenses

1 Look at the chart below and match the sentences to the information below.

present and past tenses	
a	Every year Keith and Jennifer **go** to the mountains.
b	They**'re coming** home!
c	They **were driving** home when they got stuck.
d	Keith finally **managed** to move the car.

☐ It describes a habit.
☐ It refers to an action in progress in the past.
☐ It describes something happening now.
☐ It describes a completed action in the past.

2 Refer to the chart in activity 1 and use the verb tenses in the box to complete the information below.

simple past   simple present
present progressive   past progressive

a It describes a habit: ____________

b It refers to an action in progress in the past: ____________

c It describes something happening now: ____________

d It describes a completed action in the past: ____________

3 Read the text *Mountain couple get home safely* again and provide suitable questions for these answers.

a Where ______________________?
Keith and Jennifer Lee live in Oregon, in the U.S.

b What ______________________?
They were driving home when they got stuck in the snow.

c ______________________?
No, their phones weren't working.

d Who ______________________?
Sophie did and the search began.

e ______________________
______________________?
No, only Keith is planning to go back to the mountains next year.

4 Complete the text with the correct form of the verbs in parentheses.

Vanessa Horrocks *was watching* (watch) TV in her apartment when she a ____________ (hear) a strange noise in the bathroom. She b ____________ (go) to check. She c ____________ (have) a terrible shock when she d ____________ (see) a two-meter-long python in the toilet. 'The snake e ____________ (try) to get out of the toilet,' she f ____________ (tell) our reporter, 'so I g ____________ (run) out of the bathroom because I certainly h ____________ (not want) to try and catch it. Then I i ____________ (call) Fred, our building manager. He j ____________ (arrive) quite quickly. He k ____________ (catch) the snake and I l ____________ (take) it away.'
Vanessa still m ____________ (feel) nervous when she uses her bathroom. 'And I always n ____________ (put) the toilet lid down now,' she said.
Building manager Fred Murray told us: 'Pet pythons sometimes o ____________ (escape) and p ____________ (live) in the water systems of large apartment blocks. We q ____________ (look for) the python's owner now. At the moment it r ____________ (live) in a cage in my apartment but it ____________ (grow) very fast.'

GRAMMAR GUIDE page 36

WRITING

A Description of an Accident

1 🔊 21 Read and listen to Sam's description of an accident. Put the pictures in the correct order.

Last Saturday evening, I was walking into town with my friend Jenny. It was raining really hard because there was a terrible storm. It was a bit frightening and we were thinking about going back home.
Suddenly, there was a loud noise and a big tree branch fell down into the road! We were trying to move the branch when a car appeared. The driver wasn't driving very fast, but he didn't see the branch and he drove into it. I ran to the car and looked inside. The driver wasn't conscious and there was blood on his head. Meanwhile, Jenny called an ambulance.
An ambulance arrived quite quickly and took the man to the hospital. Then, a reporter arrived when we were leaving, so we told her about the accident. The next day our story was in the newspaper – it was really exciting!

LANGUAGE FOCUS

Time Expressions

- We were watching TV. ***Suddenly***, the phone rang.
- The police evacuated the area. ***Meanwhile***, the firemen tried to stop the fire.
- We called an ambulance. ***Then***, we helped the accident victims.

2 Look at the Language Focus. Find in the text examples of the words in bold.

3 Complete the sentences with *suddenly*, *meanwhile* or *then*.

a The rescuers climbed down to the boy. ___________, they took him to the helicopter.

b We were walking through the jungle. ___________, we saw a tiger!

c I started making a fire. ___________, my friends looked for more wood.

d I was looking at the river. ___________, I heard a voice shouting, 'Help! Help!'

e Tom was walking back to the camp. ___________, his friends were looking for him.

4 Write a description of an accident (120-150 words).

Writing a Description of an Accident

Step 1 > PLAN

Think of an imaginary or a real accident. When, where and how did it happen?

Step 2 > WRITE

Write your first version. Organize the story into three paragraphs.

Step 3 > CHECK

Check your writing for errors. Try to include *suddenly*, *meanwhile* and *then*.

Step 4 > WRITE

Write your final copy and hand in your work.

VOCABULARY IN PICTURES

Prepositions

down

out of

up

around

under

through

away from

across

over

into

towards

along

-ed / *-ing* Adjectives

annoyed / annoying

frightened / frightening

bored / boring

tired / tiring

excited / exciting

worried / worrying

surprised / surprising

interested / interesting

GRAMMAR GUIDE

Simple Past and Past Progressive

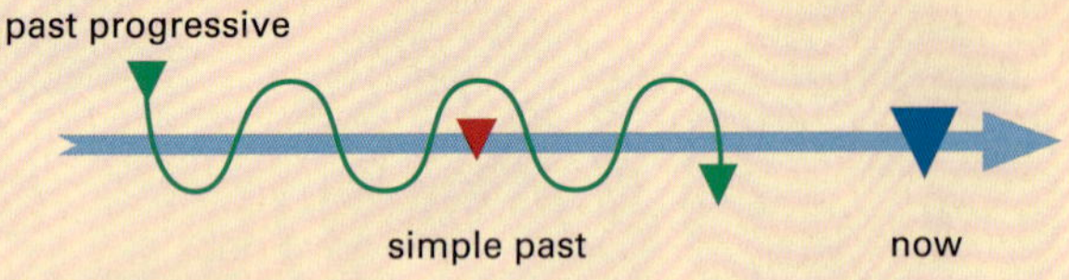

She **was falling** towards the ground when her main parachute **didn't open**.

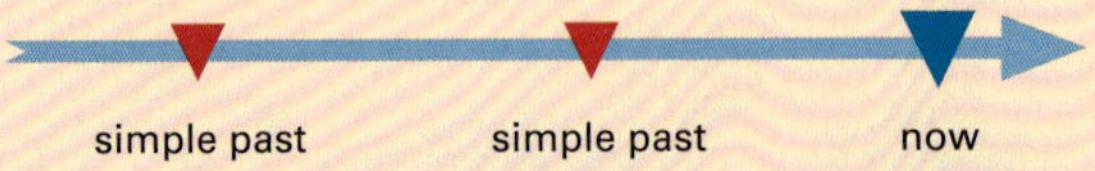

Joan **crashed** into the ground and her heart **stopped**.

- we often use the past progressive and the simple past in the same sentence
  When she **was falling**, her parachute **didn't open**.
- we use the past progressive for actions in progress in the past and the simple past for events which interrupt the action in progress
  John **was watching** TV when Beth **arrived**.
- we also use the simple past for a sequence of actions in the past
  Joan **crashed** and her heart **stopped**.

when and *while*

He was running away **when** the bear attacked.
While he was running away, the bear attacked.

- we use the simple past after *when*
- we use the past progressive after *while*

Present and Past Tenses

present		
	simple	**progressive**
+	I / You **walk** He / She / It **walks** We / You / They **walk**	I **'m walking** You **'re walking** He / She / It **'s walking** We / You / They **'re walking**
–	I / You **don't walk** He / She / It **doesn't walk** We / You / They **don't walk**	I **'m not walking** You **'re not walking** He / She / It **'s not walking** We / You / They **'re not walking**
?	**Do** I / you **walk**? **Does** he / she / it **walk**? **Do** we / you / they **walk**?	**Am** I **walking**? **Are** you **walking**? **Is** he / she / it **walking**? **Are** we / you / they **walking**?

- we use the simple present for habits and daily routines
  She **brushes** her teeth before she goes to bed.
- we use the present progressive for an action that is happening at the moment of speaking
  What **are** you **doing** now?

past	
simple	**progressive**
I / You **walked** He / She / It **walked** We / You / They **walked**	I **was walking** You **were walking** He / She / It **was walking** We / You / They **were walking**
I / You **didn't walk** He / She / It **didn't walk** We / You / They **didn't walk**	I **wasn't walking** You **weren't walking** He / She / It **wasn't walking** We / You / They **weren't walking**
Did I / you **walk**? **Did** he / she / it **walk**? **Did** we / you / they **walk**?	**Was** I **walking**? **Were** you **walking**? **Was** he / she / it **walking**? **Were** we / you / they **walking**?

- we use the simple past for a completed action or a completed sequence of actions in the past
  Last night I **had** dinner, **read** a book and **went** to bed.
- we use the past progressive for an action that was in progress in the past
  I **was watching** TV at 10 o'clock last night.

PROGRESS CHECK

Prepositions

1 Complete the sentences with the words in the box.

across into out of under up

a When John woke up, he climbed __________ his tent and ate breakfast.

b Then he walked to the river and dove __________ the water.

c While he was swimming __________ the river to the other side, it started to rain.

d When he reached the other side, he sheltered __________ a tree.

e When the rain stopped, he ran __________ a big hill.

-ed / -ing Adjectives

2 Complete the sentences with the correct form of the words in parentheses.

a They are very late. I am ________ (worry).

b The movie was really ________ (bore).

c Were you ________ (surprise) when you saw me?

d I'm reading a really ________ (interest) book.

e I can't find my smartphone. It's really ________ (annoy).

Review: Simple Past and Past Progressive

3 Complete the sentences with the correct form of the verbs in parentheses. Use the simple past or the past progressive.

a John __________ (not get up) early yesterday.

b At six o'clock yesterday I __________ (do) my homework.

c They __________ (not do) anything when I __________ (see) them.

d Kate __________ (meet) Kevin while she __________ (walk) to school.

4 Complete the questions using the simple past or the past progressive form of the verbs in parentheses.

a __________ (you / go) to a party last Saturday?

b What __________ (you / do) at 3am this morning?

c What ____________________ (you / do) last night?

d What ____________________ (your mother / do) when you __________ (wake up) this morning?

e What ____________________ (the other students / do) when your teacher ____________________ (arrive) today?

Present and Past Tenses

5 Write sentences using the simple present, present progressive, simple past or past progressive.

a Nicky / watch a DVD / when / her friend / arrive.

____

b I / look for my friends / now.

____

c They / not usually eat / meat.

____

d While / they / swim / they / see a shark.

____

Grammar Buildup 2

1 2 3 4 5 6 7 8

6 Choose the correct words.

Todd Endris **a works** / **is working** in a laboratory, but he usually **b goes** / **is going** surfing in his free time. He loves **c surfing** / **surfed**! One day last summer while he **d is surfing** / **was surfing** at Marina Beach, an enormous white shark **e attacked** / **was attacking** him. Todd **f hit** / **was hitting** the shark on the nose, but it **g didn't release** / **wasn't releasing** him. He **h got** / **was getting** desperate when suddenly six dolphins attacked the shark and Todd escaped. Two other surfers helped Todd to the beach and **i call** / **called** an ambulance. Todd **j was** / **were** in the hospital for a long time, but he recovered. After a shark attack, most people are **k frightening** / **frightened** of surfing again, but not Todd. What **l does he do** / **is he doing** at the moment? Surfing, of course!

Review 1

VOCABULARY

GRAMMAR

Start

1

He's an amazing **artist** / **lawyer**!

2

The train went **around** / **through** the tunnel.

8

They're walking **round** / **along** the seashore.

7

He's running **outside** / **towards** the bus with a cup of coffee in his hands!

9

I often **charge** / **use** my cell phone in the car.

10

He's the **mailman** / **fireman** who brings all the correspondence to the neighborhood.

16

Although the news from the hospital is very **worrying** / **worried**, I know he's going to recover soon.

15

I'm **boring** / **bored**. Let's go to the movies.

17

I trust him to do this job in the house because he's an excellent **doctor** / **construction worker**.

18

The vehicles are going **up** / **round** the traffic circle.

3

My sister's very **annoying / annoyed**! She broke my printer last night.

4

I'm reading a book about the Arctic. It's really **interesting / interested**.

6

Sorry, I need to **make / do** a phone call.

5

Can I borrow your **laptop / flash drive** to save this document?

11

They're getting **out of / into** the plane.

12

I didn't like the movie. It was very **frightening / frightened**.

14

His shelves were filled up with books, so now he only reads **e-books / emails**.

13

I'm **tiring / tired**. I think I'm going to bed.

19

She's the **lawyer / engineer** who is taking care of our court case.

20

I prefer to **store / hold** data in the cloud so I can access it anywhere.

Finish

Review 1

VOCABULARY

GRAMMAR

Simple Past

1 Complete with *was(n't)* or *were(n't)*.

It *was* my parents' 25th wedding anniversary yesterday. My mom **a** ________ excited; it was just another normal day. There **b** ________ many letters in the mail that morning, but there **c** ________ a card from my dad. When my mom opened it, there **d** ________ two airline tickets to New York in it. **e** ________ she excited then? Yes, she **f** ________. *Very* excited!

2 Complete the sentences with the simple past form of the verbs in parentheses.

I *sent* (send) you an email last night.

a Marc ______ (take) a picture with his cell phone.

b He finally ______ (read) my blog!

c My mom ______ (work) at the school.

d I ______ (do) my homework after lunch.

3 Rewrite the sentences using the negative.

You charged your cell phone.
You didn't charge your cell phone.

a They scanned the document.
____

b I wrote a letter to the politician.
____

c He met Elena online.
____

d The computer stored the data.
____

4 Complete the simple past questions with the verbs in the box. Then write the correct short answers.

make ~~send~~ take want work

Did he *send* ten emails yesterday?
✗ *No, he didn't.*

a ________ you ________ to be an actor?
✓ ________________

b ________ they ________ any pictures?
✓ ________________

c ________ your sister ________ as an artist?
✗ ________________

Past Progressive

5 Complete the sentences with the past progressive form of the verbs in parentheses.

I *was* *choosing* (choose) a new book in the library yesterday morning.

a A school boy ________ ________ (use) a computer near me.

b He ________ ________ (not do) his homework on the computer.

c He ________ ________ (play) a game.

d A man ________ ________ (wait) to use the scanner.

6 Write questions in the past progressive. Then underline the correct words in the short answers.

you / live / in Paris / last year?
Were you living in Paris last year?

No, **I was** / **wasn't**.

a it / rain / at 6 o'clock?
____

Yes, **he** / **it** was.

b Simon and Jen / work / as researchers?
____

Yes, they **was** / **were**.

c the students / download / documents?
____

No, they **were** / **weren't**.

VOCABULARY

GRAMMAR

Simple Past and Past Progressive

7 Underline the correct words.

I saw the accident while I **walked** / **was walking** to school.

a A bus was coming along the road when a dog **ran** / **was running** in front of it.

b The driver **saw** / **was seeing** the dog and tried to avoid it.

c While the driver **tried** / **was trying** to avoid the dog, he drove into a tree.

d I quickly got my cell phone and **called** / **was calling** the emergency services.

8 Complete the sentences with the correct form of the verbs in parentheses. Use the simple past or the past progressive.

Someone *went* into their room while they *were sleeping* (go / sleep).

a While Lucas __________, he __________ his leg (ski / break).

b I __________ home when I __________ a $50 bill (run / find).

c We __________ when the teacher __________ in (chat / come).

d Dad __________ a picture of us while we __________ (take / dive).

when and *while*

9 Complete the sentences with *when* or *while*.

I was surprised *when* I heard the news.

a They saw dolphins ________ they were sailing.

b We stayed inside ________ it was raining.

c ________ he saw the bear, he was walking in the forest.

d The dog was running towards me ________ it suddenly stopped.

Present and Past Tenses

10 Complete the sentences with the simple present or the present progressive form of the verbs.

My dad *gets* (get) emails every day.

a We often __________ (go) out for a meal.

b I __________ (make) a curry right now.

c What __________ your mom __________ (do)?

d She__________ (eat) an apple now.

11 Complete the text with the verbs in the box. Use the simple past or the past progressive.

~~do~~ play not know switch watch

I *was doing* my homework at 9 o'clock last night. I had to write a blog, but I **a** __________ what to write about. Then, I heard a noise outside. I **b** __________ off my light and looked out of the window. Three foxes **c** __________ in our garden. I **d** __________ them for ten minutes and then started writing my blog!

12 Number the sentences below according to the list of tenses.

1 simple present
2 present progressive
3 simple past (completed action)
4 simple past (sequence of actions)
5 past progressive (action in progress)
6 simple past and past progressive

[*3*] I slept badly last night.

a [ ] We were sleeping at 11 o'clock.

b [ ] Shhh! The baby's sleeping.

c [ ] The phone rang while I was sleeping.

d [ ] I sleep 8 hours a night.

e [ ] I got into bed and went to sleep.

3 Celebrate!

VOCABULARY 1

Clothes and Accessories

1 Look at the words in the box. How do you say them in your language?

boots coat dress jacket jeans
pants scarf shirt shorts skirt
sneakers sweater T-shirt

2 22 Listen and repeat.

3 Match descriptions a-f to pictures 1-6.

a I'm wearing a pair of jeans and a brown coat. I'm having fun with my friends. ☐

b This is my uncle and his wife at their wedding. My uncle is wearing a special Scottish skirt called kilt. ☐

c This is me on the beach. I'm wearing a pair of shorts and a T-shirt. ☐

d This is New Year's Eve. It's December so we're wearing a coat, gloves and a scarf. ☐

e This is my little brother's birthday party. He's wearing a multi-colored shirt. ☐

f It's Thanksgiving Day and my mom's wearing her favorite sweater. ☐

TIP

We often use *a pair of...* with clothes: *a pair of pants, a pair of boots*. Remember that pants and boots are plural.
These are my favorite pants. ✓

4 23 Listen to Emily and Ben. What do they usually wear on special occasions?

____

____

____

____

5 INTERFACE Work in pairs. Ask and answer questions about the clothes you wear. Use the words in the box or your own ideas.

a party a wedding school
New Year's Eve the weekend

What do you usually wear to parties?

I usually wear a pair of jeans and a black T-shirt.

READING 1

1 Skim the text and complete the headings with the words below.

a Gloves **b** Skirts **c** White

2 What genre does it illustrate?

a essay **b** feature article

Dress Properly for these Celebrations!

Men in ________________

If you're going to go to a *ceilidh*, you're going to need your dance clothes and comfortable shoes. *Ceilidhs* are traditional dances from Scotland and Ireland, and the music is fast and energetic. Everybody dances and has a good time, and *ceilidhs* are as popular as nightclubs. Girls wear what they want: jeans, skirts or pants; boys wear kilts, shirts and jackets. A kilt is similar to a skirt – it is a traditional Scottish outfit and it's perfect for dancing!

Not All Brides Wear ________________

When Indian women get married, the traditional color isn't white, it's red, because this color is the symbol of new life. So, an Indian bride doesn't wear a white wedding dress, she wears a beautiful, long, red *sari* with red and gold jewelry and red henna on her hands.

Good Fun in ________________

You can be sure it is going to be cold on New Year's Eve at Times Square, NY, so wear warm clothes! Coats, scarves and boots are best. New Year's Eve has been celebrated at Times Square since 1904. Around one million locals and tourists gather near the New York Times' building to see a huge crystal ball descend from a tower during the countdown to midnight. And no one seems to complain about the freezing weather they have to endure to take part in this celebration. The organizers recommend many layers of clothing, a good hat, winter shoes and gloves. It's a magical night of lights, fireworks and friends, but anyone who doesn't dress warmly is going to freeze!

3 24 Read and listen to the text and answer the questions.

a Where do *ceilidhs* come from?

____

b What do girls wear to a *ceilidh*?

____

c What is the traditional color at an Indian wedding? Why?

____

d Why does the text recommend coats, hats and scarves for New Year's Eve at Times Square?

____

e What do people gather to see?

____

READING STRATEGY

When you read a new word, read the context – the words around it – and try to guess the meaning.

4 Scan the text and underline words for these definitions.

a a traditional skirt from Scotland for men.

b a woman who is getting married.

c a red substance to color hair or skin.

d the counting backwards of numbers before an important event.

e colorful explosives, typical at celebrations.

5 CLASS VOTE Which is your favorite celebration?

GRAMMAR 1

be going to

1 Read these sentences. Underline the verb *be* and circle *going to* + *verb*.

- **a** You are going to need your dance shoes.
- **b** The music is going to be fast and energetic.
- **c** The Indian bride isn't going to wear white.
- **d** They are going to freeze on New Year's Eve.
- **e** We aren't going to take part in the Irish dance.

2 Look at the rules as to the use of *be going to* and complete the chart below.

- **a** The verb *be* in the simple present (am / is / are) is used before *going to*.
- **b** *going to* is followed by a verb in the base form.
- **c** The negative sentence is formed with the negative form of *be* (am not / isn't / aren't).

affirmative
I _______ going to wear a coat on New Year's Eve.
He / She / It is _______ be cold tonight.
You / We / They _______ going to take part in the dance next Saturday.
negative
I _______ going to be inside.
He / She / It _______ going to stop the dance.
You / We / They aren't going to _______ any songs.

3 Order the words to make sentences.

- **a** are / to / have / the beach / on / We / going / a party
  ____
- **b** I / to / wear / am / clothes / fancy / going / not
  ____
- **c** be / The music / to / going / great / is
  ____
- **d** is / going / not / It / to / a barbecue / be
  ____
- **e** am / sandwiches / I / take / going / cake / and / to
  ____
- **f** great time / You / to / have / are / going / a
  ____

> **TIP**
> Use time expressions with *be going to* to talk about future plans: *this August / weekend, next Tuesday / Christmas, on the weekend, tonight, tomorrow...*

4 Look at Sarah's calendar. Complete her plans with the time expressions in the box.

next Monday   on Wednesday
this Thursday   on Friday
on the weekend   tomorrow

- **a** Sarah's going to go to the movies with her friends _____________.
- **b** She's going to buy a new dress _____________.
- **c** She's going to study math _____________.
- **d** She's going to take her science exam _____________.
- **e** She's going to go to the school ball _____________.
- **f** She's going to study for the science exam _____________.

July		
Monday	8	school excursion – museum
Tuesday	9	Jack and Ellie – movies
Wednesday	10	study science
Thursday	11	science exam
Friday	12	buy new dress
Saturday	13	summer barbecue – Youth Club
Sunday	14	study math
Monday	15	last exam – math! end-of-school ball

5 Look at the sentences below. Circle the verb *be*.

a Are you going to wear a kilt? No, you aren't.

b Is it going to freeze during the night? Yes, it is.

c Are we going to enjoy the night? Yes, we are.

d Am I going to have a great time? Yes, I am.

6 Complete the chart. Note the use of *be going to* in questions and short answers.

questions and short answers	
_______ I going to have a great time?	Yes, I am. / No, I _______.
_______ you going to wear a kilt?	Yes, you _______. / No, you aren't.
_______ it going to be a cold night?	Yes, it _______. / No, it _______.
_______ he / she going to bring a friend?	Yes, he / she is. / No, he / she _______.
_______ we / you / they going to be tired?	Yes, we / you / they _______. / No, we / you / they _______.

7 Look at the sentences in the chart in activity 6 again. What is the correct order for questions?

a subject + be + going to + verb + other words?

b be + subject + going to + verb + other words?

8 Write questions using *be going to*.

Who / Sarah / go to the movies with?

Who is Sarah going to go to the movies with?

a What / she / study on Wednesday?

____

b What / she / buy this week?

____

c What / she / visit today?

____

d When / she / take / her last exam?

____

e Where / they / have a barbecue?

____

9 Answer the questions in activity 8. Use Sarah's calendar in activity 4.

She's going to go to the movies with Jack and Ellie.

a _______________

b _______________

c _______________

d _______________

e _______________

10 INTERFACE Work in pairs. Ask and answer questions about your week.

What are you going to do on Saturday?

I'm going to play tennis with Jorge.

GRAMMAR GUIDE page 54

LISTENING

Costume Party

1 🔊 25 Listen to Emma, Ethan and Conor talking about a costume party. Match the names to pictures 1-3.

2

____

1

____

3

____

2 🔊 25 Listen again and choose the correct words.

a The party is on **Friday / Saturday**.

b Emma **is / isn't** going to take her straw broom.

c The party **is / isn't** going to be at Ethan's house.

d Ethan's parrot **is / isn't** going to be real.

e Conor is going to wear his **black / brown** boots.

f Conor **is / isn't** going to wear a scarf.

CULTURAL FACT

Costume parties became popular in the US in the 19th century. Rich people dressed like historic European aristocrats and wore original accessories as a way to show off their wealth.

SPEAKING

A Birthday Party

🔊 26 Lisa is making a WhatsApp call to Emma to invite her to her birthday party. Listen and complete the dialogue.

Hi, Emma! How are you doing?

Just fine, and you?

Great! In fact, I **a** ______________ a birthday party next Saturday. Do you want to come?

Cool! What time **b** ______________?

Well, I'm having a barbecue, so I think 1 p.m. is fine.

c ________________ all our friends from school?

Not all of them, I guess, 'cause I can't spend too much money on it... But Jade and Josh **d** ________________ ... if that's what you wanted to know...

Yeah, you know me quite well. Do you need help with anything?

No, thanks! My parents **e** ________________ everything!

Well, Lisa, see you on Saturday, then... oh, no, see you tomorrow at school!

FUNCTIONAL LANGUAGE

Extending and Accepting Invitations

I'm having...
I'm going to throw / give a... party...
Do you want to come?
Cool!
What time is it going to be?

Speaking Task

Write a dialogue between you and a friend.

Step 1

Imagine it is your birthday and you are having a party. First, choose the type of party. You can use the ideas below or your own.

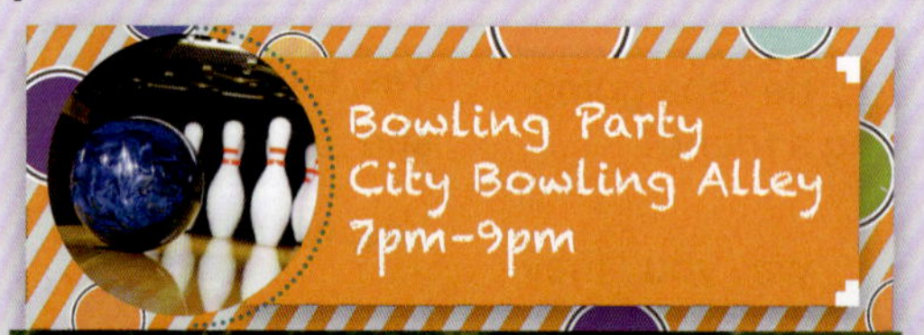

Step 2

Decide what to say.

I'm going to throw a... on...
Do you want to come? / Would you like to come?
I'm going to invite...
It is going to start at...

Think about what your friend is going to say.

Cool!
Thank you!
I'd love to!
What time is it going to start?
Who are you going to invite?
See you...

Step 3

Work with a partner. Write your dialogue. Follow the conversation above as a guide.

Step 4

Take turns practicing your dialogue.

CULTURE

Birthday Traditions in Jamaica

Miss Lou

'Appy birthday to yuh dear'

Birthday celebrations are always a festivity that warms the heart. Although people don't get a year younger, and with time, responsibilities pile up on their to-do list, they wish to be remembered on this special date.

In Jamaica, birthday celebrations are very similar to many western countries, with birthday cakes, birthday candles, sweets and drinks. However, it's not just that – some traditions in Jamaica are a chapter unto themselves:

Jamaican birthdays come down to flouring! Regardless of age, tradition calls for the birthday boy or girl to be covered with flour, often topping it with some liquid to turn the dusting into cake batter. Friends either organize it during the party or as part of an ambush.

The traditional 'Happy Birthday' song, which has only four short musical phrases and a single repetitive line of words, is sung in many languages all over the world. Jamaicans, however, have a special birthday song whose version was popularized by the Jamaican singer Miss Lou on a television show called "Ring Ding."

Jamaicans are very superstitious. A marriage superstition involves birthdays: if you want a happy, lifelong marriage, don't get married on your birthday as it may bring bad luck!

1 27 Read and listen. Then answer the questions below.

a In what ways are Jamaican birthday celebrations similar to many western countries?

____

____

____

b What birthday prank is played in Jamaica?

____

____

____

c Do Jamaicans sing the traditional Birthday Song? Explain.

____

____

____

d What superstition involves birthdays in Jamaica?

____

____

____

2 **INTERFACE** How do people celebrate birthdays in your country? Are there any funny birthday pranks? Any superstitions? Share your ideas with your friends.

VOCABULARY 2

Weather and Seasons

1 spring

2 summer

3 fall

4 winter

1 Look at the words in the box. How do you say them in your language?

cloudy cold dry hot rainy snowy stormy sunny warm wet windy

2 28 Listen and repeat.

3 Which words in activity 1 can you use to describe pictures 1-4?

1: *It's warm, dry and sunny.*

2: ______

3: ______

4: ______

4 Choose the correct words.

a In the Arctic it's **cold / hot**.

b Summer in Mexico is usually **sunny / snowy**.

c People say that the weather in England is **dry / wet**.

d There was no rain last summer so the ground is very **dry / wet**.

e It's **warm / cold** tonight so we can sit outside and eat dinner.

f Last summer in Philadelphia was very **rainy / windy** – we used our umbrellas every day!

PRONUNCIATION

/s/

1 29 Listen and repeat.

scarf snowy socks sometimes spring stormy summer sunny

2 30 Listen and repeat.

a It's sometimes sunny in spring and it's hot and stormy in summer.

b In winter you need a scarf, gloves and thick socks because sometimes it's snowy.

5 INTERFACE Work in pairs. Ask and answer questions about your favorite season.

What's your favorite season?

It's fall. It's windy and rainy, but I love the color of the trees.

Yes, I agree, but I prefer...

READING 2

1 🔊 31 Read and listen. How old is the Lollapalooza Festival?

____

Come to Lollapalooza... but Bring Your Raincoat!

The Lollapalooza Chicago Festival has been happening every summer, around July / August, since the festival started in 1991! There are going to be over 170 acts this year – rock, pop and dance music and more, including special circus, music and theater acts for children. There are 400,000 tickets but don't wait too long to buy! The tickets are going to go on sale in March, but they usually sell all the tickets in one day. Your parents must send the organizers pictures of you and the other members of your family, because all tickets are personal.

When you go to Chicago for the festival with your family, make sure to look for hotel, Airbnb or other sorts of accommodation in advance.

Also, remember to take clothes for bad weather, like ponchos, boots and especially raincoats, because it usually rains a lot and you must not enter the festival carrying an umbrella! But take your T-shirts and sunscreen too. You never know – it is summer after all!

2 Read the text again. Then write T for *true* or F for *false*.

a ☐ Lollapalooza is only a music festival.

b ☐ There are more than 500,000 tickets.

c ☐ Your parents must send the organizers a picture of you if you want a ticket.

d ☐ It's a good idea to take clothes for good and bad weather.

e ☐ Umbrellas are not allowed at Lollapalooza Chicago Festival.

GRAMMAR 2

must / must not

1 Write (O) if the sentences express *obligation* and (P) if they express *prohibition*.

a ☐ You must not enter the festival carrying an umbrella.

b ☐ Your parents must send the organizers pictures of you and the other members of your family.

2 Look at the chart and check (✓) the correct statements and mark a cross (✗) on the incorrect ones.

affirmative	
I / You	**must** purchase the ticket through Lollapalooza.com.
He / She / It	**must** comply with the search policy.
We / You / They	**must** wear the wristband on the right hand.
negative	
I / You	**must not** carry backpacks.
He / She / It	**must not** bring professional cameras.
We / You / They	**must not** bring pets.

a ☐ *Must* and *must not* are used to express ability.

b ☐ The main verb (after *must* / *must not*) is without 'to.'

c ☐ All pronouns (*I* / *you* / *he* / *she* / *it* / *we* / *you* / *they*) take *must* or *must not* + main verb.

3 Order the words to make sentences.

be / for / must not / late / You / school

You must not be late for school.

a must / Patrons / complete search / prior to entry / agree to / a

____

b do / People / must not / video recording / any / concert / at the

____

c by an adult / Children / be accompanied / must

____

d must not / with / items / enter / You / prohibited

____

GRAMMAR GUIDE page 54

CLIL

ART

Maori Music

In New Zealand, music is an important part of national culture. Wellington is the country's capital, and it is home to the New Zealand Symphony Orchestra, which sometimes tours overseas. The New Zealand School of Music is also based in Wellington.

New Zealand's most famous musical export is the opera singer Kiri Te Kanawa, who has appeared on stage around the world for five decades. She has performed with opera singer Jose Carreras and won many awards, including a Grammy in 1984. A soprano with a high singing voice, Kiri Te Kanawa is of Maori origin.

The Maoris are the native people of New Zealand and their traditional music uses special instruments, such as flutes made of animal bones – like the *nguru* flute – trumpets made of sea shells and drums made with wood and the skin of sharks.

Some of New Zealand's biggest rock, hip-hop and folk groups combine Maori music with European influences.

Nguru – Maori flutes

1 32 Read and listen. What are some of the special instruments the Maori people use to make music?

____

____

2 Choose the correct answers.

a Where is the New Zealand School of Music?

1 Auckland
2 Wellington
3 Christchurch

b What type of singer is Jose Carreras?

1 jazz
2 pop
3 opera

c When did Kiri Te Kanawa win a Grammy?

1 1994
2 1984
3 1986

d What type of singer is Kiri Te Kanawa?

1 contralto
2 soprano
3 mezzo-soprano

e Traditional Maori drums are made using...?

1 shark skin
2 animal bones
3 sea shells

VOCABULARY IN PICTURES

Clothes and Accessories

Weather and Seasons

GRAMMAR GUIDE

be going to

affirmative	contracted form
I am going to wear	'm going to wear
You are going to wear	're going to wear
He / She / It is going to wear	's going to wear
We / You / They are going to wear	're going to wear

- we use *be going to* to talk about plans or intentions in the future
- the form is subject + *be* + *going to* + verb
  I**'m going to** play tennis with my friends.
  You**'re going to** watch a movie.
  She**'s going to** buy some new clothes.

negative	contracted form
I am not going to play	'm not going to play
You are not going to play	aren't going to play
He / She / It is not going to play	isn't going to play
We / You / They are not going to play	aren't going to play

- we use *not* to form the negative
  I**'m not** (am not) **going to** wear sandals.
  He **isn't** (is not) **going to** have a party.
  They **aren't** (are not) **going to** visit their cousins.

questions and short answers	
Am I going to go?	
Yes, I am.	No, I'm not.
Are you going to go?	
Yes, you are.	No, you aren't.
Is he / she / it going to go?	
Yes, he / she / it is.	No, he / she / it isn't.
Are we / you / they going to go?	
Yes, we / you / they are.	No, we / you / they aren't.

- the word order is different in questions
  You **are going to** wear jeans.
  Are you **going to** wear jeans?

must / must not

affirmative
I / You must go
He / She / It must go
We / You / They must go

- we use *must* for obligation
  You **must** wear a uniform at this school.
- we use the same form for all subject pronouns

negative
I / You must not go
He / She / It must not go
We / You / They must not go

- we use *must not* for prohibition
  You **must not** take pictures.
- after *must / must not* we use the verb without *to*
  You **must** bring your ticket.
  You **must not** litter.

PROGRESS CHECK

Clothes

1 Complete the words with vowels.

a s c __ r f
b s n __ __ k __ r s
c c __ __ t
d j __ c k __ t
e T - s h __ r t
f s k __ r t

Weather and Seasons

2 Look at the map and complete the weather forecast.

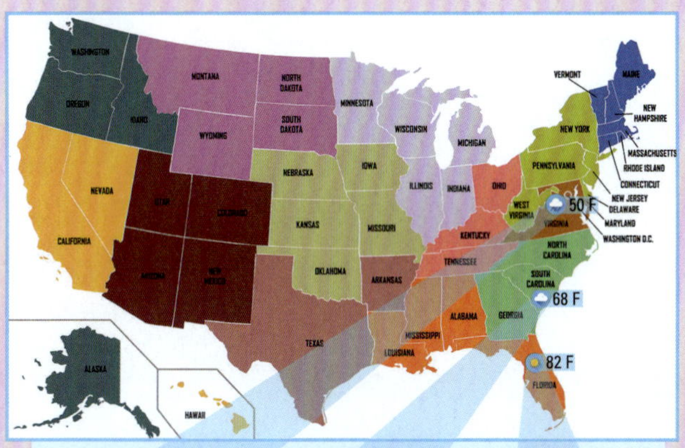

It's June, I know, but in Washington DC today it's going to be **a rainy / windy**. With maximum temperatures of 50 F, it's going to be **b warm / cold**. In South Carolina it's going to be **c warm / hot** but **d stormy / cloudy**. In Florida it's going to be **e cold / hot** and **f sunny / cloudy**.

be going to

3 Order the words to make sentences or questions.

a friends / have / a beach party / My / are / to / going
____

b not / going / wear / I / am / to / that green dress
____

c make / you / a / Are / cake / to / going ?
____

d is / Danny / dance / to / with / going / me
____

must / must not

4 Complete the sentences with *must / must not.*

a You ________ bring glass bottles.
b You ________ only camp in designated areas.
c You ________ have a ticket.
d You ________ light fires.
e You ________ put your trash in the trash cans.

Grammar Buildup 3

1 2 3 4 5 6 7 8

5 Complete the dialogue with the correct form of the verbs in parentheses.

Emily Hi, Olivia! What **a** ____________ you ____________ (do) before I arrived?
Olivia Hi, Emily. I **b** ____________ (put) these old school books in the basement.
Emily Oh yes! It's the last day of school tomorrow.
Olivia I can't wait!
Emily **c** ____________ you ____________ (wear) your black dress tomorrow night?
Olivia No, of course I'm not. Why?
Emily It's the end of year school ball. **d** ____________ you ____________ (go)?
Olivia No, I'm not. I **e** ____________ (go) last year and it **f** ____________ (be) boring.
Emily Olivia, you always **g** ____________ (go). We **h** ____________ (have) a really good time last year. You **i** ____________ (dance) with Jack, remember?
Olivia Yes, I remember. It **j** ____________ (be) awful so I **k** ____________ (not go) tomorrow.
Emily Oh please! Connor, Eric and I **l** ____________ (meet) opposite the school at 7pm. Come with us!

4 Make a Difference

VOCABULARY 1

Jobs

1 Match pictures 1-6 with the jobs in the box. Which jobs aren't in the pictures?

actor	☐	mechanic	☐
architect	☐	nurse	☐
athlete	☐	police officer	☐
electrician	☐	surgeon	☐
engineer	☐	teacher	☐
lifeguard	☐	vet	☐

2 🔊 33 Listen and repeat.

3 Complete the definitions using words from activity 1.

What do we call someone who… designs houses and buildings? *an architect*

a works in a school? ____________

b repairs vehicles and machines? ____________

c designs and builds machines and roads? ____________

d plays professional sports? ____________

e installs and repairs electrical equipment? ____________

f performs in plays and movies? ____________

READING 1

1 🔊 34 Read and listen. What do these numbers refer to?

a 1 billion
___

b 2.5 million
___

c 24,000
___
___

d 5
___

e 22
___

f 80
___
___

2 What text genre is this?

a ☐ a commercial ad.
b ☐ an institutional ad.

3 Read the text again. Then write T for *true* or F for *false*.

a ☐ Some people travel long distances to find water.
b ☐ World Water Day is celebrated in the UK only.
c ☐ Jamie Cranks is going to queue on March 22.
d ☐ Water.org is going to use Amy's Facebook status.
e ☐ Water.org sends engineers and mechanics from Hollywood to developing countries.

4 Answer the questions.

a What happens on World Water Day?
___
___

b What world record do Jamie and his friends hope to break?
___
___

c What does Water.org do?
___
___

d What is Water.org going to do on World Water Day?
___
___

TIP
Learn to recognize prefixes like *un-*. They can help you guess the meaning of a word.

5 Match the words below with their meaning.

a unclear	☐ not needed
b unsafe	☐ dangerous
c unnecessary	☐ not obvious
d unusual	☐ not normal, not ordinary

6 CLASS VOTE Which World Water Day idea do you prefer?

World Water Day
AN INTERNATIONAL DAY OF ACTION

Almost 1 billion people in the world don't have clean water to drink.
2.5 million people don't have access to a toilet.
Every day, 24,000 children under the age of 5 die because of unsafe water.
Many children can't go to school because they need to walk for hours to get water for their family.

March 22 is World Water Day, when there are events around the world focusing on the water crisis. So what should we do on World Water Day?

Stand in a toilet queue*
Jamie Cranks and his friends are from Vancouver. March 22 isn't going to be a normal school day for them because they're going to stand in an unusual queue. Their teacher is going to join them, too! In fact, people in about 80 countries are going to work together to form the world's longest toilet queue.

Donate your Facebook or Twitter status.
Amy, her friends and thousands of other people are going to donate their Facebook and Twitter status to Water.org from March 21 to 26. When Hollywood actor Matt Damon and engineer Gary White created the organization, they had a clear objective: everyone should have access to clean water to drink. Water.org works with local partners to help individuals and communities to meet their own water and sanitation needs. On World Water Day, Water.org is inviting people to donate their Facebook and Twitter statuses to tell millions about the water crisis.

GLOSSARY
*queue: a line of people waiting in a store or similar place

GRAMMAR 1

should (Affirmative and Negative)

1 Read the following sentences. Write GOOD if the recommendation / suggestion given is good and BAD if it is not appropriate.

a [ ] Everyone should have access to clean water to drink.
b [ ] Saving water shouldn't be a real concern.
c [ ] People shouldn't use less water outdoors.
d [ ] People should consider when and how much water is needed.
e [ ] Reusing and recycling water should be considered.

2 Complete the rules below with *should* or *shouldn't*.

a ________ is used to make recommendations and give advice. In a sentence, it gives the meaning of 'It is a good idea.'

b ________ is the negative form and means that you *aren't recommending or advising* something. 'It's NOT a good idea.'

c The sentence structure is: subject + ________ (or ________) + base form of the verb.

3 Complete the chart with *should* or *shouldn't*.

affirmative		
I / You	________	save water.
He / She / It	________	consider saving water.
We / You / They	________	recycle water.
negative		
I / You	________	waste water.
He / She / It	________	be left out.
We / You / They	________	drink unsafe water.

4 Look at the information about saving water at home. Complete the sentences with *should* or *shouldn't*.

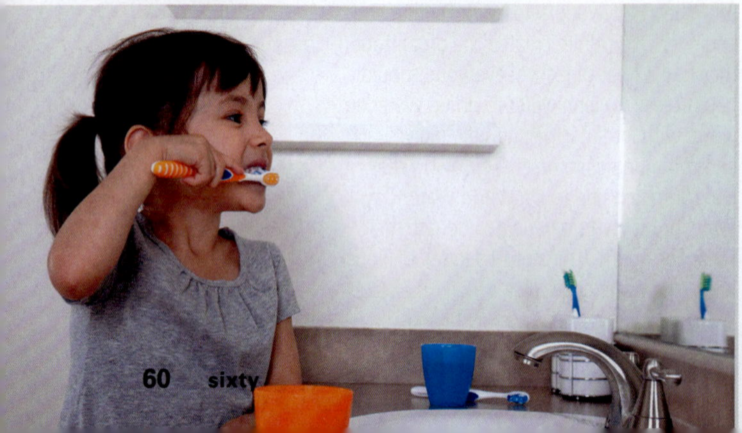

a You ________ turn off the faucet when you brush your teeth.

b You ________ take long showers.

c You ________ fix a dripping faucet.

d You ________ water your garden with a hose.

e You ________ run washing machines when they are not full.

5 Read the situations below and give people some advice / recommendation.

a You are walking down a street and you see two kids throwing trash on the sidewalk.

____
____
____
____

b Your neighbor is watering his plants with a hose. He's been doing it for two hours!

____
____
____
____

c Your friend is doing the dishes under constantly flowing water.

____
____
____
____

d Your little brother is flushing the toilet nonstop!

____
____
____
____

6 Look at the pictures below. Say what people should or shouldn't do. Use the cues to complete the sentences.

a The kids (✗) ______________________.

b People (✓) ______________________ in parks.

c Everybody (✓) ______________________ when leaving the house.

d People (✗) ______________________.

GRAMMAR GUIDE page 68

LISTENING

Heroes

1 You are going to listen to Ed, Rosie and Vicky talking about their heroes. First, look at the pictures. What do you think these people do?

____

____

2 🔊 35 Listen and match the person with their hero.

a	Ed	☐	Aunt Chantal
b	Rosie	☐	Mr. Benson
c	Vicky	☐	Tom Daley

3 🔊 35 Listen again and choose the correct words.

a Tom Daley won the world championship in **2008 / 2009**.

b Tom also helps **his local school / a charity**.

c Aunt Chantal's going to work in a camp for **700 / 100,000** people.

d She's going to work with **children / families**.

e Mr. Benson **is / isn't** going to retire next year.

4 🔊 35 Listen again and answer the questions.

a How old was Tom when he competed in the Beijing Olympics?

____

b Where is Aunt Chantal going to work?

____

c What other job does Mr. Benson have?

____

5 Who is your hero? Why?

____

____

CULTURAL FACT

The BBC gives awards to athletes every year. Tom Daley is the first person to win the Young Sports Personality of the Year award more than once.

SPEAKING

World Water Day

36 Robert and Peter are talking about World Water Day. Listen and complete the dialogue.

You know, Peter, today, in class we talked about how essential water is not only to put an end to thirst and protect **a** ________, but also for supporting economic, social and **b** ______________.

What exactly did you discuss?

Well, first we talked about **c** ______________, which puts people at risk of contracting lots of **d** ________ and dying...

Sure thing! And there's also the fact that unsafe water, **e** ______________ and hygiene cause thousands of deaths every year.

f ______________, an event celebrated every March 22, focuses on raising awareness and inspiring action to tackle water and sanitation issues.

Oh, I've heard about it! I think it's an awareness day which brings to light the inequality of access to **g** ______________, particularly in developing countries.

Yeah, I **h** ________ that an abundance of quality water can change people's jobs and **i** ________ for the better!

We **j** ________ do something to be part of it! How about starting at home and school?

Good idea! We could organize a **k** ______________!

Well, then, let's tell our friends and teachers about it.

FUNCTIONAL LANGUAGE

Giving Opinions and Suggestions

I think...
I imagine...
We should...

World Water Day

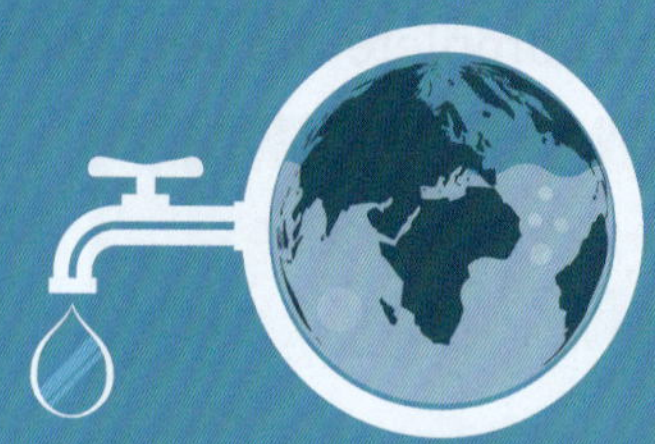

Save Water

March 22nd

Speaking Task

Write a dialogue between you and a friend.

Step 1

Choose one of the following events to write about or use an idea of your own.

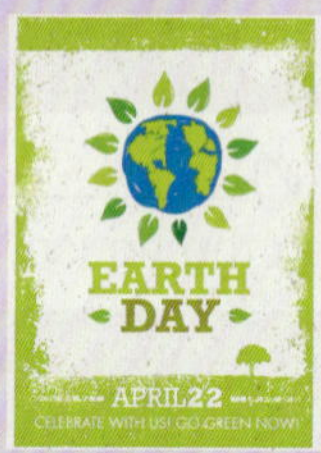

Step 2

Think about what to say. Search for information about the event.

I learned that...
In class we talked about / discussed...
It is an event celebrated...
It aims to...

Think about what your friend is going to say.

I also learned that...
I imagine...
I think...
We should / shouldn't ...

Step 3

Work with a partner. Write your dialogue. Follow the conversation above as a guide.

Step 4

Take turns practicing your dialogue.

CULTURE

Trinidad and Tobago and Its Cultural Relationship with the Ocean

Trinidad and Tobago, a two-island nation in the southern Caribbean, is home to nearly 1.4 million people whose existence is tied to the sea. Trinidadians ('Trinis,' as citizens proudly call themselves) and Tobagonians say they are blessed with a particular phenomenon in that their country consists of 15 times more ocean than land area. They firmly believe they have to pay attention to the marine and coastal environments, home to fish, sharks, turtles, coral reefs and numerous marine organisms.

Trinidadians understand that oceans are part of what it means to be a Trini. There is a traditional ritual when a baby is born: at a specific time, babies are taken to the beach to dip their feet in the saltwater so that they can grow up healthy. When you are sick or there is something wrong with you, such as an upset stomach, you should go to the beach to drink some of the salt water.

Oceans play an essential role in human well-being, producing half of the oxygen for life on the planet. Therefore, Trinidadians and Tobagonians are aware of the importance of sustainable development, which includes action on ocean-related issues such as reducing plastic pollution and addressing the impact of climate change. Protecting the ocean to protect humanity is their goal.

1 37 **Read and listen to the information. Then check (✓) the correct information.**

a Trinidad and Tobago…
- ☐ has an intimate relationship with the sea.
- ☐ consists of one island in the southern Caribbean.

b Trinis feel…
- ☐ the marine and coastal environments aren't of vital importance.
- ☐ they are blessed by living in a region where the ocean covers more area than the land.

c When babies are born…
- ☐ they are taken to the sea to dip their feet in the saltwater.
- ☐ they are blessed by a local priest.

d Trinis believe…
- ☐ boiling and bathing in seawater can heal many diseases.
- ☐ drinking sea water helps heal an upset stomach.

e Trinidadians and Tobagonians…
- ☐ know the importance of sustainable development.
- ☐ think they don't need to worry about actions on ocean-related issues.

2 **In your country, are there any cultural traditions related to nature? Describe (it / one of them) and its impact on people's lives.**

____

____

VOCABULARY 2

Health Problems

1 Read the words in the box. Which words can you use to describe pictures a-d?

broken arm	☐	insect bite	☐
cold	☐	sick	☐
cough	☐	sore throat	☐
cut	☐	stomachache	☐
earache	☐	temperature	☐
headache	☐		

2 38 Listen and repeat.

a

b

c

d

3 Choose the correct words.

a A **headache / stomachache** is when you have a pain in your head.

b He went outside without a coat in January and now he has **a cold / an insect bite**.

c She has a **sore throat / stomachache** because she ate her dinner very quickly.

d I was talking all day yesterday and now I have **a sore throat / a broken arm**.

4 Answer the questions. Use the words in the box.

drink water | have a cough drop | lie down | put on a bandage | take an aspirin

What do you do when you have…

… a headache? *I take an aspirin and I lie down.*

a … a sore throat? ________

b … a cough? ________

c … a cut? ________

d … a temperature? ________

5 INTERFACE Work in pairs. Ask and answer the questions in activity 4.

READING 2

1 39 Read and listen to the interview. What does John Martin do in his free time?

____

2 What is John Martin's advice for these situations?

a Someone feels tired.

____

b Someone has a broken leg.

____

c You need to speak to the police.

____

d Someone has an insect bite.

____

e Someone has a temperature.

____

Mountain Rescue!

John Martin works for the rescue service in the National Park.

Q: John, is this your only job?

A: No, I'm an electrician, but in my free time I'm a volunteer for the rescue service.

Q: What are the most common problems?

A: A very common problem is exhaustion. If someone in your group looks tired, you should all rest. You should also carry high energy food, like chocolate.

Q: And what should I do if someone has a broken leg or arm? Should I move them?

A: No, you shouldn't move them. You should call for help.

Q: Who should I contact?

A: You should call 911 to speak to the police. While you wait, you should keep the person warm.

Q: What about for minor things like insect bites?

A: Use cold water or a special cream, but if the person has a temperature you should contact a doctor.

GRAMMAR 2

should (Questions and Short Answers)

1 Read the questions below and choose the best answer for each one of them.

a Should you cover your mouth when you cough?
- [ ] Yes, we should.
- [ ] No, we shouldn't.

b Mark has broken his leg. Should he move it?
- [ ] Yes, he should.
- [ ] No, he shouldn't.

c The kids are sick. Should they go swimming?
- [ ] Yes, they should.
- [ ] No, they shouldn't.

d Jane has a sore throat and a cough. Should she go to the doctor?
- [ ] Yes, she should.
- [ ] No, she shouldn't.

2 Complete the rules below with the words from the box.

affirmative   questions   short answers

a In ___________, *should* comes before the subject.

b In ___________, use *should* (___________) and *shouldn't* (negative).

3 Refer to activities 1 and 2 and complete the chart below.

questions and short answers
___________ I / you go to the doctor? Yes, I / you ___________. No, I / you ___________.
___________ he / she / it move the person? Yes, he / she / it ___________. No, he / she / it ___________.
___________ we / you / they go swimming? Yes, we / you / they ___________. No, we / you / they ___________.

4 Write complete questions.

I have a terrible cold. stay at home / go to school?
Should I stay at home or should I go to school?

a I always feel terrible on buses. sit at the front / sit at the back?
____

b It's my mom's birthday. buy her a present / make her dinner?
____

c My friends want to learn a new language. study Chinese / study German?
____

d We want to try a new activity. go paintballing / go karting?
____

5 Answer the questions in activity 4 using *should* and *shouldn't.*

____
____
____
____

6 Read the information below. Then answer the questions that follow.

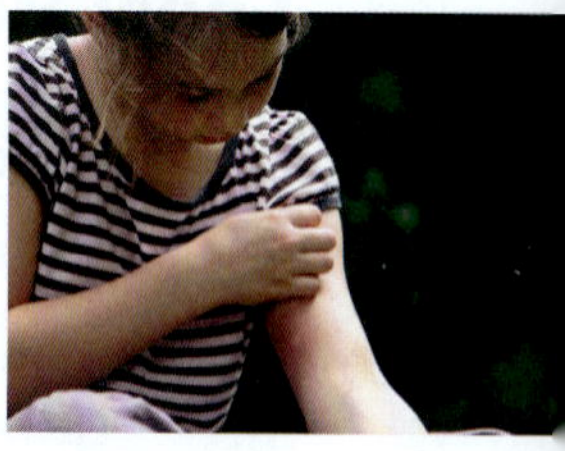

There are several things you can do to relieve pain in case of insect bites or stings. Here are a few:

- Don't panic!
- Apply an ice pack to a bite or sting for 15 to 20 minutes once an hour for the first 6 hours.
- Elevate the area of the bite or sting to decrease swelling.
- Do not use any cream on children younger than age 2 without a doctor's prescription.

In case of an insect bite or sting...

a Should we panic?
____

b Should people apply an ice pack to the sting for 15 to 20 minutes once an hour for the first 6 hours?
____

c Should we elevate the area of the bite or sting to decrease swelling?
____

d Should adults use a cream on children younger than age 2 without a doctor's prescription?
____

GRAMMAR GUIDE page 68

WRITING

A Letter

1 🔊 40 Read and listen. Who are Haley and Matt's heroes?

Local Heroes

Tell us about your hero. This could be a member of your family, a friend or someone who works in your town.

Hi!
A few years ago, my grandmother was in North Bridge Hospital for several weeks. The doctors told her, 'You should change your habits!' She began to eat a more healthy diet and she also started to play sports. Next week she's going to run a half marathon to raise money for the hospital. She's also going to work at the hospital as a volunteer. She's going to talk to patients who don't usually have visitors. What a hero!
Haley, Sacramento.

Hello!
I'm going to nominate our vet, Mr. Rodgers. Last week, our dog Maggie jumped off our balcony. She had a broken leg and a terrible cut on her face, too. Mr. Rodgers was very patient and he was also very kind. Maggie's going to be fine. Thank you, Mr. Rodgers!
Matt, Wichita.

LANGUAGE FOCUS

also* and *too
Use *also* and *too* to add new information and make your writing more interesting.

She *also* started to play sports.
He was patient and he was *also* very kind.
Maggie had a terrible cut on her face, *too*.

2 Look at the Language Focus. Where do *too* and *also* go in the sentence?

____
____

3 Rewrite the sentences including the words in parentheses.

She had a headache. She had a temperature. (too)
She had a headache. She had a temperature, too.

a We should run a marathon. We should climb Ben Nevis. (also)
____
____

b He cleaned the kitchen and the living room. He washed the floors. (also)
____
____

c They're going to look after children. They're going to look after animals. (too)
____
____

d My uncle is friendly. He is kind. (also)
____
____

4 Write a letter about your hero. Follow these steps.

Writing a Letter

Step 1 > PLAN

Make notes under three headings:
a Who is your hero?
b Why is he / she your hero?
c What is he / she going to do next?

Step 2 > WRITE

Write a first draft. Use your notes from Step 1 and the letters on this page to help you.

Step 3 > CHECK

Check your work. Try to include *too* and *also*.

Step 4 > WRITE

Write your final copy and hand in your work.

VOCABULARY IN PICTURES

Jobs

actor

architect

athlete

electrician

engineer

lifeguard

mechanic

nurse

police officer

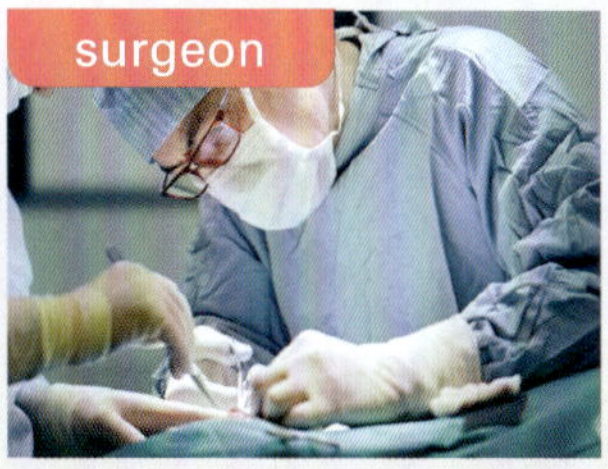
surgeon

teacher

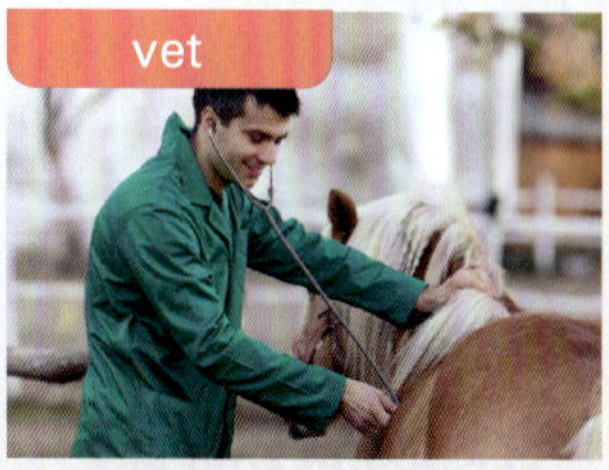
vet

Health Problems

broken arm

cold

cough

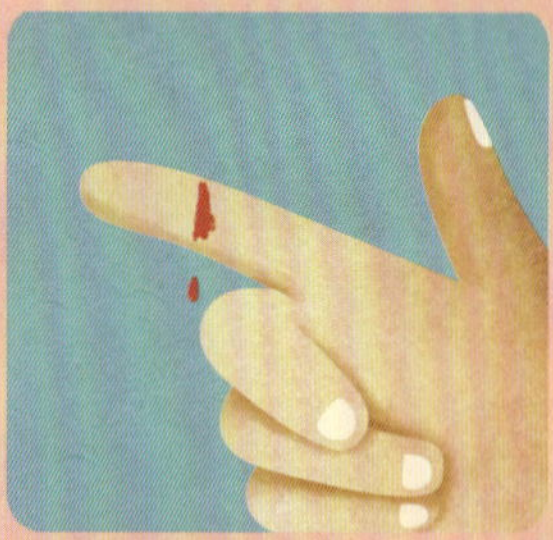
cut

earache

headache

insect bite

sick

sore throat

stomachache

temperature

GRAMMAR GUIDE

should

affirmative and negative		
+	I / You / He / She / It We / You / They	should go.
–	I / You / He / She / It We / You / They	shouldn't go.

questions and short answers	
Should I / you / go?	
Yes, I should.	No, I shouldn't.
Should he / she / it go?	
Yes, he should.	No, he shouldn't.
Should we / you / they go?	
Yes, we should.	No, we shouldn't.

- we use *should* and *shouldn't* to ask for and give advice and recommendations
  You **should** see the doctor.
  You **shouldn't** go to the party.
- the form is the same for all subject pronouns
  He **should** stop and rest.
  We **shouldn't** move.

✓ PROGRESS CHECK

Jobs

1 Identify the jobs.

a

m__________

b

p__________ o__________

c

a__________

d
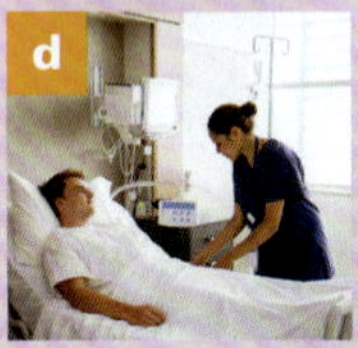
n__________

e

v__________

f

e__________

Health Problems

2 Match the symptoms with the cures.

a I have a sore throat.

b I have a temperature.

c He has a broken leg.

d I have a mosquito bite.

e I have a horrible cut.

☐ Here's some cream.
☐ Have a cough drop!
☐ Would you like a bandage?
☐ You should take an aspirin.
☐ You shouldn't move him.

should

3 Complete the sentences with *should* or *shouldn't*.

a I want to be an architect, but I'm not very good at drawing.

You __________ (✗) worry about drawing.
You __________ (✓) learn to use a drawing program on a computer.

b My sister wants to play soccer, but her friends say hockey is better.

She __________ (✓) listen to her friends.
She __________ (✗) play soccer.

c My friends are going to climb a mountain.

They __________ (✗) continue if they are tired. They __________ (✓) wear comfortable shoes.

d I have a headache and a temperature, but I want to meet my friends.

You __________ (✓) lie down. You __________ (✗) meet your friends.

Grammar Buildup 4

1 2 3 4 5 6 7 8

4 Complete the dialogue with the correct form of the verbs in parentheses.

Mom: You **a** __________ (look) awful. What **b** __________ (be) wrong?
Lou: I **c** __________ (run) home when I **d** __________ (fall).
Mom: Oh dear. **e** __________ it __________ (hurt)?
Lou: Yes, and I **f** ____________________ (play) soccer tomorrow. What should I **g** __________ (do)?
Mom: You should **h** __________ (put) some ice on it. Can you **i** __________ (move) it?
Lou: No, not really. It **j** __________ (feel) really painful.
Mom: Let's **k** __________ (call) the doctor.
Lou: OK. **l** __________ you __________ (have) the number?
Mom: Yes, here you go.
Lou: Thanks, Mom.

Review 2

VOCABULARY

GRAMMAR

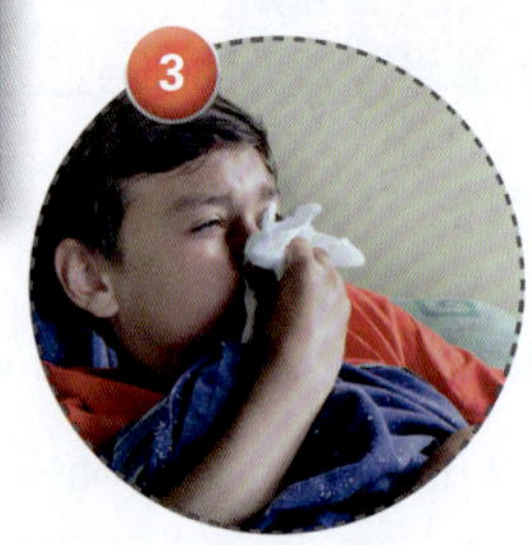

Across

3 I have a terrible ...! I have a headache, sore throat and temperature. I need to stay home today!

4 He ate too much. That's why he had a ... and couldn't go to school.

5 On ... days, use an umbrella.

7 Claire is going to take her dog Tom to the ... because he is sick.

9 A plastic ... should be prepared to operate on a patient's body.

10 A good ... should be prepared to save swimmers who are in danger.

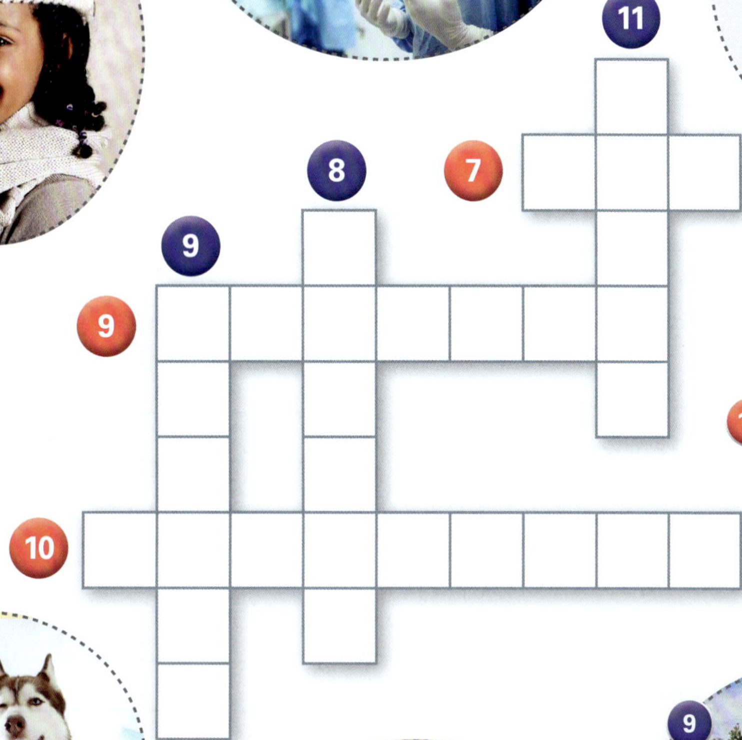

Down

1 A pain in your head is a ...

2 A ... is a warm piece of clothing that covers your upper body and arms.

3 I can hardly see the sun because the sky is ...

6 It's cold! You should wear this ... around your neck to avoid getting a sore throat.

8 He had a ... arm after he fell off his bike.

9 Let's enjoy the beautiful flowers of ..., my favorite season!

11 I usually wear a pair of ... and a white T-shirt.

Review 2

VOCABULARY | GRAMMAR

be going to

1 Write affirmative sentences with *be going to*.

my dad / arrive home late
My dad is going to arrive home late.

a we / live in Scotland
______

b my football team / win the game
______

c it / be cloudy
______

d they / wear sneakers
______

e I / study for my exams
______

f my classmates / have a party
______

2 Rewrite the sentences in the negative form.

I'm going to visit my grandmother.
I'm not going to visit my grandmother.

a They're going to read a book.
______

b Harry's going to dance at the school ball.
______

c We're going to have a terrible time.
______

d Eva's going to walk to school.
______

e You're going to call your cousin.
______

3 Complete the questions with *be going to* and the verbs in the box.

drink fly hit meet
~~play~~ sunbathe watch

Are you *going to play* basketball later?

a ______ your mom ______ orange juice for breakfast?

b ______ your friends ______ TV tonight?

c ______ your uncle ______ the airplane?

d ______ we ______ on the beach?

e ______ you ______ the ball?

f ______ I ______ you in front of the park?

4 Write short answers for the questions in activity 3.

✓ *Yes, I am.*

a ✗ ______

b ✗ ______

c ✓ ______

d ✓ ______

e ✓ ______

f ✗ ______

must / must not

5 Complete the sentences with *must* or *must not*.

You *must not* play basketball inside the classroom.

a We ______ speak English in our French class.

b I ______ do my homework every day.

c They ______ talk loudly in the library.

d Olympic athletes ______ train every day.

e You ______ take a shower before you enter the swimming pool.

f We ______ write on our desks.

should

6 Complete the sentences with *should* or *shouldn't*.

I feel tired and I have a headache. I think I *should* lie down.

- **a** Henry has a terrible stomachache. He ________ eat any more cake.
- **b** It's my friend's birthday. I ________ call her.
- **c** That old woman wants to cross the road. We ________ help her.
- **d** The party starts at 7:30pm. You ________ be late.
- **e** They use the laptop every day. They ________ sell it.
- **f** I can't understand you. You ________ speak more slowly.

7 Order the words to make questions.

I / a cream / use / Should ?
Should I use a cream?

- **a** study / my brother / Russian / Should ? ________
- **b** buy / Should / new speakers / I ? ________
- **c** we / fly / Should / to Galicia ? ________
- **d** money / they / Should / borrow ? ________
- **e** a surgeon / Rachel / be / Should ? ________
- **f** this water / Should / we / drink ? ________

8 Answer the questions in activity 7 according to the clues given.

I'm allergic.
No, I shouldn't.

- **a** He is passionate about languages. ________
- **b** My allowance money is all gone. ________
- **c** Tickets are at a super sale discount. ________
- **d** The interest rates are very low now. ________
- **e** She is scared of blood. ________
- **f** It looks a bit yellow. ________

9 Complete the how-to list using *should* or *shouldn't*.

BuzzFeed

News Testes Menu

What you *should* or *shouldn't* do when you hurt yourself while training

1. First of all, you **a** ________ panic! That can only make things worse. You **b** ________ take a deep breath and face the situation.
2. If you're on the street or at any unsafe place, you **c** ________ first check if you can walk to move to a safe place.
3. You **d** ________ ask for help to leave the unsafe spot in case you have any difficulties walking.
4. Don't try to move the injured body part on your own. You **e** ________ call your local emergency services.
5. After seeing the doctor, you **f** ________ follow their instructions carefully to heal soon!

Teens in the Tech World

- **What part does technology play in your life?**
- **Does it bring you more positive or negative things? How?**

1 Look at the picture on the right. Do you see yourself as being influenced positively or negatively by media and technology? Discuss with a classmate.

2 Media has a huge influence on teens' lives. Read and reflect on the sentences below and mark + for positive and – for negative.

a ☐ Teens can develop awareness about the world when exposed to various media outlets.

b ☐ Media can help teens make new friends from all parts of the world and be more communicative.

c ☐ Media may show a distorted body image, causing teens to want to achieve the 'perfect' body shape.

d ☐ Celebrities inspire teens and may motivate them to do good things, such as reading, eating right, etc.

e ☐ Spending too much time in front of a TV, cell phone or computer may lead to obesity.

f ☐ Video games help teens develop their coordination and motor skills.

3 Do you know the minimum age necessary to take part in any of the social media communities below? Why do you think there is a minimum age requirement?

____

____

4 Have you ever used the internet to help a cause? Check off (✓) if you have. Then give some more detail.

a ☐ Volunteered on a campaign. Which one?

____

____

b ☐ Helped a non-profit organization. How?

____

____

c ☐ Promoted an event to raise money for charity. What kind of event?

____

____

A Debate on Cyber Habits

You and a group of friends have decided to raise awareness about internet safety and solidarity in your school community. The idea is to generate a rich debate with students of all ages and school staff and, if possible, reach an agreement as to what practices could be avoided or encouraged in the school environment.

Doing

1 Decide which issues are most sensitive in your community. For example, cyber bullying, children safety on the web, privacy, cyber consumerism etc.

2 Divide the class into groups so that each group is responsible for researching information on one of the issues raised in step 1.

3 Organize the most relevant information about the issue discussed and write a few proposals, using the school community as the target audience. For example:

1. Create a school channel to report cyber bullying.

4 Share your ideas with the other groups and divide tasks in order to organize the debate with students from other grades and with school staff.

Presenting

5 One or more groups should be responsible for announcing the debate across all school communities, both online and also in posters to be hung on the school bulletin boards.

6 One or more groups should organize the debate, which involves deciding who are going to be the moderators, providing and setting up audio equipment, booking the room / auditorium / outdoor area and informing school staff and security.

7 If contradictory actions are proposed during the debate, the mediators should organize a voting system – for example, students and staff in favor of the proposal should raise their hands.

8 One or more groups should be responsible for writing down the **minutes** of the debate, that is, a document with the most important topics discussed and the decisions reached in common. Then the group(s) should make it public within the school community.

Reflecting

9 Did the school reach a conclusion that the internet can be used for good deeds? Why (not)?

10 What issues raised in the debate do you agree with the most?

11 What else can you use the experience from the debate for?

5 Ambitions

VOCABULARY 1

Life Events

1 Which of the words in the box describe the events in the pictures?

be born ☐	learn to drive ☐
buy a house ☐	leave home ☐
get a job ☐	leave school ☐
get married ☐	start school ☐
go to college ☐	train to be a... ☐
have children ☐	work ☐

2 🔊 41 Listen and repeat.

3 Complete the sentences with the correct form of the words in activity 1.

a I want to ______________ to study chemistry when I am 18.

b I ______________ when I was five years old.

c In the US, you can ______________ a car when you're 16.

d My dad ______________ in a hospital in Minneapolis in 1962.

e My aunt ______________ two ______________. Their names are Sara and Tarik.

> **TIP**
> The word *ambition* is used to talk about plans, aspirations and desires, and not only about things that we really want and are difficult to achieve.

4 Based on the sentences in activity 3, write about your story and your plans.

____

____

____

____

____

READING 1

1 Read the sentences. Then write T for *true* or F for *false*.

a ☐ British boys leave home later than girls.
b ☐ People get married younger in Spain than in Portugal.
c ☐ The Chinese have more children than people in the USA.
d ☐ The Swedes live longer than Americans.

2 42 Read the statistics, listen and check your answers.

Know Your Future

Don't read your horoscope, but instead look at the demographics for your country if you want to know your future. Demographics can tell you, for example, that if you are born in Japan, you'll probably have one child and live until you are 83. They are statistics about real people in real places, and they can be fun. Here are some more…

Leaving Home
If you're a Finnish girl, you'll probably leave home when you're about 21. The average Finnish boy won't leave home until he's nearly 23. In Spain and Portugal, a girl will leave home at about 27, but a boy won't leave until he's nearly 30. In the UK, the average girl will leave home at 23 and a boy at 25.

Getting Married
A person born in Bolivia, Portugal or the USA will get married for the first time at about 23 or 24 years old. In the UK, Spain or Japan, you'll be 29. If you want to wait, go to Finland, France or Germany – they get married at 30.

Having Children
In the USA, you'll probably have two children. But the math is more complicated in other countries. In the UK and China, a family will have 1.8 children, but in Spain they'll have 1.4 – the same as in Portugal. Do you want more? Go to Bolivia, where the average family has 3.4 children.

Age
How long will you live? Iceland is a good place to live as you'll probably live to around 82. This is similar to Sweden (81) and better than the USA (78), Turkey (72) or Russia (67).

3 Scan the text and answer the questions.

a What do demographics tell you about living in Japan?
____
b How old are Finnish girls when they leave home?
____
c In which countries do people get married at 30?
____
d How many children does the average American have?
____
e Which country has the most children per family?
____
f According to the text, is Sweden a good place to live? Why?
____

READING STRATEGY

There are many words that end in *-ics* in English. Noticing some suffix patterns can help you predict meanings and better understand some texts. For example, do you think these words are nouns, adjectives or adverbs?

____

demographics statistics mathematics

4 Look at the words in the box. How do you say them in your language?

aerobics computer graphics
economics physics politics

5 CLASS VOTE Look at the demographics in the text. Which country would you like to live in?

GRAMMAR 1

will / won't

1 Read the following sentences. Underline the verbs in the affirmative form and circle those in the negative form.

- **a** In Finland, the average girl will leave home at 21.
- **b** The average British boy won't leave home until he's 25.
- **c** In the USA, you'll probably have two children.
- **d** In China, people won't have many children.

2 Use the words in the box to complete the chart.

'll   will (x2)   won't (x2)

affirmative	negative
I / You _______ get married soon.	I / You _______ have children.
He / She / It _______ live to around 84.	He / She / It won't get married.
We / You / They _______ leave home at an older age.	We / You / They _______ live long.

3 Look at the sentences in the chart and check (✓) the rules for the use of *will / won't*.

- **a** ☐ *will / won't* are used to express past ideas.
- **b** ☐ *will / won't* are followed by the base form of the main verb.
- **c** ☐ The short form of *will* is *'ll* and the short form of *will not* is *won't*.

4 Write complete sentences. Use *will* (✓) and *won't* (✗).

a I / learn to drive / at 17. (✗)

____

____

b He / leave home / at 18. (✓)

____

____

c They / have two children. (✗)

____

____

d We / buy / a small house. (✓)

____

____

5 Complete the post with *will* and *won't* and the verbs in the box.

be   not get   go   leave
study   train   travel

Aisha Murray

I think I **a** _______ home when I'm 18 years old. I think I **b** _______ to college. I **c** _______ history, but I **d** _______ a job immediately. I think I **e** _______ around the world and when I get back I **f** _______ to be a teacher. I think I **g** _______ very adventurous!

3 likes   Comments   Share

March 1 at 8:20pm

TIP

When we make predictions, we often use time expressions like *soon, tomorrow* and *next month*. We also use phrases with *when*:
I'll work in education when I'm older.

6 Complete the sentences so they are true for you.

- **a** I hope we'll _______ tomorrow.
- **b** I won't _______ when I'm 16.
- **c** I think I'll _______ next summer.
- **d** We'll _______ one day soon.
- **e** We won't _______ this weekend.

7 Read the information below and complete the chart.

a Use *will* before the subject in questions.

b For short answers, use *will* in the affirmative form and *won't* in the negative form.

questions and short answers	
________ I / you leave home at 24?	
Yes, I / you ________.	No, I / you ________.
________ he / she / it be here soon?	
Yes, he / she / it ________.	
No, he / she / it ________.	
________ we / you / they get married next month?	
Yes, we / you / they ________.	
No, we / you / they ________.	

8 Write complete questions. Use *will.*

your family / always / live / in the same house?
Will your family always live in the same house?

a you / study / to be a vet / at college?
____

b you / have / good job / one day?
____

c your friend / play basketball / tomorrow?
____

d everybody / buy / cars?
____

PRONUNCIATION

will ('ll)

1 43 Listen to the sentences. Do you hear 1 or 2?

a **1** I go to college. **2** I'll go to college.

b **1** I have two children. **2** I'll have two children.

2 43 Listen again and repeat.

9 INTERFACE Work in pairs. Make predictions about your future using the ideas in the box.

drive a vintage car | get married | go to college | travel the world

What will you do?

I think I'll go to college.

GRAMMAR GUIDE page 88

LISTENING

Ambitions

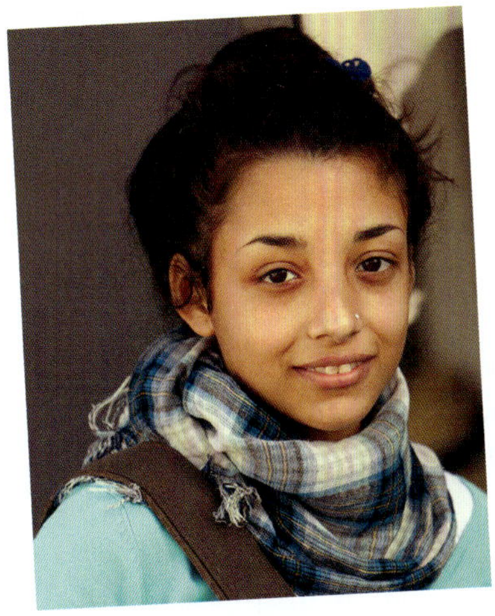

1 44 Grace and Benjamin are 13 years old and they're talking about their future. Listen and complete their ambitions with a phrase in the box.

big car | dentist | DJ | get married at 21 | India | the world

Grace

a I'll work as a ________.

b I think I'll work in ________.

c One day I'll travel ________.

Benjamin

d I'll be a ________.

e I'll buy a ________.

f I'll get married ________.

2 45 Listen to Grace and Benjamin aged 29. How many of their ambitions came true?

____
____
____
____

3 45 Listen again and answer the questions.

a What did Grace study at college?
____

b Which country does Grace frequently travel to?
____

c What is Benjamin's job?
____

d How many children does Benjamin have?
____

SPEAKING

Future Plans

46 Lou and Maggie are talking about what to do after they finish high school. Listen and complete the dialogue.

Tell me Maggie, what do you **a** __________ when you finish high school?

I don't know yet. I think **b** __________ to college. I want to **c** __________. How about you?

Well, that'll be five years from now... If I don't change my mind, **d** __________ a gap year.

A gap year? What for?

Well, I think **e** __________ an excellent way to grow personally. If I take a gap year, I'll **f** __________ abroad. It'll be a great opportunity to learn about the real world and to contribute in a community in need.

That sounds nice, but **g** __________ this is for me. I want to be at college five years from now. **h** __________live in another city, have some independence.

Well, you **i** __________ to find a job in that case.

Yeah, I know...

Well, then, how about a summer job to start saving money?

Good idea for next summer! I'm in!

FUNCTIONAL LANGUAGE

Talking about the Future

What do you want to do when you finish high school?

Five years from now, I'll...

I want to...

I think I'll...

I'll probably...

Speaking Task

Write a dialogue between you and a friend.

Step 1

First, think about things you want to do in five or six years' time. You can use the ideas below or your own.

go to college

learn to drive

study abroad

Step 2

Think about what to ask your friend and what you want to do.

What do you want to do... ?
Five years from now, I'll... / I want to...
I think I'll...
I'll probably...

Think about what your friend is going to say.

I don't know. I think I'll...
That sounds nice.
That's a good idea.

Step 3

Work with a partner. Write your dialogue. Follow the conversation above as a guide.

Step 4

Take turns practicing your dialogue.

CULTURE

Three Great Career Fields in the US

Lots of people face disappointment when job hunting. There is a lot of competition and little job growth in many fields. Taking that into consideration, what jobs can young Americans look for in the years to come? That question can be difficult to answer. You need to consider the best potential for job growth, pay, stress level, job satisfaction, among other factors. Three of the most prominent fields are:

Medical Field:
In this area, nurses are in demand. Nurse practitioners can perform some of the functions of a doctor, such as prescribing medicine and treating illnesses. Physician assistants are also climbing in America. They conduct physical exams, prescribe medicine and treat illnesses. And their pay is quite high!

Technology Sector:
This is a fast-growing field. Information technology is the #1 field in terms of expected job growth over the next decade, which makes systems engineers among the most in-demand professionals today.

Financial Services:
Many American companies are putting an end to their pension plans and employees will need help with retirement planning. Therefore, jobs in accounting are expected to grow over the next decade. As technology and business evolve quickly, new careers will come and go just as fast. So Americans understand how important it is to choose a career field that will be in high demand for the future ahead.

1 47 Read and listen. Then match.

a Americans will take into consideration the best potential for job growth, pay, stress level and job satisfaction…

b Nursing careers will be in demand…

c The #1 field in terms of expected growth…

d Accounting will be on the rise…

☐ … because employees will need help with retirement planning.

☐ … because of the need for professionals in the area who can prescribe medicine and treat illnesses.

☐ … when looking for a job in the future.

☐ … is the technology sector.

2 Which careers are on the rise in your country? Talk to some experts / family members about it.

____

____

3 Which of these areas interests you? Why? Share your ideas with your class.

____

____

VOCABULARY 2

Musical Instruments

1 Match the words in the box to the pictures.

acoustic guitar ☐ drums ☐
electric bass ☐ electric guitar ☐
flute ☐ keyboards ☐
percussion ☐ piano ☐
saxophone ☐ trumpet ☐ violin ☐

1

2

3

4

5

6

7

8

9

10

11

2 🔊 48 Listen and repeat.

3 Look at the picture and complete the sentences with words from activity 1.

a Nick plays ______________.
b Chelsea plays ______________.
c Pete plays ______________.
d Louie plays ______________.
e Liz sings and plays ______________.

READING 2

1 Skim the text below. What genre does it illustrate?

a a magazine article.
b an advice column.

2 🔊 49 Read and listen to the text and answer the questions.

a What is the minimum number of people in the band? ______________
b How often should you practice your songs? ______________
c What can make you different from other bands? ______________

I really want to be in a band but I have no idea where to start. Many friends have their own bands and I feel embarrassed to ask them. What should I do?

Bandless Musician

Dear Bandless Musician, if you want to be in a successful band, you'll need at least one singer and three friends to play the guitar, the drums and the keyboards or electric bass. It's important to practice every day. If you don't practice, you'll sound terrible and people won't like your music or buy your songs.
Your look is important, too. If you want to be famous, you'll need an image to make you different. If people don't recognize your image as well as your music, they won't remember you immediately. If you have a unique image, your fans will love you. They'll buy your songs, they'll go to your concerts and… congratulations! You will be the next big thing!

GRAMMAR 2

First Conditional

1 Read the sentences below. Underline the *if clause* and circle the *consequence.*

a If you want to be a successful band, you'll need at least one singer.
b If you don't practice, you'll sound terrible.
c You'll need an image to make you different if you want to become famous.
d Your fans will love you if you have a unique image.

2 Look at the sentences in activity 1. Choose the correct words to complete the rules for the use of the first conditional.

a We form the first conditional with *if* + **simple past** / **simple present**, *will* / *won't* + main verb in the base form.
b We use the first conditional to talk about possibilities in the **past** / **future**.
c Use a comma when the *if* clause is at **the beginning of the sentence** / **the end of the sentence**.

3 Now complete the charts with the words provided.

don't like 'll be sings won't sell

if clause	consequence
If people ___________ your image,	they won't buy your songs.
If you practice,	you'___________ a good singer.

consequence	*if* clause
You ___________ anything	if you aren't a good singer.
The singer will become famous	if he ___________ well.

4 Match the two parts to make sentences.

a If you study music every day,
b I will buy their new album
c If I don't have enough money for a guitar,
d We'll all cry tears of joy
e You won't learn any new songs
f If I say that dinner's ready,

☐ if he wins the singing contest.
☐ if you don't practice.
☐ you'll learn to play an instrument.
☐ he'll stop playing his guitar.
☐ if I have enough money.
☐ I will borrow one.

5 Write complete sentences.

If I learn German, I / be able to / work / in Switzerland.
If I learn German, I'll be able to work in Switzerland.

a He'll borrow a minibus if / he / want / to travel across the US.
____
b If you practice regularly, you / play / really well.
____
c If a group has a strong image, some of their fans / probably / copy it.
____
____
d If you share it with friends, you / enjoy / the music more.
____

6 Complete the sentences with the correct form of the verbs in parentheses.

a If you ___________ (come) to my house later, my dad ___________ (cook) us pasta.
b If I ___________ (not clean up) my room, my mom ___________ (not buy) that new computer game.
c He ___________ (not be) able to play basketball if he ___________ (arrive) late.
d If she ___________ (not arrive) before 9pm, we ___________ (go) to the concert without her.

7 Complete the sentences using your own ideas.

a If it rains on the weekend, ___________
b If I go to college, ___________
c I will visit my friends if ___________

8 INTERFACE Work in pairs. Compare your answers to activity 7.

What will you do if it rains on the weekend?

If it rains on the weekend, I'll stay home reading *The Lord of the Rings.*

GRAMMAR GUIDE page 88

CLIL

ICT

1 🔊 50 Read and listen. What do you think a dot-com company is?

___

Dot-com Companies

Silicon Valley is south of San Francisco. It's home to many large technology companies such as Apple and Hewlett-Packard, and also many dot-com companies. These are companies like Google, Facebook and eBay, which operate mainly over the internet.

But where did the dot-com company come from?

In 1985, the World Wide Web was first introduced to the world. A company called Symbolics became the first company to register its address, or URL, on the web. Today, there are 200 million websites in existence, and one domain is registered every three minutes in the UK alone. But it took a long time for the internet to become the phenomenon it is today. It was when Sir Tim Berners-Lee put up the first website in 1990 (info.cern.ch), that the internet took off.

During the 1990s, there was a dot-com boom. Many people became rich because of the World Wide Web. In 1998, PhD students Larry Page and Sergey Brin invented Google. These days, this search engine is the world's most recognizable brand and, in 2011, it was valued at $192 billion.

2 Find four ICT companies in the word search.

O	E	O	G	D	G	L	A
Y	W	W	L	O	O	F	P
F	A	C	E	B	O	O	K
A	P	S	U	M	G	F	L
C	P	G	A	P	L	L	F
E	L	O	O	G	E	B	A
R	E	R	E	B	A	Y	C

___

3 Choose the correct answers.

a What does 'www' mean?
  1 World Wide Web
  2 World World Website
  3 We Work WorldWide

b What is a URL?
  1 a computer virus
  2 a web page address
  3 an email address

c Which of these is not an internet browser?
  1 Internet Explorer
  2 Google Chrome
  3 Amazon

d What 'language' do you use to create a web page?
  1 HTML
  2 URL
  3 HTTP

VOCABULARY IN PICTURES

Life Events

be born

buy a house

get a job

get married

go to college

have children

learn to drive

leave home

leave school

start school

train to be a...

work

Musical Instruments

acoustic guitar

drums

electric bass

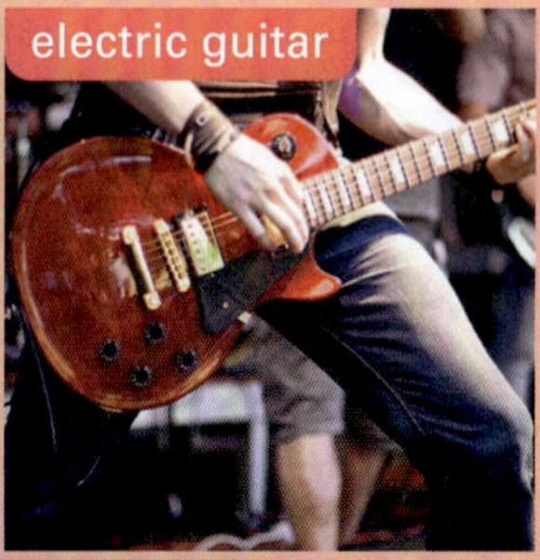
electric guitar

flute

keyboards

percussion

piano

saxophone

trumpet

violin

GRAMMAR GUIDE

will / won't

affirmative	
I / You / He / She / It / We / You / They	will have

negative	
I / You / He / She / It / We / You / They	will not (won't) have

- we use *will / won't* + the infinitive without *to* to make predictions
  I **will** have a lot of children.
  She **won't** live in Australia.
- we often use the expressions *I think, I expect, I guess* to introduce predictions
  He thinks he'**ll** be famous.
  I expect they'**ll** get married.
- *can* is never used with *will / won't*. To talk about ability in the future, use *will / won't* + *be able to*
  He'**ll be able to** learn French in Canada.
- we often use these time expressions with *will*: *one day, one day soon, soon, tomorrow, next year, when I'm older, when I finish school*
  I'**ll** buy a car **when I'm 20**.
  He'**ll** go to college **next year**.

questions and short answers	
Will I / you / he / she / it / we / you / they go?	
Yes, they will.	No, they won't.

- the word order is different in questions
  He **will** be a famous football player.
  Will he be a famous football player?
- we don't repeat the infinitive in short answers
  Will we buy a big house?
  Yes, we **will**.

First Conditional

situation	consequence
If I eat all the food,	I'll feel sick.
If she passes the exam,	she'll go to college.

consequence	situation
He won't eat popcorn	if he goes to the movies.
They will be happy	if they pass the driver's test.

- we use the first conditional to talk about possible situations and their consequences
- to form first conditional sentences we use *if* + subject + present simple (for the situation), subject + *will / won't* + infinitive without *to* (for the consequence)
- if the situation comes first, we need a comma
  If you practice, you'll get better.
- we don't use a comma if the consequence comes first
  I will be happy **if I pass** my exams.

PROGRESS CHECK

Life Events

1 Identify the life events.

1
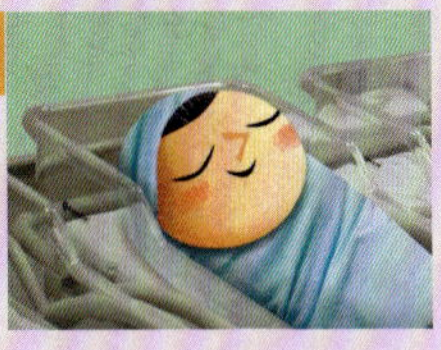

b__ b____

2

s_____
s______

3

g__
m__ri__

4

g__ a j__

5

l____
t_ d___e

6

l____
h___

Musical Instruments

2 Order the letters to write musical instruments.

a oxophsaen ____________
b mudrs ____________
c tufle ____________
d nliivo ____________
e spsrcneuoi ____________
f cusaitco tgiura ____________
g tpmtreu ____________
h ybrkedosa ____________

will / won't

3 Complete the sentences with *will / won't*.

In 2030 …

a more people __________ (be) older than 65.
b I __________ (have) a good job.
c we__________ (use) only computers to study.
d more people __________ (not get) married.
e I __________ (not drive) a car, but I __________ (ride) a bike to work.
f The population of the world __________ (be) 9 billion.

4 Order the words to make questions.

a you / when you're older / Will / live abroad
____
b go to college / when you are 18 / you / Will
____
c you / one day / train / Will / to be a doctor
____

First Conditional

5 Write complete sentences.

a If / he / want / to be an actor / he / go / to drama school.
____
b If / he / go / to drama school / they / teach him to speak clearly.
____
____
c He / live / in Hollywood / if / he / become / a successful actor.
____

Grammar Buildup 5

1 2 3 4 5 6 7 8

6 Complete the dialogue. Use the correct form of the verbs in parentheses.

Dad What **a** ________ you ________ (look) at?
Lizie I **b** ________ (think) about my future and I **c** ________ (not be) sure what subjects to choose.
Dad Oh! What **d** ________ (be) the options?
Lizie I **e** ________ (look) at the options right now. All my friends **f** ________ (go) to do biology and chemistry.
Dad Well, what do you want to do in the future?
Lizie That's the problem. I **g** ________ (want) to work with animals two years ago. Now I think I **h** ________ (work) with people.
Dad If you **i** ________ (write) a list of your favorite subjects, you **j** ________ (know) which subjects to do.
Lizie Thanks a lot, Dad. That's a really good idea.

6 On Screen

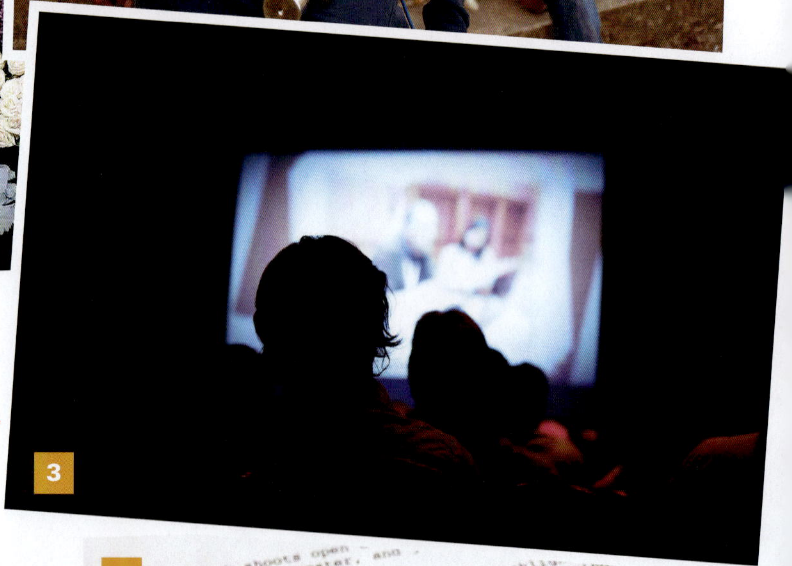

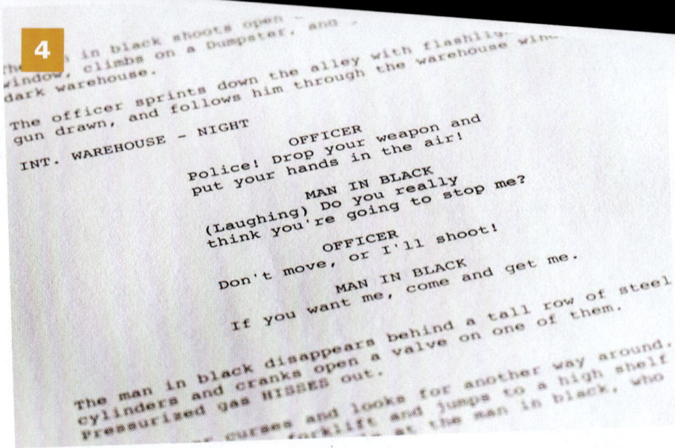

VOCABULARY 1

Movies

1 Look at the words in the box. Which words can you use to describe the pictures?

director ☐	script ☐
film a scene ☐	soundtrack ☐
movie star ☐	special effects ☐
plot ☐	star in a movie ☐
producer ☐	stunt ☐
release a movie ☐	stunt man / woman / double ☐
screen ☐	win an award ☐

2 🔊 51 Listen and repeat.

3 Complete the chart with the words in activity 1.

people	verbs related to movies	other movie words
director	*star in a movie*	*stunt*
________	________	________
________	________	________
________	________	________
________	________	________
________	________	________

4 Complete the sentences with the correct form of the words and phrases in activity 1.

The *director* wants to film the action scenes tomorrow.

a The ________ is wonderful – the dialogue is great.

b The music is great, too – I love the ________.

c Lupita Nyong'o ________ in the film. I hope she wins an ________ at the next Oscars.

d A ________ does all the dangerous scenes in a movie instead of the actor.

e The ________ in that science-fiction movie are wonderful. They look really realistic.

READING 1

1 52 Skim the news article. Then match predictions a-e with paragraphs 1-5.

a ☐ All movies will be 3D.
b ☐ People will stop watching movies.
c ☐ There won't be any actors in the future.
d ☐ Movies will be interactive.
e ☐ There will be 4D movie theaters.

READING STRATEGY

Look at the layout, the title and the pictures of the text in order to make some predictions about it.

The Future of Movies

What will movies and movie theaters be like in the future? Here are our answers to your predictions!

1 Ever since the release of the extremely popular *Avatar* in 2009, 3D movies have become more and more common.
In 2011, there were more than 60 3D movies released, and producers are planning many more for the next few years.
In fact, some directors, such as James Cameron and Steven Spielberg, are re-releasing 3D versions of some of their best known old movies, too. For example, you can now see classics like *Titanic*, *Indiana Jones* and *Top Gun* in 3D. The famous director Martin Scorsese released his very first 3D movie in 2011 – the film was called *Hugo*, and it won 5 Academy Awards. Today, 3D movies are so popular that many people even have special 3D televisions so they can enjoy these special effects at home as well as at the movie theater.

2 There are already interactive TV shows on the internet. You can choose what happens, help to write the dialogue and plot and even appear in a show! Will movies ever be interactive? Who knows!

3 Will computer-generated images of actors replace human actors? Computer programmers can create action scenes using digital actors – they are so realistic that audiences don't realize they aren't human. This new technology is very expensive, so movie-makers have decided that they are only going to use it to film dangerous stunts and to re-film some scenes. They are not going to stop using real actors, so we'll definitely have human actors for many more years!

4 Companies have already tried extra special effects inside the movie theater, such as smells and moving chairs, without much success. People are more interested in realistic special effects on screen. Producers are investing a lot of money to create better special effects. For this reason, the special effects are going to get more exciting and realistic – but movie theaters themselves probably won't change much.

5 Since the first movie in 1895, people have loved cinema. Audiences everywhere enjoy good stories and they want entertainment. Movie technology will change and perhaps we'll all watch hologram movies in a few years. But one thing is certain, people definitely won't stop watching movies!

2 Read the text again and choose the correct answers.

a In the future, human actors will …
  1 disappear. 2 still exist.
b There are … more 3D movies now compared to a year ago.
  1 many 2 a few
c Interactive movies …
  1 already exist. 2 are only a possibility.
d In the future, movie theaters will …
  1 be similar to now. 2 be very different.
e People … movies now.
  1 still enjoy 2 prefer holograms to

3 Find words in the text that mean …

a well-known movies (paragraph 1) ____________
b people who watch the movie (paragraph 3) ____________
c odors (paragraph 4) ____________
d lifelike (paragraph 4) ____________
e performances that people enjoy (paragraph 5) ____________

CULTURAL FACT

In the past, people used the word *actor* for men and *actress* for women.
Now, we usually say *actor* for men and women. What about in your country?

GRAMMAR 1

Future Tense: *will*

1 Read the sentences and complete the chart below.

a Most movies will probably be 3D.
b We'll definitely have human actors for many years.
c Movie theaters themselves probably won't change much.
d People definitely won't stop watching movies.
e Special effects will be much more advanced, according to experts.

will / won't
Make predictions about the future __________ __________
When you are sure about something in the future __________ __________
If you think something is likely to happen __________ __________

2 What will movie theaters be like in the future? Complete the sentences with the correct form of *will* and the verbs in parentheses.

In the future, technology a __________ (do away) with the old-school movie screen. Movies b __________ (not be) events to see at the movie theater during two hours. Instead, they c __________ (be) gamified and d __________ (unfold) in real time around you. You e __________ (literally / become) part of the action. Events f __________ (change) as you 'act,' and smells, tastes and sensations g __________ (be) experienced live. Actors h __________ (be) your own avatars and you i __________ (turn into) a star! What about all those movie stars? What j __________ (they / do)?

3 Choose the most appropriate verb form to fill in the blanks in the sentences below.

a In the future, there __________ lots of programs to create special effects.
☐ be ☐ will be ☐ will

b I don't think Spielberg __________ that movie.
☐ won't ☐ 'll ☐ will direct

c How many people __________ movies on DVD in ten years' time?
☐ will watch ☐ watch ☐ won't

d __________ a CD of the soundtrack?
☐ They will release ☐ Will they release
☐ They won't release

e I think that movie __________ a lot of awards.
☐ will win ☐ win ☐ will

Future Tense: *be going to*

4 Read the sentences below and write (A) if they talk about future plans and intentions or (B) if there is evidence in the present for future events or actions.

a ☐ James Cameron is going to release 3D versions of some old movies.
b ☐ Those actors are really good. They aren't going to be fired.
c ☐ The director is going to use stunt doubles for that scene. The actors may get hurt if they shoot it.
d ☐ Meryl Streep is going to take a break after that movie.

5 What was used to indicate the future events in activity 4?

____

6 Use the words below to complete the chart.

Are they going to | aren't going to use | is going to

	be going to
+	Spielberg __________ release a new movie.
–	Movie makers __________ new technology so much.
?	__________ use stunt doubles instead of actors for that scene?

7 Match 1-5 with a-e to make sentences.

a ☐ The director has asked for silence because
b ☐ They are not going to do the stunts
c ☐ He has earned so much money
d ☐ I lost my purse last week so
e ☐ Are you going to book the seats at the movie theater

1 I'm going to buy another one.
2 filming is going to start.
3 before next Thursday?
4 because they think they are too dangerous.
5 that he is going to retire now.

8 Complete the sentences with the correct form of the verbs in the box. Use *be going to.*

download give invite leave (not) ask travel

a I love that song! I ________________ it to my phone right now.
b ________________ around the world during her gap year before university.
c They ________________ her to sing because she has a terrible voice.
d Jim ________________ because he didn't get the new job.
e ________________ you ________________ me your homework before tomorrow?
f I ________________ Paul to my birthday party.

9 Choose the correct words.

a In the future, I think people **will live / are going to live** in space.
b I don't think that I **will learn / am going to learn** Chinese in the future.
c I **will meet / am going to meet** my friends on the weekend.
d In my opinion, that movie **won't / isn't going to** win an award.
e What **will you do / are you going to do** after school today?

PRONUNCIATION

Sentence Stress and Weak Forms

1 53 Listen and repeat the sentences. Which two syllables have the main stress in each sentence? What happens to the words in bold?
a I'm **going to** download that song.
b We're **going to** invite **them** to the party.
c They aren't **going to** buy a house.

2 53 Listen and repeat the sentences.

GRAMMAR GUIDE page 102

LISTENING

3D Movies

1 Look at the picture below. What 3D movies have you seen?

2 INTERFACE Work in pairs. Ask and answer the questions.

Have you seen any 3D movies? Which ones? Did you like them?

Yes, I have. I've seen *Avatar* and *Alice in Wonderland.* They were great!

3 What do you know about 3D movies? Do you think the statements are true or false?

a ☐ 3D technology first appeared in 1994.
b ☐ In 3D movies, two images are combined into one image to create a sensation of depth.
c ☐ The first 3D movies were for children.
d ☐ The movie *Monster House* came out in 2007.
e ☐ The movie *Beowulf* was the second 3D movie for adults.
f ☐ Next year, at least 15 3D movies are going to be released.
g ☐ Jane thinks that one day we'll be able to watch 3D movies without glasses.
h ☐ Jane believes TVs that can show 3D movies will never be cheap.

4 54 Listen and check your answers.

SPEAKING

3D Movies Are Awesome!

55 Dan and Rita are talking about 3D movies. Listen and complete the dialogue.

Rita, what a ____________ next Saturday afternoon?

Well, I b ____________ to the movies. Do you want to come?

Good idea! What are you c ____________?

In fact, I'm planning to go for *Star Wars: the Last Jedi* in 3D.

You love d ____________, don't you?

Yeah, you know, I love sci-fi, fantasy, adventures in galaxies... As for *Star Wars*, I've read e ____________ quite a bit of focus on Luke Skywalker... we f ____________ to see Rey wielding a lightsaber and we g ____________ something in our eyes when Princess Leia shows up.

It sounds awesome!

3D movies are the most spectacular way to enjoy some big-screen thrills, in my opinion. That's why I like them!

The only problem is that tickets for h ____________ are a bit expensive...

I know, but some of these i ____________ are worth watching anyway!

FUNCTIONAL LANGUAGE

Talking about Going to the Movies

What are you doing ...?
You like ..., don't you?
I love ...
What are you going to watch? What do you want to see?

Speaking Task

Write a dialogue between you and a friend.

Step 1

What kind of movies do you like? Choose one of your favorite movies to talk about.

Step 2

Ask your friend about movies he or she would like to watch.

Would you like to go to the movies?
What about watching ...?
What are you doing ...?
What are you going to watch?

Think about what your friend is going to say.

I don't know. I think I'll ...
I like ...
I'd love to see ...
I'm planning ...
I'd like to see ...
I'll probably ...

Step 3

Work with a partner. Write your dialogue. Follow the conversation above as a guide.

Step 4

Take turns practicing your dialogue.

CULTURE

Steven Spielberg

Steven Allan Spielberg is one of the finest Hollywood directors in the history of the movie industry and also one of the founding pioneers of the new Hollywood era. He has directed many popular and significant movies in the recent Hollywood history, such as *E.T. the Extra-Terrestrial*, *Jurassic Park*, *Close Encounters of the Third Kind*, *Schindler's List* and *Saving Private Ryan*. In a career spanning more than four decades, Spielberg's movies have covered many themes and genres (science fiction, action-adventure and high drama). Is he thinking about retiring? No way! Spielberg likes to stay busy. He is either planning his next step as an iconic moviemaker, thinking about the next massive blockbuster, or producing something we'll probably watch and enjoy immensely.

Right now, he is developing a new feature-movie adaptation of the classic musical *West Side Story*. However, he announced that *Indiana Jones 5* has been added to his production schedule, with Harrison Ford returning for one more adventure in the title role. He is going to start shooting it in 2019 for a 2020 release.

1 🔊 56 Read and listen to the information about Steven Spielberg and complete the chart.

Steven Spielberg	
Job	
Famous movies	
Movie genres	
Plans for the future	

2 Think of a famous person in the movie industry in your country (a director, an actor, etc.) and fill in the chart below.

Name:	
Job	
Famous movies	
Movie genres	
Plans for the future	

VOCABULARY 2

Suffixes *-ion* and *-ment*

1 Complete the chart with the verbs in the box. Then make the verbs into nouns by adding the suffixes *-ion* or *-ment*.

advertise argue compete connect decorate develop educate enjoy equip excite inform possess predict suggest

verbs	nouns
compete	*competition*
advertise	*advertisement*

2 🔊 57 Listen and repeat.

3 Complete the sentences with nouns from activity 1.

I don't know what to write in the script. Do you have a good *suggestion*?

a You need a lot of e________ to make a movie.

b What is the c________ between these two things?

c I think e________ is important. I want to get a good job, so I study a lot.

d Can you send me some i________ about the movie course?

e I get a lot of e________ from reading – I love it!

4 Complete the questions with nouns from activity 1.

What's your favorite *possession*?

a What's the funniest __________ on TV in your opinion?

b Do you put up __________ at Christmas?

c When was the last time you had an __________? Why did you argue?

d Do you need any special __________ to go camping?

5 INTERFACE Work in pairs. Ask and answer the questions in activity 4.

What's your favorite possession?

My favorite possession is a T-shirt with Brad Pitt's autograph on it.

TIP

Use your dictionary to find out how the suffix *-less* changes the meaning of these nouns: *use, help, job, home.*

READING 2

1 Skim the advertisement. Then choose the correct words.

a Fresh Films has a competition for **teenagers** / **directors**.

b The winners make a movie with **new actors** / **Hollywood stars**.

Make a Movie in Hollywood!

Many teenagers only dream of making a movie or becoming the next big name in Hollywood. Fresh Films gives some of them the opportunity to do exactly that! Fresh Films is opening a movie-making competition soon. This film school is giving those teens the training, equipment and connections to make their dreams come true. They are inviting talented teens to spend a week in Hollywood in December.

The competition is open to anyone aged 13-18. All you have to do is explain why the organizers should choose you. If they choose you, you'll spend a week in Hollywood and you'll produce, film and edit movies with real Hollywood movie stars! This year, *Lost* star Dominic Monaghan and Bobb'e J. Thompson (from *30 Rock*) are just two of the actors you could work with.

Sixteen-year-old Gina has always wanted to be a movie-maker and she is registering for the competition tomorrow. "If I am successful, I'll get to work with professionals. It's a fantastic opportunity! I really want to go to film school, but my parents want me to go to college. They'll let me go to film school if I win, I'm sure."

Since it started in 2002, Fresh Films has produced over 80 movies and shown movies at over 20 festivals. Some of the past winners now have careers in movies.

So, what are you waiting for?
There's still time to apply!
You never know, you could soon be on your way to Hollywood!

2 🔊 58 Read and listen. Check your answers.

3 Read the text again. Then write T for *true* or F for *false*. Correct the false sentences.

a ☐ This is the first year Fresh Films has organized the competition.

____

____

b ☐ Dominic Monaghan will appear in a film made by the winners this year.

____

____

c ☐ Gina's parents think she should go to college, not to film school.

____

____

d ☐ All of the movies made by teenagers have been in movie festivals.

____

____

GRAMMAR 2

Review: Present Progressive for Future Arrangements

1 Read the following sentences. Underline the verb and circle the time expression.

a Fresh Films is opening a movie-making competition soon.

b They are inviting talented teens to spend a week in Hollywood in December.

c This film school is giving those teens the training, equipment and connections to make their dreams come true.

d Sixteen-year-old Gina is registering for the competition tomorrow.

2 Complete the rules for the use of the present progressive for future arrangements. Use the words in the box.

always | future arrangements | It is not | organization | plan

a An arrangement is a _______________ decided between two people, or a person and a group of people, an _______________ or company.

b _______________ necessary to state who the arrangement is with.

c Time expressions are often (but not _______________) used when the present progressive is used to talk about _______________.

3 Complete the sentences with the correct form of the words in parentheses. Use the present progressive.

a Tomorrow I __________ (travel) to the festival by train.

b __________ you __________ (give) me a lift to the station?

c My friend Alex __________ (meet) me at 11am.

d I __________ (not take) the 10am train.

e __________ we __________ (eat) before I leave?

4 Complete the sentences with the verbs in parentheses in the present progressive.

Singaporeans a __________ (take part) in movie-making activities by the end of the month. Who b __________ (encourage) them to make movies? The Chinese clan! The competition co-chairman c __________ (expect) lots of entries. The Singapore-born, new citizens and residents d __________ (make) movies that are no longer than 10 minutes. They e __________ (not film) with professional cameras; they f __________ (use) a smartphone – that's all they need. Those Singaporeans who only speak English are invited, too!

5 INTERFACE Work in pairs. Ask and answer questions about your plans for the weekend. Ask about Friday night, Saturday morning and Saturday night.

Are you doing anything on Saturday morning?

GRAMMAR GUIDE page 102

WRITING

A Movie Review

1 59 Read and listen.
Does the writer like the movie?

____

2 Read the review again and match descriptions a-d with paragraphs 1-4.

a ☐ conclusion: your opinion and recommendation

b ☐ information about what was good about the movie and what was the best thing

c ☐ introduction: general information, director's name, actors' names, when the movie came out

d ☐ information about the story

LANGUAGE FOCUS

Giving Opinions
One of my favorite movies is *Black Panther*.
For me, it is one of the best Marvel movies.
I think the best thing about the movie is the computer-generated images.
In my opinion, *Black Panther* is a fantastic movie.

3 Order the words to make sentences.

a I / very / the / was / script / funny / thought

____

b romantic comedy / It / a / is / but / makes / you / it / think / really

____

c I / think / the / thing / was / the plot / best / about / the movie

____

d to / recommend / I / it / everyone / would

____

e it / a / fantastic / In / opinion, / movie / my / is

____

4 Write a movie review (120-150 words) about a movie you have seen recently.

My Favorite Movie

1 One of my favorite movies is *Black Panther*. It's a superhero movie that came out in 2018. The director was Ryan Coogler and he co-wrote the script with Joe Robert Cole. The main actors are Chadwick Boseman, Michael B. Jordan and Lupita Nyong'o.

2 The plot is based on the Marvel Comics story about the same character, T'Challa, who became the king of Wakanda – a technologically advanced nation in Africa – after his father's death. He must fight against an enemy who also wants to be the king of Wakanda. For me, *Black Panther* is one of the best Marvel movies.

3 The actors were very good. I thought the soundtrack (by Ludwig Göransson) was also amazing. I think the best thing about the movie is the computer-generated images – they are really fantastic. It's a 3D movie and you really feel like you are part of the action.

4 In my opinion, *Black Panther* is a fantastic movie. The special effects are fantastic and it also makes you think. I would recommend it to everyone.

Writing a Movie Review

Step 1 > PLAN
Choose a movie. Think about the setting, plot, actors, soundtrack and special effects.

Step 2 > WRITE
Write a first version. Organize your information into four paragraphs.

Step 3 > CHECK
Check your writing for errors. Have you given your opinion?

Step 4 > WRITE
Write your final copy and hand in your work.

VOCABULARY IN PICTURES

Movies

director

film a scene

movie star

plot

producer

release a movie

screen

script

soundtrack

special effects

star in a movie

stunt

stunt man / woman / double

win an award

Suffixes *-ion* and *-ment*

advertisement

argument

competition

connection

decoration

development

education

enjoyment

equipment

excitement

information

possession

prediction

suggestion

GRAMMAR GUIDE

Future Tense: *will*

+	I / You / He / She / It / We / You / They	'll go.
–	I / You / He / She / It / We / You / They	won't go.
?	Will I / you / he / she / it / we / you / they Yes, he will. / No, he won't.	go?

- we use *will* / *won't* + the infinitive without *to* to make predictions about the future
  I think that movie **will** win a lot of awards.
- we can use *definitely* when we are certain about something in the future and *probably* when we think something is likely
  That film **definitely** won't win any awards!
  Most films will **probably** be in 3D in future.

Future Tense: *be going to*

+	I	'm going to come.
	You	're going to come.
	He / She / It	's going to come.
	We / You / They	're going to come.

–	I	'm not going to come.
	You	aren't going to come.
	He / She / It	isn't going to come.
	We / You / They	aren't going to come.

?	Is he / she / it going to come? Yes, he is. / No, he isn't.

- we use *be going to* to talk about future intentions
- we also use *be going to* when there is evidence in the present that something is very likely to happen
- we form sentences with *be* + (*not*) + *going to* + infinitive without *to*
  They **aren't going to** watch a movie.

Present Progressive for Future Arrangements

- we use the present progressive for definite plans and arrangements in the future.
- we use it with future time expressions, such as *this evening, tomorrow, on Friday, next week*
  I'm meeting my friends **on Friday**.
- we form the present progressive with *be* + verb + *-ing*

PROGRESS CHECK

Movies

1 Complete the sentences with the words in the box.

awards	plot	screen	script	soundtrack

a Can you move your head? I can't see the ___________.

b Who wrote the ___________ for that movie? The dialogue is really funny.

c Meryl Streep has won many ___________, including three Oscars.

d The ___________ of the movie was confusing. It's a very complicated story.

e The music in the movie was great. I loved the ___________.

Suffixes *-ion* and *-ment*

2 Complete the sentences with the correct form of the words in parentheses.

a I didn't agree with him and we had an ___________ (argue) about it.

b If you need any more ___________ (inform), just ask me.

c What is your favorite ___________ (advertise) on TV?

d Does anyone have a good ___________ (suggest) about where to go tonight?

Future Tense: *will*

3 Complete the sentences with the correct form of *will*.

a Where do you think you ___________ (live) in the future?

b That movie definitely ___________ (not win) an award. It was terrible!

c Do you think they ___________ (make) another film together?

d Perhaps they ___________ (film) those scenes in Scotland, I'm not sure.

e ___________ (he / write) the music for the movie?

Future Tense: *be going to*

4 Order the words to make sentences and questions.

a going / be / hot / It's / to / today

____

b they / to England / Are / to / going / fly ?

____

c not / going / tonight / I'm / go out / to

____

Review: Present Progressive for Future Arrangements

5 Make sentences and questions with the words below.

a What / you / do / next weekend?

____

b Where / you / stay / during vacation?

____

c He / not study / Chinese / tomorrow.

____

Grammar Buildup 6

1 2 3 4 5 6 7 8

6 Complete the interview with the correct form of the verbs in parentheses.

Interviewer: Congratulations on your new movie. Do you think **a** ___________ (it / win) an award?

Monica: Thanks. I hope it will get a nomination.

Interviewer: What **b** ___________ (you / do) if you win?

Monica: If I win, I **c** ___________ (celebrate) with my friends.

Interviewer: And what about your plans for the future? What **d** ___________ (you / do) next?

Monica: I **e** ___________ (start) work on a new movie next week. After that I'm not sure. Perhaps I **f** ___________ (take) a vacation!

Review 3

VOCABULARY **GRAMMAR**

Start

1 Which A tries to sell you things?
a ___ ___ ___ ___ ___ ___ ___ ___ ___ ___ ___ ___

6 Which C involves people or teams and has a winner?
c ___ ___ ___ ___ ___ ___ ___ ___ ___ ___

7 Which P is to guess the future?
p ___ ___ ___ ___ ___ ___ ___ ___ ___

12 Which B is an electric musical instrument with 4 strings?
b ___ ___ ___

13 Which E are often special in movies?
e ___ ___ ___ ___ ___ ___

14 Which C do you go to when you finish high school?
c ___ ___ ___ ___ ___ ___ ___

18 Which K is the electric equivalent to a piano?
k ___ ___ ___ ___ ___ ___ ___ ___

19 Which S is the written text of a movie?
s ___ ___ ___ ___ ___ ___

Finish

2
Which H do you leave when you become independent?
h ___ ___ ___

3
Which T did Dizzy Gillespie play?
t ___ ___ ___ ___ ___ ___

4
Which P is the story of a movie?
p ___ ___ ___

5
Which D is a percussion instrument you play with two sticks?
d ___ ___ ___ ___

8
Which A can a movie win?
a ___ ___ ___ ___

9
Which F is a musical instrument that you blow?
f ___ ___ ___ ___

10
Which S do you start to learn how to read?
s ___ ___ ___ ___ ___

11
Which S is the music of a movie?
s ___ ___ ___ ___ ___ ___ ___ ___ ___

15
Which G is an acoustic musical instrument with 6 strings?
g ___ ___ ___ ___ ___

16
Which D do you need to have a license to do with a car?
d ___ ___ ___ ___

17
Which I means knowledge or facts about something?
i ___ ___ ___ ___ ___ ___ ___ ___ ___ ___

Review 3

VOCABULARY

GRAMMAR

will / won't

1 Complete the sentences with *will* and the verbs in the box.

~~be~~ eat feel get leave play

I *'ll be* an architect when I'm older.

a My sister ________ home soon.

b I ________ married when I'm 30.

c You ________ tired tomorrow morning.

d Jack ________ the guitar in a famous band one day.

e We ________ pasta when we go to Italy.

2 Write complete sentences with *won't* and the verbs in parentheses.

We *won't have* a good time on the beach. It's cold. (have)

a I ________ as a doctor because I don't like needles very much. (work)

b My best friend ________ dancing because she's ill. (go)

c My family ________ by plane. It's very expensive. (travel)

d You ________ your exams. You always study a lot. (fail)

e Your cousin ________ the movie. It's a western. (like)

f It ________ cold tomorrow. It's summer. (be)

3 Choose the correct answers to complete the sentences.

My brother's only eight. He'll get married …

1 soon. **2** next month. **3** one day.

a It's March. We'll finish school …

1 next week. **2** in June. **3** tomorrow.

b I'm 14. I won't leave school …

1 tomorrow. **2** one day. **3** when I'm older.

c My sister loves drawing. She'll be an architect …

1 tomorrow. **2** when she's older. **3** soon.

d The best player on my team has a broken leg. We won't win the game …

1 next week. **2** one day. **3** soon.

e It's snowing a lot. School will be closed …

1 one day. **2** tomorrow. **3** in May.

4 Write questions and short answers about Jess', Tom's, Fred's and Julia's future.

	Jess	Tom	Fred and Julia
transportation	motorcycle	fast car	bicycle
job	engineer	police officer	actor
home	Paris	London	Hollywood

Jess / drive / a fast car

Will Jess drive a fast car?

No, she won't.

a Tom / work / as a police officer?

b Jess / study / to be an engineer?

c Fred and Julia / ride / a bicycle?

d Jess / live / in Hollywood?

e Fred and Julia / live / in Paris?

VOCABULARY

GRAMMAR

First Conditional

5 Write sentences with the first conditional. Add commas when needed.

If / Mike / fail / his exams / his dad / be / angry
If Mike fails his exams, his dad will be angry.

a Our teacher / be / happy / if / we / tidy / our desks
______

b If / the sun / shines / we / go / to the lake
______

c If / Mom / not come / home soon I / cook / dinner
______

d We / cross / the Atlantic / if / we / sail / to New York
______

Future Tenses: *will* and *be going to*

6 Write predictions for the future with *will* or *won't*. Include the words in parentheses.

people / live / on the moon (probably)
People will probably live on the moon.

a My brother / be / a movie star (definitely)
______

b That movie / not win / an award (definitely)
______

c Schoolchildren / not use / books (probably)
______

7 Write questions with *will*. Then write true short answers.

(your dad) be Prime Minister
Will your dad be Prime Minister?
No, he won't.

a (you and your friends) make a charity CD
______
______

b (you) go out for a meal on Saturday
______
______

c (your school) be open tomorrow
______
______

8 Complete the sentences with the correct form of *be going to* and the verbs in parentheses.

They're *going to build* a new movie theater. (build)

a I ______ any more DVDs. (not buy)

b Look out! Your book ______ on the floor. (fall)

c ______ Sara ______ as a stuntwoman? (work)

d Matt ______ math at university. (not study)

Present Progressive for Future Arrangements

9 Look at Kate's diary and complete the sentences about her weekend. Use the present progressive.

Kate has a lot of arrangements this weekend.

Saturday		Sunday	
10am	play tennis with Dan	11am	Grandma & Grandpa come
2pm	meet friends in town	3pm	do a sponsored swim
7pm	go out for a pizza with Emma	6pm	watch a movie at Joe's house

She *'s playing tennis* with Dan at 10 o'clock on Saturday. In the afternoon, she a ______. Then, in the evening, Emma and Kate b ______. On Sunday morning, Kate's grandparents c ______. Kate d ______ at 3 o'clock that afternoon, and then at 6 o'clock she e ______ at Joe's house.

7 The World We Live in

VOCABULARY 1

Materials and Containers

1 Look at the words in the box. Which of the words are containers (C)? Which are materials (M)?

aluminum ☐ bag ☐ bottle ☐ box ☐
can ☐ cardboard ☐ carton ☐
cotton ☐ glass ☐ jar ☐ metal ☐
paper ☐ plastic ☐ wool ☐

2 🔊 60 Listen and repeat.

3 Match the words in activity 1 with pictures 1-10. Some items have more than one answer.

a ☐ aluminum		**h** ☐ glass	
b ☐ bottle		**i** ☐ jar	
c ☐ box		**j** ☐ metal	
d ☐ can		**k** ☐ paper	
e ☐ cardboard		**l** ☐ plastic	
f ☐ carton		**m** ☐ wool	
g ☐ cotton			

4 Complete the sign with words in activity 1.

Welcome to Red Forest Recycling Center

The **BLUE** bin is for **a** ___________ and **b** ___________. Put your boxes and newspapers in here!

YELLOW is for **c** _________ and **d** _________. All your soft drink bottles and cans go here.

GREEN is for **e** _________. Use this for bottles and jars.

BROWN is for clothes. Please wash your **f** _________ T-shirts and **g** _________ sweaters first.

READING 1

1 Skim the text below. What do the entrants' texts express?

a tips

b testimonials

Every year for five years we've organized the *It's Your World!* competition for under-16s to give tips to save the planet. This year, Imran Chopra is our winner, with Jake Burns and Leanne Morris as runners-up. Their tips are simple but effective – have a look! Congratulations to Imran, Jake and Leanne!

Theme: Reduce, refuse, reuse, recycle

How many hours have you spent outside today? Outdoor activities are healthier than indoor entertainment and they save electricity. If you reduce your 'screen time,' you'll do your planet a favor.
So switch off lights, the TV and gaming consoles and get out there!

Imran Chopra, Eureka, CA

'I haven't worn this for years!' You haven't? Don't throw away old clothes. Put everything into two piles: clothes someone can wear and clothes no one can wear. Take the first pile to thrift shops or give them to friends. Take the rest to a recycling center. You can also reuse wool or cotton clothes to clean your house with.

Jake Burns, Erie, PA

Refuse to buy products with a lot of plastic! Even better, write to the company and explain why you haven't bought their product. Also, when you buy food (for example, chocolate or cans of soft drinks), look for the Fairtrade symbol or support local companies. This is better for the environment and helps local communities.

Leanne Morris, Pueblo, CO

2 🔊 61 Read and listen. Match the people with the words.

a Imran ☐ reuse and recycle

b Jake ☐ refuse

c Leanne ☐ reduce

3 Scan the text. Then write T for *true* or F for *false*.

a ☐ The *It's Your World!* competition is for people younger than 16.

b ☐ Imran suggests an alternative way to generate electricity.

c ☐ Jake gives three suggestions for old clothes.

d ☐ Leanne tells you to write to companies and ask them to recycle plastic.

e ☐ All three entrants ask you to reduce how much you consume of something.

4 Answer the questions.

a What does Imran want people to do?

____

____

b What does Jake want people to do?

____

____

c What does Leanne want people to do?

____

____

READING STRATEGY

Learning the meaning of prefixes like *re-* can help you guess the meaning of a word. The context around the word will help you, too.

5 How do you say the words in the box in your language?

rebuild	resend	restart	rewrite

6 CLASS VOTE Which of the three tips do you think is the best?

GRAMMAR 1

Present Perfect (Affirmative and Negative)

1 Look at the following sentences and underline the verb form.

- **a** Some children have spent too many hours in front of the TV.
- **b** My mom has given our old clothes to charity organizations.
- **c** I have tried to be eco-friendly.
- **d** At school, we have organized a recycling event.

2 Read the rules below and complete the chart with the words provided.

- **a** We form the *present perfect* with *have* (I / you / we / they) or *has* (he / she / it) + *the past participle of the main verb.*
- **b** The past participle of *regular* verbs is formed by adding *-d* or *-ed* to the main verb.
- **c** Some verbs have *irregular* past participles.
- **d** *'ve* is the contracted form of *have* and *'s* is the contracted form of *has*.
- **e** The *present perfect* is used to express an action that happened at *an indefinite time in the past* but is important at the time of speaking.

has He 've bought 've organized

affirmative form	
I / You	________ some Fairtrade coffee.
________ / She / (It)	________ reduced screen time.
We / You / They	________ a recycling event.

3 Complete the sentences with the present perfect form of the verbs in parentheses. Use the spelling rules on page 120 to help you.

- **a** I________ (recycle) my old clothes.
- **b** She________ (decide) to recycle at school.
- **c** My father________ (try) a new organic shampoo.
- **d** We________ (reduce) our screen time.

4 Complete the text with the present perfect form of the verbs in parentheses.

Eco-tourism **a** ________ (become) quite popular in the last few years. People **b** ________ (build) eco-hotels all over the world. The public reaction **c** ________ (be) very positive. The hotels **d** ________ (provide) 100 percent organic cotton towels and they **e** ________ (use) solar energy for their visitors. In general, water and electricity consumption in the hotels **f** ________ (fall).

5 Write complete sentences. Use the present perfect affirmative.

a

They / turn off / all the lights.

____

____

b

She / pass / the exam.

____

____

c

She / break / the window.

____

____

d

The boy / eat / all the chocolate.

____

____

e

He / steal / the car.

____

____

f

He / throw away / the old toys.

____

____

6 *Hasn't / has not* and *haven't / have not* are the negative forms of *has* and *have* respectively. Complete the chart below.

negative form
I / You ________ purchased anything new in the past month.
He / She / (It) ________ worn that T-shirt anymore.
We / You / They ________ bought any plastic products recently.

7 Choose the correct words.

a We **haven't** / **hasn't** had meat for lunch today.
b My school **haven't** / **hasn't** stopped using paper.
c I **haven't** / **hasn't** tried Fairtrade chocolate.
d My friends **haven't** / **hasn't** left school.

8 Complete the text with the present perfect form of the verbs in parentheses.

Brad Pitt didn't study architecture, but he **a** ______________ (create) a foundation to help build 150 special eco-houses in New Orleans.
Twenty top architects **b** ______________ (choose) to help him. Pitt **c** ______________ (promise) to complete the project because a terrible hurricane hit New Orleans in 2005 and he saw the destruction it caused. House by house, families **d** ______________ (rebuild) their lives. The project **e** ______________ (not finish), and the architects and their builders **f** ______________ (not stop) working.

9 Write sentences that are true for you using the present perfect affirmative and negative. Use the words in the box or your own ideas.

eat finish read see visit

I haven't finished that series.
____
____
____
____

10 INTERFACE Work in pairs. Compare your sentences in activity 9.

I haven't finished that series.

Lost in Space? I loved it!!!

GRAMMAR GUIDE page 120

LISTENING

Eco Family

1 Look at the headline. What do you think the radio show is about?

____
____

2 62 Listen and check your answer to activity 1.

3 62 Listen again. Then write T for *true* or F for *false*.

a ☐ The family has started growing vegetables.
b ☐ The family is vegetarian.
c ☐ The local stores give them special plastic boxes.
d ☐ They put used coffee grounds in the garden.
e ☐ The family gives old toys to hospitals.

4 Answer the questions.

a Where does the Carter family live?
____
b Where do they buy their food?
____
c What do they do with their old clothes?
____

CULTURAL FACT

Did you know that high-income countries produce the most waste per person? The United States leads the statistics (over 760kg per person per year), followed by Australia, Denmark, Switzerland and Canada.

SPEAKING

A Fundraising Bike Ride

63 Ed and Adam are talking about a bike ride for a charity. Listen and complete the dialogue.

You know, Adam, a ____________ to take part in the ReCycle event which is going to happen next month.

What is it for?

It is to b ____________ for children with cancer.

Cool! How is it organized?

They say on this website that, this year, the organizers c ____________ a route of 15 miles. They carry your gear, and provide d ____________ and food along the way.

Let me check! Look, some riders e ____________ it for over 10 years! Besides helping, they f ____________ lots of fun. Many of them g ____________ much farther than ever imagined... Cyclists and volunteers on the way cheer and encourage the group rides.

It sounds great!

The only thing is, it requires lots of training...

Yeah, but pedaling for a h ____________ is a rewarding experience...

You're right... Well, let's go for it, then!

FUNCTIONAL LANGUAGE

Talking about Charity Events

I've decided to take part in ...
What is it for?
When is it?
How is it organized?

Speaking Task

Write a dialogue between you and a friend.

Step 1

Decide which fundraising event to take part in. Choose one of the following:

A walking fundraising event

A race event

Step 2

Talk to your friend about the event

I've decided to take part in ...
It is for...
The organizers...
Many people have taken part / helped etc.

Think about what your friend is going to ask.

What is it for?
When is it?
How is it organized?

Step 3

Work with a partner. Write your dialogue. Follow the conversation above as a guide.

Step 4

Take turns practicing your dialogue.

CULTURE

New Zealand Loves Cycling

In New Zealand, cycling offers great Kiwi experiences such as traveling through time to gold mining days, visiting famous movie locations and diving into a thermal pool. It is a popular sport, with many quiet roads, forest trails and cycling tracks, with easy riding for the less experienced.

'Love 'em or hate 'em, bikes are here to stay', New Zealanders say. From the law graduate running a cargo bike delivery company to the velodrome track racer, the cycling culture is spreading all around. In addition to the commuter and the bike tourist, some other people have cycled lately:

The e-biker:

Some people, particularly those who are older or suffer from some diseases, have purchased an electric bike which gives them a power boost on hills, is fast, offers no parking problems and is easy to get around on.

The cargo bike courier:

They can deliver packages weighing up to 80 kilos. The bike's easy to maneuver and a 'green' way to get goods from A to B. Biking in the winter? No problem: wear a waterproof jacket and keep moving to stave off the cold!

The trendy campaigner:

Riding a vintage-style bike can be a great way of drawing people's attention, especially adults, to get into cycling. According to these bike riders, the main barrier to adult cycling is not cycling itself, but changing their habits. They believe people need to make changes to their lives in order to make cycling work.

1 64 Read and listen. Then answer the questions.

a Which experiences does cycling offer in New Zealand?

____

b What are the advantages of an e-bike?

____

c List the advantages of the cargo bike.

____

d What is the objective of the trendy campaigner?

____

2 Is riding bikes popular in your city? Where do people cycle?

____

3 Do you have a bike? How often do you cycle?

____

VOCABULARY 2

Endangered Animals

1 Match pictures 1-10 with the words in the box.

dolphin ☐ elephant ☐ leopard ☐ orangutan ☐ panda ☐ polar bear ☐ rhinoceros ☐ snake ☐ tiger ☐ turtle ☐

2 65 Listen and repeat.

3 Complete the sentences with words from activity 1.

Why are all these animals in danger of extinction?

a The ________ is a mammal. It lives in the Arctic, but the ice is disappearing.

b The ________ is a very intelligent marine mammal. It lives in the sea, but thousands die in fishing nets every year.

c The ________ is the world's largest cat, but there are only 3,200 of them in the world.

d The ________ is the second biggest land mammal after the elephant. Humans hunt them for their horns.

e The ________ lives in trees in the forest, and we're destroying their habitat.

f Many species of sea ________ are hunted for their meat, eggs, skin and shells and are now endangered.

4 Copy and complete the chart with the words from activity 1. Can you add more animals to each habitat?

forest	savannah
orangutan	

water	other

1

2

3

4

READING 2

1 Look up the meaning of the words in the box.

adopt hunt ivory rain forest territory

2 66 Read and listen to a social environmental ad. Would you like to adopt an animal?

3 Answer the questions.

a How much does it cost to adopt an animal?

____

b Which animals do humans hunt for meat?

____

c Which two animals are losing their natural habitats?

____

d What is an elephant's tusk made of?

____

Adopt an Animal!

For just US$36 a year you can adopt an animal. All these animals are in danger of extinction, but you can adopt them and help them to survive.

Adopt a Turtle!

Have you eaten turtle soup? Some people hunt turtles for their meat and their eggs. Turtles are older than dinosaurs, but they could soon disappear if we don't act fast!

Adopt an Asian Elephant!

African elephants are the largest land animals, but their Asian cousins are in danger of extinction. Their natural habitat is getting smaller because we – humans – are moving into their territory. People also hunt these animals for their tusks, which are made of ivory.

Adopt an Orangutan!

Have you ever wanted an unusual pet? Did you know that people hunt orangutans for pets? They also hunt them for meat. However, the greatest danger to orangutans is the destruction of their rain forest habitat.

GRAMMAR 2

Present Perfect (Questions and Short Answers)

1 Complete the questions and short answers in the chart below. Use *have / haven't / has / hasn't.*

questions and short answers
________ I / you eaten turtle soup? Yes, I ________. No, I ________.
________ he / she / (it) adopted an unusual animal? Yes, he ________. No, he ________.
________ we / you / they hunted elephants? Yes, we ________. No, we ________.
How many hours ________ you spent outside today?

2 Order the words to make questions.

a you / Europe / have / been / to ?

____

____

b abroad / worked / your dad / has ?

____

____

c present / you / bought / an unusual / have / your parents ?

____

____

d adopted / a / you / have / recently / pet ?

____

____

3 INTERFACE Work in pairs. Ask your friend the questions in activity 2. He or she is supposed to give short answers.

CLIL

HISTORY

Apartheid

From 1948 to 1991, South Africa had a policy of legal racial discrimination called apartheid. From the Afrikaans word meaning 'separation,' this law enforced racial, social and economic segregation on the native people of South Africa. When the National Party won the general election in 1948, the government passed many laws that gave white people dominance over other races. The non-white population of South Africa became second-class citizens. Over the years there was a lot of national and international resistance to these laws, and a key person was Nelson Mandela, a native South African.

In 1964, he was sentenced to life imprisonment for his opposition to apartheid. He was released on February 11, 1990.

On April 27, 1994, South Africa celebrated its first democratic elections, and Mandela became the country's first black president. He won the Nobel Peace Prize in 1993 and, today, even after his death in 2013, he remains a symbol of freedom and equality in the world, inspiring many generations to come.

Nelson Mandela

Black citizens were forbidden from using the same facilities as white (or 'European') people.

1 67 Read and listen. When did Nelson Mandela win the Nobel Peace Prize?

____

2 Nelson Mandela had many names. Read the box and guess which of the names all South African people called him.

Rolihlahla: birth name given by his father
Nelson: English name given by his school teacher
Madiba: family 'clan' name
Dalibhunga: name given when he was 16
Tata: nickname, this means 'father' in Mandela's language, Xhosa
Khulu: nickname, this means 'grandfather' in Xhosa

____

3 Complete the text about Nelson Mandela with the correct dates in the box.

2013 1918 1994 1964

Nelson Mandela was born in **a** ______ in the village of Mvezo, in South Africa. As a young man, he became a lawyer and a political activist. He fought against apartheid. In **b** ______ he was put in prison. He spent 26 years in prison and he left prison in 1990. Four years later, in **c** ______, he became the president of South Africa. He was the first black president of South Africa. He stopped being president in 1999 but he was still politically active for many years. He died in **d** ______.

VOCABULARY IN PICTURES

Materials and Containers

aluminum

bag

bottle

box

can

cardboard

carton

cotton

glass

jar

metal

paper

plastic

wool

Endangered Animals

dolphin

elephant

leopard

orangutan

panda

polar bear

rhinoceros

snake

tiger

turtle

GRAMMAR GUIDE

Present Perfect

affirmative	
I've (have) You've (have) He / She / It's (has) We've (have) You've (have) They've (have)	bought local food.

negative		
I	haven't (have not)	used plastic bags.
You	haven't (have not)	
He / She / It	hasn't (has not)	
We	haven't (have not)	
You	haven't (have not)	
They	haven't (have not)	

- we use the present perfect to talk about experiences or actions in the past when we don't mention (or we don't know) the exact time
  I **have organized** a competition.
- we also use the present perfect to talk about past events that have an effect or a reflection in the present
  She **has painted** the house.
- we form the affirmative of the present perfect with *have* / *has* + the past participle of the verb
  He **has tried** a new organic shampoo.
- we form the negative with *haven't* / *hasn't* + the past participle of the verb
  They **haven't reduced** their screen time.
- the regular past participle ending is *-ed*
  use → us*ed*

questions			short answers affirmative	negative
Have	I	seen a snake?	Yes, I have.	No, I haven't.
Have	you		Yes, you have.	No, you haven't.
Has	he / she / it		Yes, he / she / it has.	No, he / she / it hasn't.
Have	we		Yes, we have.	No, we haven't.
Have	you		Yes, you have.	No, you haven't.
Have	they		Yes, they have.	No, they haven't.

- the word order is different in questions
  You **have seen** a tiger.
  Have you **seen** a tiger?
- we don't repeat the past participle in short answers
  Have you **touched** a polar bear?
  Yes, I have. / No, I haven't.

Spelling: Past Participle Regular Verbs

- for most verbs, add *-ed*
  want → want*ed*
- for verbs that end in *-e*, add *-d*
  like → like*d*
- for verbs that end in a consonant + *y*, omit the *y* and add *-ied*
  study → stud*ied*
- for verbs that end in a stressed vowel + a consonant, double the final consonant and add *-ed*
  stop → stop*ped*

Past Participle Irregular Verbs

- for the Irregular verbs list, see page 142.

PROGRESS CHECK

Materials and Containers

1 Find nine words in the word search.

P	A	B	A	G	C	P	M	V	J
W	O	O	L	E	A	J	E	Q	A
S	O	X	A	H	R	T	T	W	R
G	L	A	S	S	T	M	A	C	K
D	G	Y	K	R	O	O	L	A	U
U	Z	B	G	H	N	Y	D	N	L
C	A	R	D	B	O	A	R	D	K

Endangered Animals

2 Identify the animals.

a p _ _ _ _

b r _ _ _ _ _ _ _ _ _

c l _ _ _ _ _ _

d d _ _ _ _ _ _

e p _ _ _ _ b _ _ _

f o _ _ _ _ _ _ _ _

Present Perfect

3 Complete the sentences with the present perfect form of the verbs in parentheses.

a My brother ________ (swim) with dolphins in Florida.

b I ________ (ride) on the backs of elephants in India.

c We ________ (have) a lot of turtles as pets.

d My neighbor ________ (feed) polar bears in Alaska.

4 Rewrite the sentences from activity 3 in the negative form to indicate that they are not animal friendly.

a ________________________

b ________________________

c ________________________

d ________________________

5 Write complete questions. Use the present perfect.

a you / reuse / paper / this week?

____

b your school / recycle / old test papers?

____

c your local supermarket / reduce / packaging?

____

Grammar Buildup 7

1 2 3 4 5 6 7 8

6 Complete the dialogue with the correct form of the verbs in parentheses.

Boy: Hi. You **a** ________ (look) lost.
Ava: Yes, I am.
Boy: Can I **b** ________ (help) you?
Ava: I **c** ________ (look) for the animal sanctuary.
Boy: **d** ________ (go) straight ahead past the bank. Then **e** ________ (turn) right onto Park Street.
Ava: Park Street?
Boy: Yes. The sanctuary **f** ________ (be) on your left.
Ava: **g** ________ you ________ (be) there?
Boy: Yes, I **h** ________. It's great.
Ava: What **i** ________ you ________ (see)?
Boy: Lots of things. But you have to **j** ________ (see) the donkeys!

8 Altruism

VOCABULARY 1

Fundraising Ideas

1 Match pictures 1-4 with fundraising ideas in the box.

- collect money ☐
- do a sponsored swim ☐
- have a rummage sale ☐
- make a charity CD ☐
- organize a concert ☐
- sell badges ☐
- sell candy ☐
- sell raffle tickets ☐
- wash cars ☐

2 🔊 68 Listen and repeat.

3 Complete the text with words from activity 1.

After the earthquake in Haiti, lots of people from around the world wanted to help. People collected money in the street and sold **a** ______________ for people to wear. Schoolchildren sold candy, they did **b** ______________ walks and swims, and washed **c** ______________ to raise money. They also had **d** ______________ with their old toys. In the USA, one family had a **e** ______________ in their garden. Their neighbors bought tickets for $5 and listened to some great music. In many countries, pop stars worked together to make **f** ______________ CDs. Everyone wanted to help.

READING 1

1 69 Skim the article and listen. Choose the best title for the text.

☐ How to Build your Own School

☐ **Young Woman in School Fundraising Project**

Have you ever considered living abroad to set up a charity project? If so, Felicity's story will inspire you.

Felicity Marks is a busy young woman. In 2002 she spent four months teaching street children at The Street Academy school in Accra, Ghana. When she came home, she decided that she wanted to do more to help educate the city's children. So, in 2003, she set up a charity called The Street Academy Annexe Project.

In Ghana, most parents have to pay to send their children to school, but The Street Academy offers free education to children aged 8-18, as well as uniforms, books and a decent meal each day. But the conditions are very basic. The building is a wooden hut with three different classes in the same room and no other facilities. The aim of Felicity's Street Academy Annexe Project is to raise enough money to build a bigger school with at least four classrooms, toilets, a soccer field and an auditorium.

So what has Felicity done to raise money for this ambitious project? She's already done many different things: 'First we had a big party to launch the charity. We've already organized quiz nights and on-line competitions, we've sold cakes and I've done sponsored walks and skydives. Other people have just helped raise money on our behalf, which really helps'. So how much money has she raised?

'We haven't raised enough money yet! We need enough money to build a school where the kids can learn in proper conditions. We've received the architect's plans and we love them because they've taken the kids' ideas into consideration. For example, the windows are in the shape of triangles and stars!' Does Felicity recommend a project like this? 'Yes, but this type of project isn't easy. It has taken a long time and there have been problems and obstacles. But in the end, it's been worth it.'

2 Read the text again. Then write T for *true* or F for *false*. Correct the false sentences.

a ☐ Felicity worked in a school in Ghana.

______

b ☐ The school was well equipped.

______

c ☐ She wants to build a new school for the children.

______

d ☐ She has raised all the money they need to build the school

______

e ☐ It is not difficult to organize a project like this.

______

3 What six things did Felicity do to raise money for the school? Write a list.

______

______

______

4 Read and answer the questions.

a How long was Felicity at the Street Academy School?

______

b Why is the Street Academy School different from other schools in Ghana?

______

c What facilities does the new school have?

______

______

d What shape are the new windows?

______

5 Find words a-d in the text and match them with definitions 1-4.

a hut	1 for us
b aim	2 objective
c launch	3 a small, simple building
d on our behalf	4 initiate (a product or project)

GRAMMAR 1

Present Perfect: *ever, never, yet, already, just*

1 Read the sentences below. Write (A) in case of affirmative sentences, (B) in case of negative sentences and (C) for questions. Underline the adverbs.

a ☐ Have you ever done a sponsored swim?
b ☐ My sister has already sold all the raffle tickets.
c ☐ I've never given any money to charity organizations.
d ☐ We haven't finished the charity badges yet.
e ☐ The sponsored swim has just started.

2 Complete the rules with *ever, never, already, yet* or *just*. Then complete the chart with these words.

The words *ever, never, already, yet* and *just* are often used with the present perfect.

a ______ is used to talk about something which is expected to happen. It means 'at any time up to now.' It is used in questions and negative sentences. It is placed at the end of sentences.
b ______ is used to express a negative idea.
c ______ is usually used with the present perfect tense and means 'a short time ago.' It comes before the main verb.
d We often use ______ to ask if something has happened at any time before now.
e ______ is used to say that something has happened early. It usually comes before the main verb.

present perfect with *ever, never, yet, already, just*	
+	Felicity has ______ done lots of things for the project. I have ______ finished helping Felicity.
–	The charity hasn't raised enough money for the new building ______. My friend Jill has ______ taken part in a sponsored swim. She'll do it next time.
?	Have you ______ been to Ghana? Have the kids sold all the badges ______?

3 Write complete sentences in the present perfect affirmative, negative or interrogative. Note where to insert the adverbs.

a I / do / a sponsored swim / yet. ✗
____
b My friends / organized / lots of barbecues / already ✓
____
c Mark / buy / a raffle ticket / just ✓
____
d you / organize / a rummage sale / ever ?
____
e My mom / raise / so much money / for charity / never ✗
____
f Maggie / sell / the cakes / for charity / yet ?
____

4 Complete the text with the present perfect form of the verbs in parentheses and the adverbs provided.

To: Barbara
From: Petra
Subject: Raising money for charity

Hi, Barbara,
a ____________ you ____________ (ever / raise) money for charity? I **b** ____________ (not do) anything before, but I really want to be a volunteer. My brother **c** ____________ (just / finish) organizing a raffle to raise money for cancer research and he **d** ____________ (already / buy) lots of charity badges. My sisters **e** ____________ (make) cakes and **f** ____________ (just / sell) them outside school to raise money for the Red Cross. I **g** ____________ a charity CD ____________ (not buy / yet)! I want to do a sponsored swim because I think it is a good way to raise money. My brother and sisters **h** ____________ any money for an animal charity ____________ (not collect / yet), so I want to raise money for the ASPCA. Do you think that's a good idea? Oh, God, I **i** ____________ (never be) so happy! Will you help me organize the sponsored swim?

Petra

PRONUNCIATION

Contractions

70 Listen and repeat the sentences.

a I've done a sponsored swim.
b You haven't finished your homework.
c She hasn't got a badge.
d He's raised over $1,000.

5 Choose the correct answer.

Gina Have you **a ever / never** ridden a horse, Colin?
Colin No, I **b have / haven't**. **c Have / Had** you?
Gina No, I haven't. I've **d ever / never** done anything interesting.
Colin I don't believe you. Everyone's **e done / doing** something interesting.
Gina I **f haven't / hasn't**.
Colin OK, have you ever **g meet / met** a famous person?
Gina No. Have **h you / she**?
Colin Erm... yes. I know, **i have you / you have** ever eaten Indian food?
Gina No, I've **j ever / never** eaten it.
Colin Have you ever **k been / being** in a movie?
Gina You mean as an actor?
Colin Yes. Well, **l had / have** you?
Gina Yes, I **m have / did**. But years ago. I've **n forgotten / forgetted** all about it.

6 71 Listen and check your answers.

GRAMMAR GUIDE page 134

LISTENING

Charity Appeals

1 Work in pairs.
Write a list of famous charities and what they do.

2 72 Listen to the radio program. Which charities do the speakers mention?

a The Red Cross
b Oxfam
c The Red Crescent
d Médecins Sans Frontières
e Comic Relief
f ASPCA

3 72 Listen again and choose the correct words.

a Oxfam helps **animals / hungry people / sick people**.
b MSF helps **animals / hungry people / sick people.**
c The ASPCA helps **animals / hungry people / sick people**.

4 72 Listen again. Then write T for *true* or F for *false*. Correct the false sentences.

a ☐ Oxfam wants people to give money for their stores.
____

b ☐ Oxfam has 15,000 stores worldwide.
____

c ☐ A group of Spanish doctors started MSF.
____

d ☐ MSF needs people to volunteer for them.
____

e ☐ The ASPCA looks after animals all over the world
____

f ☐ The ASPCA gets money from donations.
____

5 INTERFACE Work in pairs. Which charity is the most important?

I think Oxfam is the most important because it helps people who are hungry in emergency situations.

SPEAKING

A Yard Sale

73 Martina and Ed are planning a yard sale. Listen and complete the dialogue.

Well, I think I'a ______________ all the items for our yard sale.

Good! b ______________ all the goods?

Yeah, but it wasn't an easy task. You know, shoppers look for bargains; we can't go high on c ______________...

Our plan is get rid of all this stuff and donate the money for the local church homeless program. That means we have to sell everything to d ______________ as much as we can.

For the 'more valuable' items, I e ______________ about writing 'make an offer' on the price tag.

Good idea! The next step is setting the date and time.

I believe we should start at 8 in the morning, from 8am to 6pm, what do you think?

Perfect! Let's check the f ______________ to choose the best sunny Saturday or Sunday...

That's really important! Next step: g ______________ it!

I'll post it on the local newspaper and all h ______________ platforms. I'm sure our friends will help us, too!

FUNCTIONAL LANGUAGE

Planning a Sale

I've already gathered...
Have you priced...?
Our plan is...

Speaking Task

Write a dialogue between you and a friend.

Step 1

Choose one of the informal events:

A yard sale

A garage sale

A swap meet

A bric-a-brac sale

Step 2

Talk about the organization of the event.

I've already gathered...
I've decided on the date and time...
We need to advertise...

Think about what your friend is going to ask.

How much...?
Have you priced...?
What time should we start?
What date should we choose?
Have you advertised it yet?

Step 3

Work with a partner. Write your dialogue. Follow the conversation above as a guide.

Step 4

Take turns practicing your dialogue.

CULTURE

Good Deeds Day in India

Good Deeds Day is a global celebration which unites people from over 100 countries to do good deeds for the benefit of others and the planet: every single person can do something good to improve the lives of others and, therefore, help change the world for the better.
In addition to changing some groups' attitudes during Good Deeds Day, the NVP (Non-Violence Project Foundation) in India wants to inspire, engage and motivate young people to understand how to solve conflicts peacefully. They focus on two areas: Education and Raising Awareness.
They believe in education and follow Mahatma Gandhi's words: "If you want to change the world, you must start with the children." Inspiring youth through education is their philosophy. They understand education has the power to build and ensure a strong base for tolerance, acceptance and respect for human rights.
Their approach is based on interaction and creativity and they count on teachers, sport coaches and youth leaders to interact with young people face-to-face, or through e-learning.
Good Deeds Day is, then, a great opportunity to share such good deeds with the world!

1 74 **Read and listen to the information. Then match the two parts to make sentences.**

- **a** Good Deeds Day seeks to call people's attention to the importance ...
- **b** The NVP in India wishes to inspire and motivate ...
- **c** Their philosophy is ...
- **d** Education, in the NVP's view, has the power ...
- **e** They count on teachers, sport coaches and youth leaders to interact ...

- ☐ ... 'inspiring through education.'
- ☐ ... of doing something good to improve the lives of others.
- ☐ ... with young people face-to-face or through e-learning.
- ☐ ... young people to understand how to solve conflicts without using violence.
- ☐ ... to build tolerance, acceptance and respect for everyone.

2 Is Good Deeds Day celebrated in your country? What do people do on this day?

____

____

3 Have you done any good deed recently? Read some good deed ideas. Check (✓) the ones you have done. Share your answers with your class.

- **a** ☐ Help a friend in need.
- **b** ☐ Volunteer for an hour at an organization of your choice.
- **c** ☐ Write a thank-you note to someone who won't expect it.
- **d** ☐ Find unneeded items in your house and donate them to a charitable organization.
- **e** ☐ Plant a tree.
- **f** ☐ Think of something you do well, and use your talent to benefit others – for example, perform magic tricks at a children's hospital.
- **g** ☐ Teach an elderly person to use a computer to surf the net.
- **h** ☐ Collect stuffed animals or toys from family members, friends and neighbors and donate them to an organization that helps children.
- **i** ☐ Donate supplies to children from underprivileged homes.

VOCABULARY 2

make and *do*

1 Do we use *make* or *do* with the phrases in the box? Write the correct answers.

_____ a decision _____ a mistake
_____ charity work _____exercise
_____ friends _____homework
_____ money _____ nothing
_____ someone a favor
_____ someone happy
_____ someone laugh _____ your best

2 75 Listen, check and repeat.

3 Match pictures 1-5 with phrases from activity 1.

1

____

2

____

3

____

4

____

5

____

4 Complete the questions with the correct form of *make* or *do*.

Have you ever *done* any charity work?

a What ________ you happy?

b Which people ________ you laugh?

c What's the biggest mistake you have ever ________?

d How often do you ________ someone a favor?

e How often do you ________ exercise?

f What's the most difficult decision you have ever ________?

g Where do you usually ________ your homework?

h What's the best way to ________ a lot of money?

5 INTERFACE Work in pairs. Ask and answer the questions in activity 4.

READING 2

1 Look at the picture of Selena Gomez and answer the questions.

a Have you ever heard of Selena Gomez?

b What do you know about her?

2 76 Skim the personal profile and listen. Why is Selena Gomez famous?

____

SELENA GOMEZ,
Goodwill Ambassador

Selena Gomez has been famous for over ten years. She's an actress and a pop singer.
She's starred in a hit TV series and her band, Selena Gomez and the Scene, have released a hit album. She's a busy girl and she makes a lot of money!
But Selena finds time to do lots of charity work, too. She supports Island Dog, a charity that helps dogs in Puerto Rico, and RAISE Hope for Congo, a charity that campaigns against violence against Congolese women.
Since August 2009, Selena has been a UNICEF Goodwill ambassador. She has been to Ghana to visit children who are living without enough food or clean water. She realized that she was publicizing their problems by visiting Ghana. This is what being a Goodwill Ambassador is all about – making people aware of the world's problems and encouraging them to help.

3 Read the text again and answer the questions.

a How long has Selena been famous?
____

b What charities does she work for?
____

c When did she become a UNICEF Goodwill Ambassador?
____

d Why did she visit Ghana for UNICEF?
____
____

e Why are Goodwill Ambassadors important?
____
____

CULTURAL FACT

Other UNICEF Goodwill Ambassadors include Argentinian soccer player Lionel Messi and Colombian singer Shakira.

4 INTERFACE Work in pairs. Do Goodwill Ambassadors do an important job?

Yes, because they publicize problems around the world.

No, because they are rich and famous. They don't really help poor people.

GRAMMAR 2

Present Perfect: *for* and *since*

1 Read the sentences below. Underline the verbs in the present perfect and circle the time expressions.

- **a** Selena Gomez has been famous for over ten years.
- **b** Selena has been a UNICEF Goodwill ambassador since August 2009.
- **c** Her fans have loved her since she started singing.
- **d** Selena has worked as an actress for some time now.
- **e** How long has she supported Island Dog?

2 Look at the sentences in activity 1 again and complete these rules with the words in the box.

for   How long   since

- **a** We often use a clause with ________ to show when something started in the past.
- **b** We often use a clause with ________ to indicate periods of time.
- **c** ________ is used in questions to ask about the duration of an activity.

3 Now, complete the chart.

Present perfect with *for* and *since*
________ has she been a Goodwill Ambassador?
She has been an Ambassador ________ 2009. She has been an ambassador _______ over ten years.

4 Copy and complete the chart with the time expressions in the box.

2010   2pm   a long time   a month
April   I was born   last night   Saturday
this morning   three weeks   two hours

since	for
________	________
________	________
________	________
________	________
________	________
________	________
________	________

5 Complete the text using *for* or *since*.

My hero is my grandfather. He's 80 years old. He loves soccer and he has watched every Arsenal game **a** ________ 1951. He hasn't missed a game **b** ________ the day he got married – it was a Saturday. He's been married **c** ________ over 60 years and he and my grandma have lived with us **d** ________ five years. He loves music and he's been a fan of hip hop **e** ________ 2011 when I played him one of my hip hop CDs. He's the coolest grandfather in the world.

6 Write questions with *How long*.

you / be / at this school

How long have you been at this school?

- **a** he / know / his best friend
  ____
- **b** you / study / English
  ____
- **c** you / have / your cell phone
  ____
- **d** you / live / in your apartment
  ____
- **e** they / have / their dog
  ____

7 INTERFACE Work in pairs. Ask and answer the questions in activity 6.

How long have you known your best friend?

I've known him for ten years.

GRAMMAR GUIDE page 134

WRITING

A Magazine Article

1 77 Read and listen. What have the students done to raise money for charity?

____

2 Read again and answer the questions.

a Which charity did they want to help? Why?

____

b Why did the students want to raise money?

____

c Why did they do a sponsored walk?

____

LANGUAGE FOCUS

so* and *because

We all enjoy walking, **so** we decided to do a sponsored walk.
We wanted to do something to help animals **because** many of us have pets.
300 people have promised sponsorship money, **so** the total will probably be more than $2,000.
I hope it will become an annual event **because** it has been such a success.

3 Look at the Language Focus and complete the rules with the words *so* and *because*.

a We use ________ to show the result.

b We use ________ to give a reason.

4 Join the sentences with *because* or *so*.

a We don't have any milk. I'm going to the supermarket.

____

____

b I'm going to buy a raffle ticket. I want to support that charity.

____

____

c Dave wants to raise money. He's going to do a sponsored walk.

____

____

d I can't go to Sally's party. We're going away this weekend.

____

____

10th grade students from St. Anne School have raised over $1,500 for the ASPCA

Organizer Harry Jones said, 'We wanted to do something to help animals because many of us have pets and we are all animal lovers. We all enjoy walking, so we decided to do a sponsored walk at the local park.' Over 200 parents and friends were at the park to support the students. More than 300 people have promised sponsorship money, so the total will probably be more than $2,000 when the students have collected all the money. Principal Marion Kemp is very proud of the students. 'We've never done a sponsored walk before. I hope it will become an annual event because it has been such a success.'

5 Write a magazine article (120-150 words) about a charity event.

Writing a Magazine Article

Step 1 > PLAN

Think about a charity event. Who organized it? Which charity was it for?

Step 2 > WRITE

Write a first draft. Include information about the organizers, location and activity. Include a quote.

Step 3 > CHECK

Check your work. Make sure you have used *so* and *because* correctly.

Step 4 > WRITE

Write your final version.

VOCABULARY IN PICTURES

Fundraising Ideas

collect money

do a sponsored swim

have a rummage sale

make a charity CD

organize a concert

sell badges

sell raffle tickets

sell candies

wash cars

make and *do*

make a decision

make a mistake

make friends

make money

make someone happy

make someone laugh

do charity work

do exercise

do homework

do nothing

do someone a favor

do your best

GRAMMAR GUIDE

Present Perfect: *ever, never, yet, already, just*

Have you **ever** lived in France?
I have **never** lived in France.
Have you lived in France **yet**?
I haven't lived in France **yet**.
I have **already** lived in France.
The sponsored swim has **just** started.

- we often use the adverb *ever* to ask if something has happened at any time before now.
- we use *never* to express a negative idea.
- we use *already* to say that something has happened early. It usually comes before the main verb.
- we use *yet* to talk about something which is expected to happen. It means 'at any time up to now.' It is used in questions and negative sentences. It is placed at the end of sentences.
- we usually use *just* with the present perfect tense, and it means 'a short time ago.' It comes before the main verb.

Present Perfect: *for* and *since*

How long has she been a Goodwill Ambassador?
She's been an Ambassador **since** August 2009. She's been an Ambassador **for** more than a year.

for (a period in time)	since (a point in time)
ten minutes	2010
two hours	2pm
four days	April
three weeks	this morning
a month	I was born
a year	Saturday
a long time	last night

- we use *How long* with present perfect questions to ask about the duration of an activity or situation
  How long has she been a doctor?
- we use *for* with durations of time
  She's been a doctor **for more than a year**.
- we use *since* with starting points in time (when the activity commenced)
  She's been a doctor **since August 2009**.

PROGRESS CHECK

Fundraising Ideas

1 Match a-f with 1-6 to make sentences.

a ☐ Dan and Rita are doing
b ☐ I bought a charity
c ☐ Pop stars are making a
d ☐ My friends are washing
e ☐ There was a woman collecting
f ☐ We've organized

1 money for the Red Cross.
2 charity CD to raise money for famine victims.
3 a sponsored swim this weekend.
4 raffle ticket to help Haiti.
5 a rummage sale for the ASPCA.
6 cars for charity.

make and *do*

2 Complete the sentences with the correct form of *make* or *do*.

a I've just ______ some exercise. I'm really tired.
b I always ______ my homework before I watch TV.
c Ken is so funny. He really ______ me laugh.
d Can you ______ me a favor? I really need some help.
e Robin wants to ______ some charity work in Africa for a year.
f I think I failed the test. I ______ too many mistakes.

Present Perfect: *ever, never, yet, already, just*

3 Complete the sentences with *ever, never, yet, already* or *just*.

a Beth has ______ done a sponsored swim.
b My brother has ______ met some people.
c Have you ______ raised money for charity?
d I haven't visited India ______, but I want to.
e Have you seen the new adventure movie ______?
f Alex has ______ collected lots of money for charity.

Present Perfect: *for* and *since*

4 Complete the sentences with *for* or *since*.

a I've known my best friend ______ 2006.
b Carla's done charity work ______ she was 12.
c Rafael Nadal has been famous ______ many years.
d You've studied ______ three hours. Well done!
e I haven't eaten ______ this morning. I'm hungry.
f Tom's been here ______ a long time. He arrived early.

Grammar Buildup 8

1 2 3 4 5 6 7 8

5 Choose the correct answers.

a ________ you know someone you really admire? I do. My best friend, Jenny. We've known each other since we **b** ________ primary school and we've been best friends **c** ________ five years. Jenny loves **d** ________ other people. She **e** ________ lots of money for charity.

She's washed cars and **f** ________ cakes. I've done some events with her. For example, we've done a sponsored swim to raise money for the ASPCA.

We think it's the **g** ________ important charity in the world. The only thing Jenny has **h** ________ done is a sponsored walk, but she's going to do one this summer. She's fantastic!

a	**1** Do	**2** Have
b	**1** start	**2** started
c	**1** for	**2** since
d	**1** help	**2** helping
e	**1** is raising	**2** has raised
f	**1** sells	**2** sold
g	**1** more	**2** most
h	**1** never	**2** ever

Review 4

VOCABULARY

GRAMMAR

Start

1

Have you ever sold _________ for charity?

2

The _________ lives in the Arctic Circle.

9

Have you ever done a _________ swim?

10

Do you _________ some exercise everyday?

11

The _________ is a mammal that lives in the sea.

12

How do you _________ someone happy?

13

Have you ever seen a _________ in the wild?

14

Honey is usually sold in _________.

15

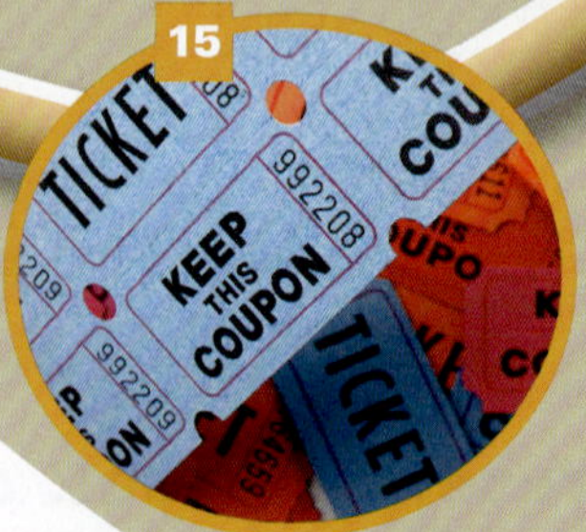

How often do you buy charity _________?

3

What _________ you laugh?

4

This cake takes a whole _________ of milk.

5

The _________ is the biggest land animal.

6

When I'm tired, I like _________ nothing.

7

Have you ever bought something at a _________ sale?

8

_________ is made from wood.

16

Sweaters, gloves and scarves are often made of _________.

17

Do you always _________ your homework?

18

You should recycle your used _________.

Finish

Review 4

VOCABULARY

GRAMMAR

Present Perfect

1 Write the past participles of the regular and irregular verbs.

organize	*organized*	e	have	______
see	*seen*	f	choose	______
a stop	______	g	read	______
b play	______	h	become	______
c try	______	i	do	______
d open	______	j	make	______

2 Complete the sentences with *have* or *has* and the past participle form of one of the verbs in the box.

build buy do have make see

They *have built* the new library.

a I ________ a mistake.

b Gemma ________ a new bag.

c The students ________ voluntary work.

d I ________ my hair cut this month.

e My brother ________ the Tower of London.

3 Write sentences in the present perfect affirmative.

I / read / a great book
I have read a great book.

a my sister / promise / to take me to the concert
____

b my uncle and aunt / open / a new hotel
____

c I / meet / several famous people
____

d we / have / fish for lunch
____

e they / arrive / early for the game
____

f you / become / very brave
____

4 Rewrite the sentences in the negative form.

I've seen this film five times.
I haven't seen this film five times.

a My uncle has sailed around the world alone.
____

b I have finished this activity.
____

c My friend Dan has bought my old desktop.
____

d At school we have reduced our waste.
____

5 Look at Kate's to-do list. Write questions and short answers using the present perfect affirmative and negative.

a recycle plastic bottles ...	✓
b turn off the TV ...	✗
c throw away clothes ...	✗
d buy local food ...	✓
e become vegetarian ...	✓

a ________________
____

b ________________
____

c ________________
____

d ________________
____

e ________________
____

VOCABULARY

GRAMMAR

Present Perfect: *ever, never, yet, already, just*

6 Complete the sentences using the present perfect tense of the verbs in parentheses. Add *already* or *just*, according to the clues given.

They _have already built_ (build) the new hospital. (It was ready earlier than expected.)

a My dad __________ (break) his leg. (He can't walk right now.)

b She __________ (have) lunch. (She doesn't need to eat for at least three hours.)

c We __________ (organize) a concert. (We have been through this experience before.)

d Louie __________ (post) a new picture. (The Facebook status says "just now.")

7 Complete these sentences with *ever* and *never*.

I've _never_ played the trumpet.

a Have you ______ swum in a lake?

b My boyfriend has ______ driven a car.

c Have your friends ______ played rugby?

d She's ridden an elephant but she's ______ ridden a camel.

8 Write questions in the present perfect.

you / ever / meet / a scientist?
Have you ever met a scientist?

a your parents / sell / yet / their house?

____

b Miss Martinez / ever / give / you a bad grade?

____

c you / ever / eat / shark?

____

d Charlie / yet / wash / his dad's car?

____

9 Write answers for the questions in activity 8.

✗ _No, I have never met a scientist._

a ✓ __________

b ✗ __________

c ✓ __________

for and *since*

10 Complete the chart with the time expressions in the box.

~~2009~~ last year a year eight months a few minutes 9 o'clock February a long time hours

for	*since*
	2009

11 Complete the sentences with *for* or *since*.

My dad hasn't worked _for_ ten years.

a 'How long has there been a cathedral here? ______ more than five centuries.'

b We've known each other ______ last summer.

c Henry has wanted to be an actor ______ he was young.

d They haven't seen Katy ______ two weeks.

e Tuvalu has been an independent country ______ 1978.

f Europeans have inhabited this island ______ over 400 years.

Go Green!

- **What do you think is going to happen to the environment in the next few years?**
- **And in the next hundred years?**
- **How can we contribute to the environment's health and longevity?**

1 Match the pictures with the information provided. Then, discuss the situations presented with your classmates.

a About 70% of the world's marine species are at risk of extinction.

b Animals raised for food currently generate between 15% and 20% of methane emissions globally.

c 2.12 billion tons of waste are dumped every year around the globe.

d Each year, over 63,000 square miles of tropical forest are destroyed, resulting in more than half the world's tropical forests being lost.

 ☐

 ☐

 ☐

 ☐

2 Read the text about the 3 R's below. Then read the questions in the box and write each question next to the action it relates to.

Can the material be made into something new?
Can I or someone else make use of it in a different way?
Do I really need it?

Reduce: Waste happens because products are used inefficiently or due to bad planning. For example, when we buy food we don't need on impulse, or because there's a special offer, and then waste it.
Ask yourself: ______________________________

Reuse: Using a product more than once, either for the same purpose (for example, returnable glass bottles) or for a different purpose (such as old jam jars for food storage); repairing products, selling or donating them to charity / community groups.
Ask yourself: ______________________________

Recycle: This can involve turning old material into a new version of the same thing or into something completely different. For example, used glass bottles can be recycled into new bottles, used paper can be recycled into new paper and even composting can be considered a form of recycling – turning biodegradable waste into new substances to fertilize the soil.
Ask yourself: ______________________________

3 **Do you know there is a 4th R? What does it stand for? Check (✓) the correct answer.**

☐ After reducing, reusing and recycling (including composting) as much as possible, the garbage left can be used to generate heat and power. This is known as 'Recovery,' the 4th R.

☐ The fourth R is just meant for industries; they 'refuse' to manufacture products that pollute the environment.

4 **Classify the sentences below under the most appropriate column of the chart. Work with a partner.**

a Separate glass, paper and plastic into different trash cans.

b Borrow instead of buying.

c Take quick showers.

d Use old shirts or towels as rags.

e Buy products made of recycled material.

f Bring hazardous items (such as batteries) to a collection site.

g Use dish cloths instead of paper towels.

h Save paper and plastic bags.

i Turn off all the lights when leaving the room.

j Donate old items.

reduce	reuse	recycle
c		

A Stopwaste School Campaign

You and your classmates have decided to investigate how much waste goes on at your school to help fight it.

Doing

1 Get together in groups of four or five students.

2 During some days, walk around the school and find out if…

- lights are turned off when students leave the classroom;
- snacks / sandwiches brought from home are packed in reusable containers;
- snacks / sandwiches aren't thrown away;
- the school provides recycling bins;
- students do not throw napkins, plastic bags, etc. on the floor during recess;
- students use both sides of notebook pages when they take notes during classes or do homework;
- students use school supplies wisely;
- a projector or blackboard is used to help reduce the amount of photocopied information.

Presenting

3 Create a STOPWASTE foldable booklet with top tips to reduce waste at school. Make your booklet attractive and appealing. You can look at examples of how to build your booklet typing "hot dog booklet" or "foldable templates" on a search engine.

4 Talk to your teacher / school principal about a booklet display during recess and / or parents' meetings.

5 Be a waste watcher at school, at home, everywhere you go!

Reflecting

6 Did you change your attitudes towards waste?

7 Do you think your ideas have reached many students at school?

8 Did you notice any changes in students' behavior in school?

Irregular Verbs

Infinitive	Simple Past	Past Participle
78 **be** /bi/	was / were /wɑz/, /wɜr/	been /bin/, /bɪn/
begin /bɪ'gɪn/	began /bɪ'gæn/	begun /bɪ'gʌn/
break /breɪk/	broke /broʊk/	broken /'broʊkən/
bring /brɪŋ/	brought /brɔt/	brought /brɔt/
build /bɪld/	built /bɪlt/	built /bɪlt/
buy /baɪ/	bought /bɔt/	bought /bɔt/
choose /tʃuz/	chose /tʃoʊz/	chosen /'tʃoʊz(ə)n/
come /kʌm/	came /keɪm/	come /kʌm/
do /du/	did /dɪd/	done /dʌn/
drink /drɪŋk/	drank /dræŋk/	drunk /drʌŋk/
drive /draɪv/	drove /droʊv/	driven /'drɪv(ə)n/
eat /it/	ate /eɪt/	eaten /'it(ə)n/
fall /fɔl/	fell /fel/	fallen /'fɔlən/
find /faɪnd/	found /faʊnd/	found /faʊnd/
fly /flaɪ/	flew /flu/	flown /floʊn/
forget /fər'get/	forgot /fər'gɑt/	forgotten /fər'gɑt(ə)n/
get /get/	got /gɑt/	got /gɑt/, gotten /'gɑt(ə)n/
give /gɪv/	gave /geɪv/	given /'gɪv(ə)n/
go /goʊ/	went /went/	gone /gɔn/
have /hæv/	had /həd/	had /həd/
hear /hɪr/	heard /hɜrd/	heard /hɜrd/
know /noʊ/	knew /nu/	known /noʊn/
learn /lɜrn/	learnt / learned /lɜrnt/, /'lɜrnəd/	learnt / learned /lɜrnt/, /'lɜrnəd/
leave /liv/	left /left/	left /left/
lose /luz/	lost /lɔst/	lost /lɔst/
make /meɪk/	made /meɪd/	made /meɪd/
meet /mit/	met /met/	met /met/
pay /peɪ/	paid /peɪd/	paid /peɪd/
put /pʊt/	put /pʊt/	put /pʊt/
read /rid/	read /red/	read /red/
run /rʌn/	ran /ræn/	run /rʌn/
say /seɪ/	said /sed/	said /sed/
see /si/	saw /sɔ/	seen /sin/
sell /sel/	sold /soʊld/	sold /soʊld/
sing /sɪŋ/	sang /sæŋ/	sung /sʌŋ/
sit /sɪt/	sat /sæt/	sat /sæt/
speak /spik/	spoke /spoʊk/	spoken /'spoʊkən/
take /teɪk/	took /tʊk/	taken /'teɪkən/
teach /titʃ/	taught /tɔt/	taught /tɔt/
tell /tel/	told /toʊld/	told /toʊld/
think /θɪŋk/	thought /θɔt/	thought /θɔt/
wear /wer/	wore /wɔr/	worn /wɔrn/
win /wɪn/	won /wʌn/	won /wʌn/
write /raɪt/	wrote /roʊt/	written /'rɪt(ə)n/

Workbook

CONTENTS

Starter

Free-time Activities

1 Complete the sentences with the words in the box.

do (2x)	go to (2x)	play (2x)

a My parents ________ volunteer work at an urban wildlife rehabilitation center.

b I love to ________ video games with my younger cousins at my grandma's house.

c John and Mike ________ judo and it really helps them to be more focused and relaxed.

d One of my favorite free-time activities is to ________ my guitar.

e My friends and I like to ________ the movies on Saturday evenings.

f We often meet our neighbors when we ________ the gym.

Character Adjectives and Formation of Adverbs

2 Complete with the opposite adjectives and write their adverb form.

a dishonest ___*honest*___ ___*honestly*___

b bad ____________ ____________

c sad ____________ ____________

d shy ____________ ____________

e talkative ____________ ____________

3 Complete the adverbs with the missing letters.

a ___ u i ___ ___ l ___

b h a ___ ___ ___ l y

c c ___ r ___ f ___ ___ l y

d ___ n g ___ ___ ___ y

Rooms, Furniture and Gadgets

4 Label the furniture and gadgets and the room where you usually find them.

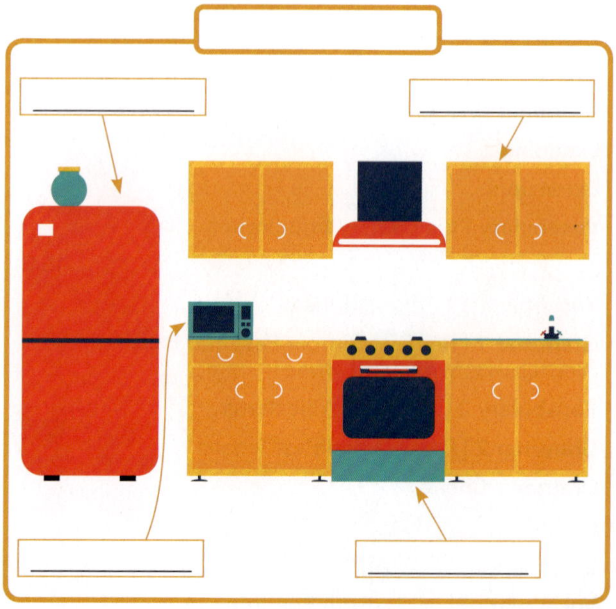

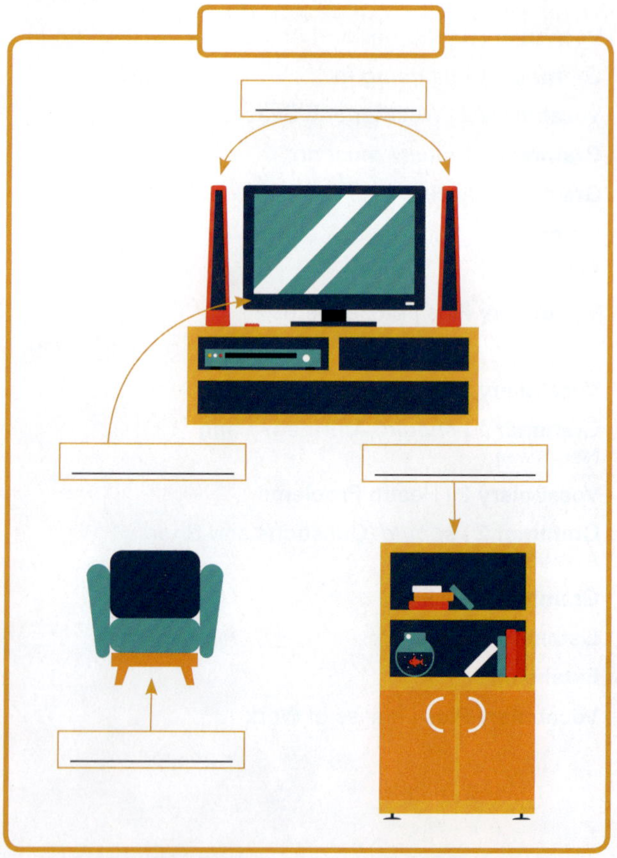

Places to Visit

5 Write the place each person should visit, according to their interests.

art gallery campground cave safari park

a Maria wants to observe freely roaming animals: ______

b Edward is fascinated by paintings and sculptures: ______

c Lavaughn is really curious about underground formations: ______

d Jeremy likes nature and wants to learn some outdoor skills: ______

Comparatives and Superlatives

6 Look at the picture and complete the sentences with the comparative or the superlative form of the words in the box.

long old short tall young

a Dean is ______ person in the family.

b Sarah's hair is ______ than Karen's.

c Frank is ______ than Lisa.

d Laura is Dean's and Sarah's ______ daughter.

e Sue is ______ than Larry.

Simple Present and Present Progressive

7 Complete the questions with the simple present or present progressive. Then find the answers in the box.

I thought of something really funny. On the weekends. Yes, I do. To the library. No, I'm studying.

a Where ______ you ______ (go)?
______

b When ______ you usually ______ (play) video games?
______

c ______ you ______ (watch) TV now?
______

d ______ you usually ______ (go) to school in the morning?
______

e Why ______ you ______ (laugh)?
______

Simple Past and Past Progressive

8 Write questions for the answers.

a ______
______

Last night I had dinner at 9:00.

b ______
______

When the teacher arrived I was talking to my friend.

c ______
______

Yesterday I watched the new episode of *Greenhouse Academy* on TV.

d ______
______

The person I was talking to is my cousin Dan.

e ______
______

The most interesting book I read last year was *Around the World in Eighty Days*, by Jules Verne.

1 Technology

VOCABULARY 1

IT Activities

1 Order the letters and write the words.

d s n e a n i m l a e ___*send an email*___

a d a e r a n o k b o e- ______________

b i t n p r a m t u n e o d c ______________

c l o d u p a a e d i o v l c p i ______________

d l u p g i n a h a f s l r v i e d ______________

2 Look at the pictures and find six IT activities in the wordsnake.

a

b

c

d

e

f

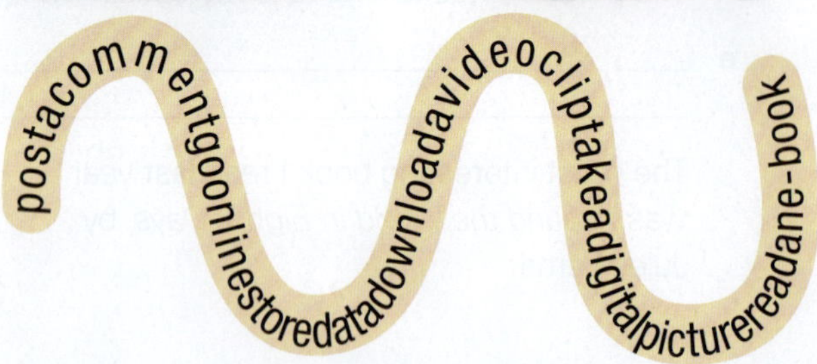

3 Match the verbs with the phrases.

a	*3*	scan	**1** a blog
b	☐	write	**2** a phone call
c	☐	charge	**3** a picture
d	☐	play	**4** a video game
e	☐	make	**5** a cell phone

4 Complete the sentences with the words in the box.

blog charge data online post print read scan send store ~~upload~~

I have a video clip on my camera. How can I ___*upload*___ it onto the internet?

a There's an interesting story on this website. I want to __________ a comment.

b I always __________ my cell phone at night when I go to bed.

c I love movies. I have a __________ called Movie Zone and I write two posts on it every week.

d I don't want to lose this __________. I have it on my computer and on my flash drive.

e Can you __________ music files on your cell phone?

f When you buy a ticket __________, you usually need to __________ a copy.

g These are my grandma's old black and white pictures. I want to __________ them and give them back to her.

h I need the PDF files from that book to write my part in the project. Can you __________ them to me via email, please?

i This e-book is too long for me to __________ it on my cell phone. I need to get an e-reader.

GRAMMAR 1

Review: Simple Past

1 Underline the correct words.

The video clip **was / were** really boring.

a Where **was** / **were** you last night?

b Who **was** / **were** that girl at the internet café?

c Adam and Layla **wasn't** / **weren't** pleased about the comments on their blog.

d There **was** / **were** an amazing picture on that website.

e My digital camera **wasn't** / **weren't** a birthday present.

f **Was** / **Were** there a lot of free games on that site?

2 Complete the sentences with *was* or *were*.

How old *were* you in 2013?

a Where ________ Andy's flash drive?

b Where ________ you during the video conference?

c I ________ annoyed with her about the pictures of me on Facebook.

d There ________ a great blog about zombie movies by a French guy.

e What ________ Kate's digital pictures like?

3 Correct the sentences. Write one negative and one affirmative sentence.

My video clips were on my digital camera. (✗ cell phone)
My video clips weren't on my digital camera.
They were on my cell phone.

a My cell phone was under the bed. (✗ the sofa)

____

____

b We were at the computer store yesterday afternoon. (✗ park)

____

____

c The text message was from Adam. (✗ Alice)

____

____

d The games on that site were terrible. (✗ great)

____

____

4 Complete the text with the simple past form of the verbs in parentheses.

We *visited* (visit) the Computer History Museum in California last year. First, we **a** ________ (watch) a movie about the history of computers. They **b** ________ (show) us a strange computer from 1939 – the Atanasoff-Berry computer. It **c** ________ (look) like lots of light bulbs on a metal plate! In the movie there was also a huge calculator from 1940. They **d** ________ (call) it the Complex Number Calculator. George Stibitz **e** ________ (design) it. It **f** ________ (use) telephone wires to send the calculations to a machine in another city. After the movie, we **g** ________ (walk) around the museum with a guide. She **h** ________ (talk) about all the old computers.

5 Complete the text with the simple past form of the regular verbs in the box.

~~arrive~~ call charge chat learn play stay store try use

My new cell phone *arrived* by mail yesterday. I **a** ________ at home in the afternoon and **b** ________ how to use it. First, I **c** ________ the battery. Then I **d** ________ all the data from my old phone on it – names, telephone numbers and email addresses. Then I **e** ________ Marianne and **f** ________ with her for ten minutes. After that, I **g** ________ two games. They were both excellent! Then I **h** ________ taking some pictures with the camera. It's fantastic. Finally, I **i** ________ a special flash memory card to upload some pictures and music files from my computer. Technology! I love it!

6 Complete the text with the simple past form of the irregular verbs in parentheses.

I *had* (have) an amazing vacation last year. My grandmother **a** ________ (give) me some money and I **b** ________ (go) traveling with my friend, Adam. Our vacation **c** ________ (begin) badly because Adam **d** ________ (lose) his passport in Paris. Luckily, the police **e** ________ (find) it for him. We **f** ________ (take) a train from Paris to the south of France. Then we **g** ________ (get) a boat to the island of Corsica. We **h** ________ (swim) every day, **i** ________ (eat) lots of delicious French food and **j** ________ (make) friends with some Spanish people at the campground. Then we **k** ________ (fly) back to Austin.

7 Match the sentence beginnings with the endings. Write the sentences in the simple past negative form.

a [*3*] I (not visit) you
b [ ] I (not call) you
c [ ] We (not watch) all of the movie
d [ ] I (not scan) his pictures
e [ ] We (not chat) to her online
f [ ] We (not go) to the internet café

1 because I (not have) my cell phone.
2 because we (not like) it.
3 because I (not have) your address.
4 because we (not know) her.
5 because he (not want) me to.
6 because we (not need) to.

a *I didn't visit you because I didn't have your address.*
b ________________
c ________________
d ________________
e ________________
f ________________

8 Complete the questions and answers with the simple past form of the verbs in parentheses.

Ross Where *did you get* (you / get) your new cell phone?
Jane I **a** ________ (buy) it at the store on Creekside Way.
Ross How much **b** ________ (it / cost)?
Jane I **c** ________ (pay) US$200 for it.
Pete **d** ________ (you / call) Ellie?
Carol No, I **e** ________ (send) her a text.
Pete What **f** ________ (you / say) in it?
Carol I **g** ________ (invite) her to a concert.
Sue When **h** ________ (Jo / break) her e-reader?
Paul She **i** ________ (not break) it. She **j** ________ (leave) it at her cousin's house on Saturday.
Guy When **k** ________ (Tom download) all this music?
Jen He **l** ________ (do) it yesterday. It **m** ________ (not take) long.

9 Write a short answer and an extra sentence for each question.

Did you wake up early yesterday?
Yes, I did. (short answer)
I woke up at 6:30. (extra sentence)
No, I didn't. (short answer)
I woke up at 10:30. (extra sentence)

a Did you have breakfast this morning?
____
____

b Did your teacher give you homework yesterday?
____
____

c Did you get any text messages yesterday?
____
____

d Did you leave your flash drive in the school computer?
____
____

VOCABULARY 2

Jobs

1 Match the jobs with the pictures.

- **a** [5] construction worker
- **b** [ ] scientist
- **c** [ ] mailman
- **d** [ ] doctor
- **e** [ ] fireman
- **f** [ ] policewoman
- **g** [ ] lawyer
- **h** [ ] artist

1

2

3

4

5

6

7

8

2 Match the word beginnings and endings to make jobs.

- **a** journal [ ] ian
- **b** politic [ ] er
- **c** research [ ] ist
- **d** techni [ ] cian

3 Read what the people say and write their jobs.

Open your mouth please. I need to check your throat.
doctor

a Someone dropped a cigarette and that's how the fire started. We managed to put it out and luckily nobody died.
____

b The police say he did it. He says he didn't do it. I'm speaking for him in court.
____

c I did these paintings ten years ago. It was my blue period and, as you can see, the main color in all of them is blue.
____

d We're asking a million cell phone users to answer these questions. We want to find out: are cell phones bad for us?
____

e In our laboratory we're trying to make new kinds of sunscreen.
____

f I'm arresting you on suspicion of robbery.
____

GRAMMAR 2

Review: Past Progressive

1 Underline the correct words.

I was / **were** waiting for you outside.

a You **was** / **were** using the computer for a long time.

b She **was** / **were** writing an email when I arrived.

c We **was** / **were** chatting online.

d Josh and Lisa **was** / **were** downloading music this morning.

e It **was** / **were** raining early this morning when I woke up.

f You and Vicki **was** / **were** playing loud music last night.

2 Write sentences using the negative and affirmative form of the past progressive.

Liam (✗ chat) online. He (✓ do) his history project.
Liam wasn't chatting online. He was doing his history project.

a I (✗ read) a blog. I (✓ watch) a video clip.

____
____

b He (✗ hang out) with his friends. He (✓ buy) a flash drive.

____
____

c They (✓ download) music. They (✗ do) their homework.

____
____

d We (✓ upload) pictures. We (✗ use) the scanner.

____
____

e You (✗ talk) on your cell phone. You (✓ take) a picture.

____
____

f She (✗ send) a message. She (✓ call) Josie.

____
____

3 Complete the questions and the answers with the past progressive form of the verbs in parentheses. Then match the questions with the answers.

a [2] Why *were you shouting* (you / shout) at the dog?

b [ ] Who ________________ (make) that noise last night?

c [ ] Where ________________ (you / sit) in the concert?

d [ ] What ________________ (your friends / do) on the computer?

e [ ] Why ________________ (Rosie / stand) in the street with her cell phone?

1 I ________________ (not sit).
I ________________ (stand) at the back.

2 Because he *was eating* (eat) my dinner.

3 She ________________ (use) it to make a video.

4 Steve. He ________________ (listen) to very loud rock music.

5 They ________________ (look) at their Facebook pages.

4 Write questions using the past progressive. Then write answers for you.

What / you do / at five o'clock / on Saturday afternoon?
What were you doing at five o'clock on Saturday afternoon?
I was playing basketball in the park.

a What / you do / at ten o'clock / last night?

____
____
____

b Where / you live / five years ago?

____
____
____

c What / you wear / yesterday?

____
____
____

d What / you think about / five minutes ago?

____
____
____

e Who / you sit / next to / in the last math class?

____
____
____

GRAMMAR CHECK

1 Read the interview and circle the correct answers.

Julie Brinton tells Mark at *#Instaenglish* about her experience with an online gym.

Mark Why **a** ______ you join it?

Julie I didn't **b** ______ time to go to the gym last summer. A friend told me about an online gym and I **c** ______ to try it. First, I **d** ______ questions about my height, weight and age. Then a virtual trainer **e** ______ an exercise program for me.

Mark **f** ______ you get in shape?

Julie Yes, I **g** ______ . But there **h** ______ some problems.

Mark What kind of problems?

Julie When I **i** ______ exercises, it was often hard to see the screen. Then once, when I was lying on the floor, my cat **j** ______ on my face!

	1	2	3
a	have	(did)	do
b	had	has	have
c	was deciding	is deciding	decided
d	is answering	answered	was answering
e	chose	was choosing	choosed
f	Do	Were	Did
g	did	was	do
h	was	were being	were
i	was doing	did	am doing
j	jumped	jumps	was jumping

2 79 Listen and check your answers.

LISTENING

1 80 Listen to five teenagers talking about their ideal jobs. Match the letters a-e with the names.

Who …

a wants to be a scientist?

b wants to work in the music business?

c wants to work for justice in the world?

d wants to work with computers?

e wants to be a reporter?

1 ☐ Andrea

2 ☐ Joel

3 ☐ Tom

4 ☐ Mark

5 ☐ Rose

2 80 Listen again. Then write T for *true* or F for *false*.

a ☐ Andrea prefers TV to radio and newspapers.

b ☐ Joel is scared of blood.

c ☐ Mark can't act.

d ☐ Rose only wants to work in the USA.

e ☐ Tom is interested in spaceships.

EXTENSION

Circle the correct words to complete the text.

'What **a do / are** you want to be?' Why do people **b always ask / ask always** this question? My answer is always, 'I **c didn't / don't** know.' At age six, the answer **d were / was** easy for me – astronaut! Now, I **e like / liked** the idea of being a web designer. I'm **f always happy / happy always** to help friends with their computer problems. And I love **g do / doing** fun things with my computer. Yesterday, for example, I **h was / am** surfing the net when I found some great design ideas. So I scanned some old pictures. Then I **i drew / was drawing** some sketches on them with my digital pen and I **j was writing / wrote** words in a balloon coming out of someone's mouth. At the moment, I'm **k designing / design** a website for a friend. But my mom **l came / comes** into my room every ten minutes and **m says / said** helpful things like, 'Why **n are you / you are** staying inside on a lovely day like today?' So things **o is / are** going very well!

VOCABULARY PLUS

Safety Equipment

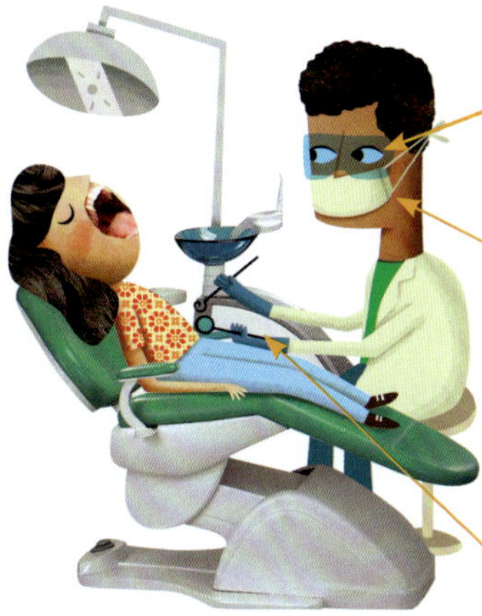

1 🔊 81 Complete the chart with the words above. Then listen and repeat.

head	eyes/ face	ears	hands	body
hat				

2 Underline the correct words.

An artist usually wears **<u>overalls</u>** / **a bulletproof vest**.

- **a** A fireman usually wears **a helmet** / **ear muffs**.
- **b** A scientist often wears **a high visibility jacket** / **safety glasses**.
- **c** A security guard usually wears a **bulletproof vest** / **face mask**.
- **d** A doctor often wears **disposable gloves** / **a cap**.
- **e** A construction worker often wears a **visor** / **high visibility jacket**.

3 Read the definitions and write the words.

These are plastic and they come in pairs.
disposable gloves

- **a** This is made of paper and it covers your mouth. ______
- **b** This is always a bright color like yellow or orange. ______
- **c** This is a head covering, but it isn't hard. ______
- **d** This is plastic and it covers your face. ______
- **e** These are plastic and they cover your eyes. ______

2 Strange but True!

VOCABULARY 1

Prepositions

1 Match the words with numbers 1-12 in the pictures.

a *11* climb **out of**
b ☐ dive **into**
c ☐ climb **up**
d ☐ walk **along**
e ☐ sail **around**
f ☐ jump **over**
g ☐ run **towards**
h ☐ parachute **down**
i ☐ drive **away from**
j ☐ jump **through**
k ☐ swim **across**
l ☐ walk **under**

a

b

c

2 Complete the text with the prepositions in the box.

across along ~~around~~ away from down into out of over under up

I had a strange dream last night. I was looking at a beautiful lake with an island in the middle. A boat was sailing *around* the island. I felt hot, so I dove **a** ________ the lake and started swimming **b** ________ it. When I got to the other side, I climbed **c** ________ the lake and lay in the sun. Then a plane flew **d** ________ me and a man parachuted **e** ________ to the grass. It was Simon. I waved at him, but he got into a car and drove **f** ________ the lake. Then I saw a river. There was a path next to the river and a bridge over the river. I started walking **g** ________ the path next to the river. I walked **h** ________ the bridge and found a mountain in front of me. My best friend was at the top of the mountain, so I wanted to run **i** ________ it, but suddenly I couldn't move. That's when I woke up.

GRAMMAR 1

Review: Simple Past and Past Progressive; *when* and *while*

1 Circle the correct words.

We were sleeping on the beach **while** / **when** somebody stole our camera.

a **While** / **When** they were cooking sausages on the beach, it started to rain.

b Where were you going **while** / **when** we met you?

c Were you watching the game **while** / **when** I called you?

d **While** / **When** I wasn't watching, she jumped out of the tree.

e We were cycling in the forest **while** / **when** we saw the bear.

2 Complete the sentences with the past progressive form of the verbs in parentheses.

I *was diving* (dive) into the lake when I hit my head.

a She fell over while she __________ (run) to catch the bus.

b Who __________ (you / talk) to when I saw you this morning?

c He lost his keys while he __________ (climb) over the wall.

d __________ (she / play) soccer when she hurt her leg?

e What __________ (you / do) while he __________ (make) dinner?

f __________ (they / sit) in their living room when the thief broke the window?

3 Circle the correct words.

I **fixed** / **was fixing** my bike when Fred **sent** / **was sending** me a text.

a She **found** / **was finding** the letter from Alex while she **cleaned** / **was cleaning** her room.

b They **played** / **were playing** soccer when she **broke** / **was breaking** her leg.

c He **fell** / **was falling** out of the tree while he **picked** / **was picking** fruit.

d He **did** / **was doing** the dishes when he **cut** / **was cutting** his finger on a knife.

e While we **watched** / **were watching** TV, somebody **knocked** / **was knocking** on the door.

4 Order the words to make sentences.

living / Martin / met / were / when / Where / you / you ?

Where were you living when you met Martin?

a A bird / my breakfast / flew / having / I / into / the kitchen / was / while

____

b at / her bag / bus stop / a man / She / standing / stole / the / was / when

____

c engine trouble / flying / over / the sea / started / the / The plane / was / when

____

d saw / shark / swimming / the / the island / to / We / we / were / when

____

e getting / I / I / into / saw / snake / my tent / a / was / While

____

f the beach / they / some treasure / were / found / While / along / walking / they

____

5 **Complete the sentences with the simple past or past progressive form of the verbs in parentheses.**

It *started* (start) to rain while we *were having* (have) a picnic.

a I ________ (not answer) the phone because I ________ (have) my dinner.

b ________ (you / see) anything strange while you ________ (walk) by the river?

c I ________ (woke) you up because you ________ (talk) in your sleep.

d What ________ (Katrin / wear) when you ________ (see) her yesterday?

e She ________ (not hear) the bell because she ________ (listen) to very loud music.

f While she ________ (write) an email, the computer ________ (stop) working.

6 **Write sentences using the past progressive or simple past form of the verbs.**

While / I get / a glass of water / the cat / eat / my lunch

While I was getting a glass of water, the cat ate my lunch.

a My pet hamster / hide / in my suitcase / while / I pack / it

____

b He crash / into another car / because / he talk / on his cell phone

____

c Who drive / when / they have / the accident ?

____

d Where you sit / when / you see / the spaceship ?

____

e We dance / at a party / when / we hear / a terrible crash

____

7 **Complete the text with the past progressive or simple past form of the verbs in parentheses.**

Andrew Philips *was surfing* (surf) with a friend in California when a shark **a** ________ (attack) him. 'I **b** ________ (lie) on my surfboard, because I was tired, when suddenly a huge black shape **c** ________ (appear) in the water,' Andrew said. Andrew **d** ________ (shout) to his friend, Tom, but Tom **e** ________ (not understand). So Andrew **f** ________ (start) to swim very fast. 'I **g** ________ (try) not to think about the danger while I **h** ________ (swim),' he told newspaper reporters. The shark **i** ________ (bite) Andrew's arm twice. 'It **j** ________ (not hurt) very much, but there was a lot of blood and I was very frightened. Then, suddenly, six or seven dolphins **k** ________ (swim) towards me. They **l** ________ (make) a circle around me and **m** ________ (stop) the shark from getting near me. While I **n** ________ (swim) towards the shore, the dolphins **o** ________ (keep) me safe.' Andrew **p** ________ (get) very weak and tired when, luckily, Neil Turner, of the coast guard, **q** ________ (see) him.

'I **r** ________ (get) into my boat immediately and **s** ________ (go) to help him,' Neil said. 'The water around Andrew was very red because he **t** ________ (still lose) a lot of blood. I **u** ________ (lift) him out of the water immediately and **v** ________ (take) him back to the shore. When the boat **w** ________ (arrive) at the shore, a medical team **x** ________ (already wait) for Andrew. They **y** ________ (give) him first aid and **z** ________ (drive) him to hospital.

VOCABULARY 2

-ed / -ing Adjectives

1 Look at the pictures and complete the words.

a bor__________

b bor____*ing*____

c annoy__________

d annoy__________

e excit__________

f excit__________

g tir__________

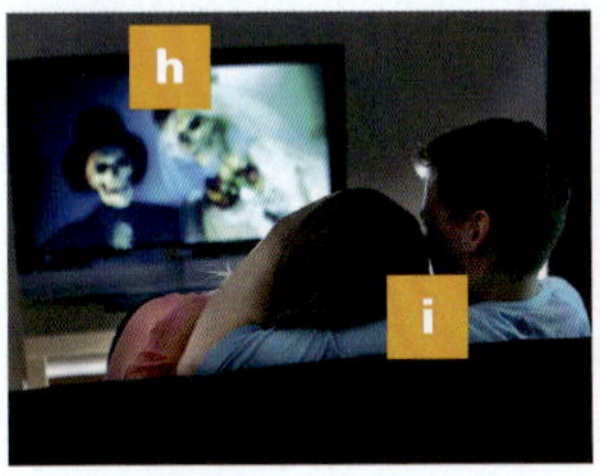

h frighten__________

i frighten__________

j tir__________

k worr__________

l worr__________

m interest__________

n surprise__________

o surpris__________

p interest__________

2 Circle the correct words.

She borrows my things and doesn't give them back. It's very **annoyed** / **annoying**.

a He travels a lot and tells great stories. He's a very **interested** / **interesting** person.

b We're going on vacation tomorrow. I'm really **excited** / **exciting**.

c I'm very **worried** / **worrying** because I can't find my passport anywhere.

d I didn't expect to get a good grade. I was very **surprised** / **surprising**.

e The waves were really big and I'm not a good swimmer. It was **frightened** / **frightening**.

3 Complete the sentences with the words in the box.

annoyed bored boring exciting frightened frightening ~~interested~~ tired tiring

Are you ___*interested*___ in birds? There's a big green one in that tree.

a Let's take the elevator to the seventh floor. Walking up the stairs is too __________.

b I got __________ with my brother last night. He was making a lot of noise and I couldn't sleep.

c I don't watch horror movies. They're too __________ for me.

d I was __________ in that class, so I started to think about the holidays.

e I'm __________ because I didn't sleep last night. I must go to bed early tonight.

f This book is very __________. I can't stop reading it.

g The bull started to run at me and I was really __________.

h The movie was really __________. I fell asleep in the middle of it.

4 Complete the sentences so they are true for you.

a I am frightened of __________.

b I think __________ is boring.

c When I'm annoyed, I __________.

d I was surprised when __________.

e I'm interested in __________.

GRAMMAR 2

Present and Past Tenses

1 **What tenses are the underlined verbs? Write *simple present, present progressive, simple past* or *past progressive*.**

Why are you wearing that silly hat?
present progressive

a I always wear a hat in the sun.
____

b Did you get it in Florida?
____

c Yes, I bought it at a market.
____

d What were you doing in Florida?
____

e My parents took me there for vacation.
____

f Do you go there every year?
____

g No. We went there last year because my uncle was living there.
____

h Where's he living now?
____

i Scotland. I want to go there for New Year.
____

2 **Match the sentence beginnings with the endings. Then complete the beginnings with the correct form of the verbs in parentheses.**

a [3] While I *wasn't looking* (not look),
b [ ] What ______________ (you / do)
c [ ] She ______________ (drop) all the plates
d [ ] He always ______________ (wear) a suit and tie
e [ ] Look at them! They ______________ (smile)
f [ ] I ______________ (crash) the car last year
g [ ] Josie ______________ (not speak) today

1 because I was driving too fast.
2 because someone is taking their picture.
3 my little sister hid my keys under my bed.
4 when he goes to work.
5 because she has a sore throat.
6 when she heard the terrible news.
7 when you found the scorpion in your tent?

3 **Complete the text with the correct form of the verbs in parentheses. Use the simple present, present progressive, simple past or past progressive.**

Last summer, I *was staying* (stay) in my little house by the sea when something very strange **a** ______________ (happen). I **b** ______________ (watch) the sunset when, suddenly, a boy of about ten **c** ______________ (appear) from nowhere. He **d** ______________ (hold) a big white towel and his hair was wet. I **e** ______________ (notice) a chain around his neck with the letter 'C' on it. He said, 'My sister, Gaby, swam out to Burnt Island. Now she **f** ______________ (try) to swim back, but the current is very strong. She **g** ______________ (drown). Please do something.' I **h** ______________ (go) to my boat but the boy **i** ______________ (not come) with me. Suddenly, he wasn't there. I **j** ______________ (take) the boat towards Burnt Island and **k** ______________ (find) Gaby. She **l** ______________ (not swim) and she **m** ______________ (lie) with her face in the water. I **n** ______________ (pull) her into the boat. She was very weak, but she was alive. 'Thank you,' she said, 'I **o** ______________ (drown). You **p** ______________ (save) my life.' 'Your brother did,' I **q** ______________ (answer). 'He **r** ______________ (tell) me to help you.' Gaby **s** ______________ (start) to cry. 'I don't have a brother,' she said. 'Charlie **t** ______________ (drown) near Burnt Island last year. He was only ten years old. I **u** ______________ (think) about him every day. This was his chain. I always **v** ______________ (wear) it now.' She **w** ______________ (show) me the chain around her neck. It was the same chain as the boy's.

GRAMMAR CHECK

1 Read the text and circle the correct answers.

You probably know about hypnotists. They **a** ______ into a person's eyes and that person **b** ______ to sleep. Tanya Brooks, a talented hypnotist, and her friend **c** ______ a picnic in Yellowstone National Park when a dangerous bear came up to them. They were both so frightened, they **d** ______ away. But then, Tanya **e** ______ an excellent idea. She **f** ______ up and looked into the eyes of the bear. While she was doing this, it suddenly **g** ______ asleep. Then, Tanya and her friend **h** ______ into their car and drove away. Now, she **i** ______ a book about hypnotizing dangerous animals. But be careful! It usually **j** ______ .

	1	2	3
a	are looking	(look)	were looking
b	went	is going	goes
c	are having	had	were having
d	aren't running	didn't run	weren't running
e	was having	has	had
f	stood	was standing	stands
g	is falling	fell	was falling
h	were getting	did get	got
i	writes	is write	is writing
j	doesn't work	wasn't working	isn't working

2 82 Listen and check your answers.

LISTENING

1 83 Listen and number the events in the correct order.

- **a** ☐ Joss got her sweater from her bedroom.
- **b** ☐ Joss met a girl on the stairs.
- **c** ☐ Joss saw a light in her bedroom window.
- **d** ☐ Joss took a picture of a girl in her window.
- **e** ☐ Joss took some pictures of the lake.
- **f** ☐ Joss walked around the garden.
- **g** ☐ Joss went to stay with Leonie.
- **h** ☐ Joss looked for her picture of Betsy.
- **i** ☐ Leonie started practicing the piano.
- **j** ☐ Leonie told Joss about Betsy.

2 83 Listen again and circle T for *true*, F for *false* or DK for *don't know*.

- **a** There were usually a lot of visitors at Leonie's house. T / F / DK
- **b** Joss doesn't have any brothers or sisters. T / F / DK
- **c** Joss didn't know the girl on the stairs. T / F / DK
- **d** Joss was not surprised to see the light in her room. T / F / DK
- **e** The girl with the pink flower was trying to use Joss's camera. T / F / DK
- **f** Betsy was one of Leonie's cousins. T / F / DK
- **g** Joss's picture did not show Betsy. T / F / DK

EXTENSION

Underline the correct words to complete the text.

Last weekend, I **a was staying / stayed** at Gary's house in the country. Gary and I **b was / were** lying in the sun in the garden. I was trying to read a difficult philosophy book, but Gary's dog was making noise, so I **c didn't / don't** understand anything. Gary's dog loves **d to chase / chasing** after his ball, so I **e threw / was throwing** it for him. I was surprised because he **f didn't / wasn't** come back to me with it. After a bit, I **g was going / went** to look for him. He **h was / is** under a tree with a very long white bone. I got Gary to look at it. He **i studies / is studying** medicine now, so he knows about bones. Gary **j said / was saying** it's definitely a human bone. My question is: where **k did / does** the dog find it? And how and when did that person **l die / died**?

VOCABULARY PLUS

Natural Phenomena

1 🔊 84 Label the pictures with the words in the box. Then listen and repeat.

avalanche blizzard cyclone drought hailstorm heat wave landslide thunderstorm tsunami wildfire

2 Underline the correct words.

There is often **a drought** / **an avalanche** in hot countries in the summer.

- **a** It was snowing and then it became a **blizzard** / **landslide**.
- **b** The **tsunami** / **wildfire** started in the forest.
- **c** The **drought** / **cyclone** destroyed everything in its path.
- **d** The dark clouds were followed by a **hailstorm** / **wildfire**.
- **e** **Thunderstorms** / **Blizzards** often occur in very hot weather.

3 Complete the definitions with the correct words.

A *tsunami* is an enormous wave in the sea.

- **a** An __________ is when a lot of snow moves down a mountain.
- **b** A __________ is an extremely strong rotating wind.
- **c** A __________ is when it is unusually hot for several days or weeks.
- **d** A __________ is when there isn't any rain for months.
- **e** A __________ is when a lot of earth moves down a mountain.

4 Complete these sentences for you. Try to use words from activity 1.

- **a** In my country, there are sometimes ________________.
- **b** I have never seen ________________.
- **c** I am scared of ________________.

3 Celebrate!

VOCABULARY 1

Clothes and Accessories

1 Order the letters and write the words. Then match them with the pictures.

[*4*] h t s r i - T *T-shirt*

a [ ] k j e t a c ______

b [ ] s i r k t ______

c [ ] r k s n e s a e ______

d [ ] r s f a c ______

e [ ] n j s a e ______

f [ ] t s o b o ______

g [ ] t s r i h ______

h [ ] r s d e s ______

i [ ] t w s e r e a ______

j [ ] o t a c ______

k [ ] s t n p a ______

l [ ] t s s r h o ______

2 Where do the clothes go? Write the words from activity 1 in the correct group.

a on your neck ______

b on your body ______

c on your legs ______

d on your feet ______

3 Read the clues and complete the crossword.

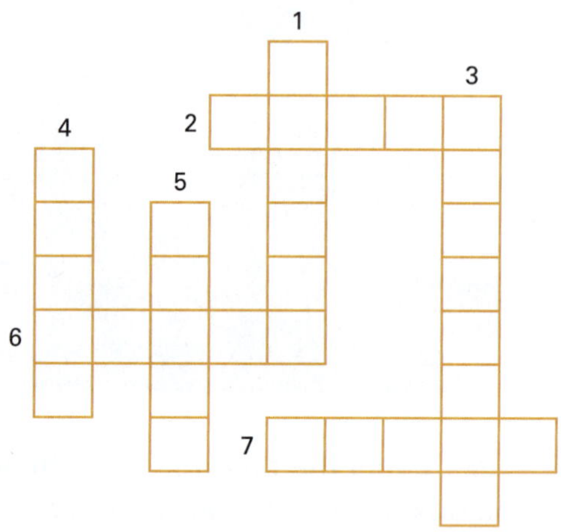

Down

1 A light coat.

3 You wear a pair of these on your feet when you're doing exercise.

4 It's only one piece and it covers your body.

5 You wear this on the top of your body. It's light and has buttons on the front.

Across

2 Jeans are an example of a pair of these.

6 Men don't usually wear this.

7 You wear this on your neck to keep warm.

4 Complete the sentences for you.

a Today I'm wearing ______.

b Yesterday I wore ______.

c On weekends I usually wear ______.

GRAMMAR 1

be going to

1 Underline the correct words.

I'm really excited. It's my brother Ned's birthday on Saturday. He **a 's / 're** going to be 18! Ned thinks we **b isn't / aren't** going to do anything special, but in fact we **c 'm / 're** going to have a big party. It **d 's / 're** going to be at home and lots of family and friends **e is / are** going to come. A DJ **f am not / isn't** going to be there, but it's OK. I **g 'm / 's** going to play music on Ned's music streaming app.

It's going to be great! ☺

2 Rewrite the sentences using the information in parentheses.

Ned's going to be unhappy on Saturday night. (happy)

Ned isn't going to be unhappy on Saturday night.

He's going to be happy.

a One thousand people are going to come to the party. (one hundred)

______

______

b Ned's going to receive two presents. (lots of)

______

______

c I'm going to wear a dress. (pants)

______

______

d The party's going to finish at 10 o'clock. (11 o'clock)

______

______

3 Complete the text with the *going to* form of the verbs in parentheses.

We have a big problem. We **a** ______ (have) Ned's party in the garden, but the weather forecast says it **b** ______ (rain) on Saturday evening. My parents **c** ______ (not change) their plans. Instead, they **d** ______ (buy) lots of umbrellas. That's silly! I **e** ______ (tell) them to think again, but I know my dad **f** ______ (not listen) to me. Poor Ned! The party **g** ______ (be) a disaster in the rain! ☹

4 Look at Mark's diary and write sentences with the affirmative or negative form of *going to*.

MONDAY (today)	get up early do judo 7:00 pm
TUESDAY	no school! go to the movies
WEDNESDAY	meet Sarah – play basketball ☺
THURSDAY	buy new jeans
FRIDAY	go swimming with Leo
SATURDAY	visit grandparents
SUNDAY	

a Mark / get up early / today

______

b he / do judo / tonight

______

c he / go to school / on Tuesday

______

d Mark and Sarah / play basketball / on Wednesday

______

e Mark / buy new sneakers / on Thursday

______

f Mark and Leo / go surfing / on Friday

______

g he / visit grandparents / on the weekend

______

5 Write sentences about your future plans.

a Tonight ______.

b Next Thursday ______.

c On the weekend ______.

6 Complete the questions with *is* or *are*. Then match and write the answers in the box with the correct questions.

No, he isn't. No, we aren't.
Some soccer shoes.
~~Yes, I am.~~ Yes, it is. Yes, they are.

Are you going to go shopping this Saturday?
Yes, I am.

a What ___ you going to look for?
______

b ______ your dad going to drive you to the mall?
______

c ______ you and Ed going to play soccer next Sunday?
______

d ______ your parents going to buy the shoes?
______

e ______ it going to be an expensive day for them?
______

7 Order the words to make questions. Then write short answers.

going / Gemma / sunbathe / Is / to ? (✓)
Is Gemma going to sunbathe?
Yes, she is.

a swim / Are / to / going / they ? (✓)
______
______

b to / play / they / going / Are / tennis ? (✗)
______
______

c Is / rain / to / going / it ? (✓)
______
______

d cook / she / to / Is / going ? (✗)
______
______

e your dad / go / going / Is / skiing / to ? (✓)
______
______

f a coat / she / going / Is / to / wear ? (✗)
______
______

8 Complete the questions with the correct *going to* form of the verbs in parentheses. Complete the short answers.

Ted What **a** ______ (you / do) this Saturday night, Dad?

Dad Your mom and I are going to go to a party at Emma's house at eight o'clock.

Ted What type of party **b** ______ (it / be)?

Dad A costume party.

Ted Really? **c** ______ (you / buy) a costume?

Dad No, **d** ______. I'm going to make a cowboy costume. I'm going to wear a red shirt, boots, and a big hat.

Ted A cowboy! **e** ______ (Mom / go) as a cowgirl?

Dad Yes, **f** ______. She will wear boots, too.

Ted **g** ______ (all the men / go) in costumes?

Dad Yes, **h** ______.
i ______ (you / see) your friends on Saturday night, Ted?

Ted Yes, **j** ______, but not before eight.

Dad Why not?

Ted Because I want to take some pictures of you – as a cowboy!

9 Answer the questions for you. Write full sentences.

a What are you going to do this weekend?
______

b Where are you going to go?
______

c Who are you going to see?
______

d What are you going to wear?
______

VOCABULARY 2

Weather and Seasons

1 Write the words in the box under the correct picture.

cloudy cold dry hot mild rainy
snowy stormy sunny warm ~~wet~~ windy

wet ______

a

______

b

______

c

______

d

______

e

______

f

______

g

______

h

______

i

______

j

______

k

______

2 Complete the sentences with the seasons in the north hemisphere.

March, April and May are in *spring*.

a December, January and February are in ______.

b September, October and November are in ______.

c June, July and August are in ______.

3 Look at the pictures and write sentences about the weather in the countries.

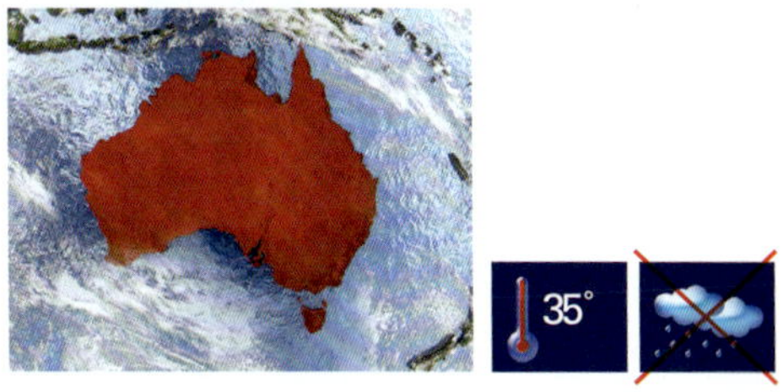

In Australia *it's hot and dry*.

a In France ______.

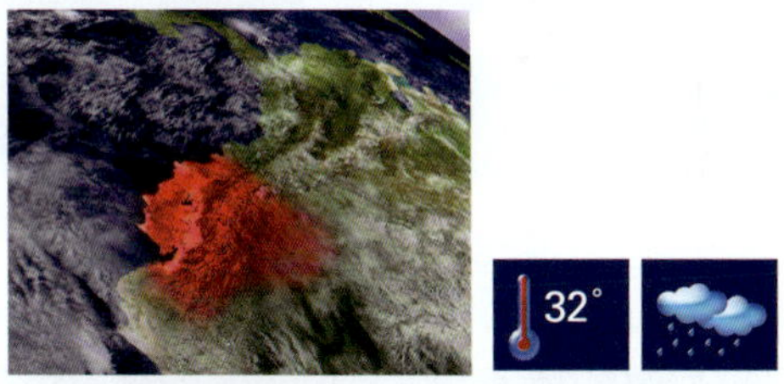

b In Ecuador ______.

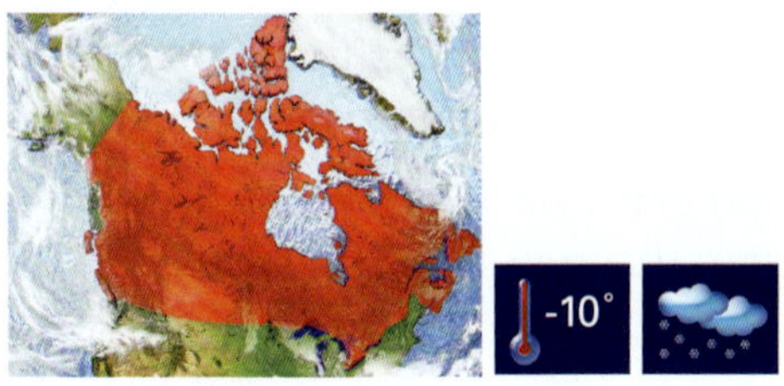

c In Canada ______.

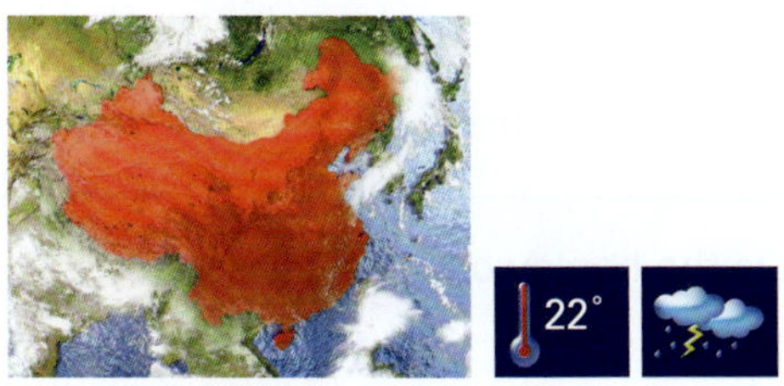

d In China ______.

GRAMMAR 2

must / must not

1 Complete the rules with *must* or *must not*.

POOL RULES

You *must* wear a hat.

a You ________ eat food.

b People ________ run.

c You ________ swim in the correct lane.

d You ________ listen to the lifeguard.

e Swimmers ________ play ball games.

2 Rewrite the sentences using the pronouns in parentheses and *must* or *must not*.

Sit next to the window. (She)

She must sit next to the window.

a Don't eat in class. (You)

____

b Don't touch the video projector. (They)

____

c Listen to the teacher. (We)

____

d Do the homework again. (He)

____

e Don't wear these sneakers to school. (I)

____

3 Look at the pictures and match the beginnings a-f to the endings 1-6. Then write sentences with the phrases *You must* or *You must not*.

a [2] take pictures
b [ ] drive on the left
c [ ] talk on the phone
d [ ] give any food
e [ ] take dogs
f [ ] wear a seatbelt

1 on the plane
2 in the museum
3 in the movie theater
4 into the store
5 in Australia
6 to the animals

a *You must not take pictures in the museum.*

b ________________________________

c ________________________________

d ________________________________

e ________________________________

f ________________________________

GRAMMAR CHECK

1 Read the dialogue and circle the correct answers.

Tina Hi, Mom.
Mom Hi, Tina. What time **a** … going to be home?
Tina I'm just trying on a T-shirt and then I **b** … to come home.
Mom A T-shirt? Are you going **c** … it?
Tina Yes, **d** … . It's really cool.
Mom What color **e** … to get?
Tina Black.
Mom Black? **f** … a black one, Tina. That **g**… going to be good for summer. How about a yellow one?
Tina No, Mom. I **h** … going to buy a yellow T-shirt. I hate yellow! Look! I **i** … pay for the T-shirt so I can leave the store and go home. I have to go now. Bye!
Mom Tina? Wait a minute! Tina!

	1	2	3
a	you	you are	(are you)
b	'm going	'm go	going
c	buy	to buy	buys
d	am	I do	I am
e	are you going	are going you	you are going
f	Get	Don't get	Doesn't get
g	no	is aren't	isn't
h	isn't	'm not	aren't
i	must not	have not	must

2 🔊 85 Listen and check your answers.

LISTENING

1 🔊 86 Listen to the dialogue and check (✓) the picture of Phoebe. Which city is she going to visit next month?

____

☐ 

☐ 

2 🔊 86 Listen again and answer the questions.

a Who is Phoebe going to go away with?
____

b When did she go to Vancouver?
____

c Why didn't she go skiing there?
____

d What's the weather like in Aspen today?
____

e Where does Phoebe look at the weather forecast?
____

f Which clothes does Matt think she's going to need?
____

EXTENSION

Underline the correct words to complete the text.

a **You love / Do you love** skiing and also going to pop concerts? If the answer is *yes*, then you should go to Méribel in March next year. Why? Because b **is / there's** a music festival there called the *Little World Festival*. For five days c **they / you** can ski or snowboard during the day and then listen to some of the top DJs and pop bands at night. Méribel is a beautiful ski resort in the French Alps. d **Ago a few years / A few years ago**, the band The Feeling went skiing there. During their vacation, they e **played / 're playing** a free concert outdoors on the piste for around 6,000 people. Everyone f **was loving / loved** it, so the band decided to create a new annual music festival. The first Little World Festival g **was / were** in March 2010. I h **learn / 'm learning** to ski right now. I i **don't go / 'm not** skiing outdoors because it doesn't often snow where I live in the US. I can ski j **fast / fastly** now! I think the *Little World Festival* sounds great! I k **'m going to go / go** there next year with some friends.

VOCABULARY PLUS

Closet Items

1 🔊 87 Translate these words into your language. Then listen and repeat.

earrings flip-flops gloves sandals
slippers sun hat tie umbrella
waterproof jacket rain boots

2 Label the picture with the words from activity 1.

3 Do you wear these accessories on your feet (F), hands (H) or body (B)?

[F] flip-flops

a [ ] gloves

b [ ] sandals

c [ ] a tie

d [ ] waterproof jacket

e [ ] rain boots

4 Complete the sentences with words from activity 1.

When you come into the house, take off your shoes and put on your *slippers*.

a It's rainy, put on your ______ and a ______. Don't forget your ______.

b We're going to the beach. Bring your ______ for your head, and wear ______ on your feet.

c In many schools, you can't wear very long ______ in your ears.

d At weddings, the groom wears a ______ and the bride sometimes wears white ______.

5 Complete the sentences for you. Try to use words from activity 1.

a If I go to a birthday party, I'll wear ______.

b In winter, I usually wear ______.

c If it is raining, I always put on my ______.

4 Make a Difference

VOCABULARY 1

Jobs

1 Look at the pictures and complete the crossword.

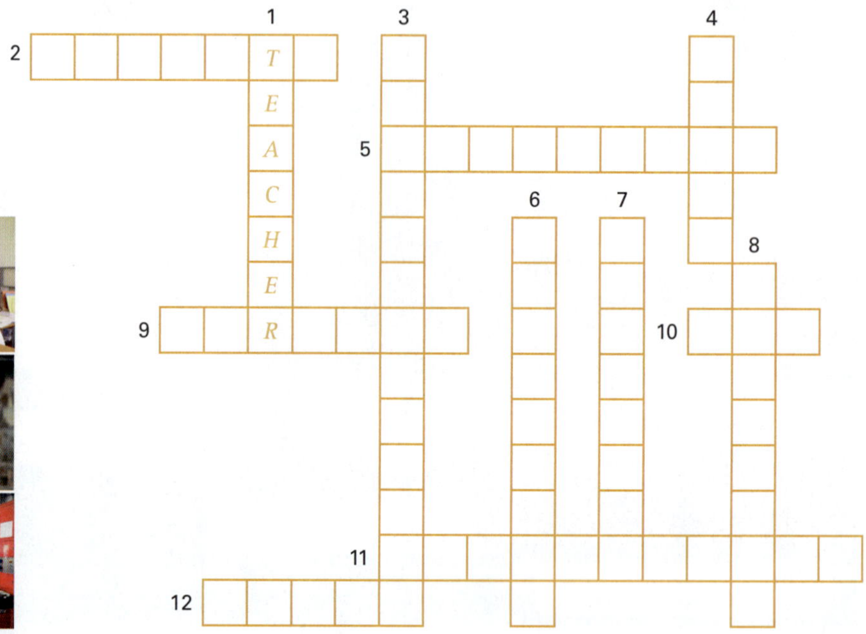

Down

Across

2 Match the words in the box with the places where the people work.

actor	lifeguard	mechanic
nurse	~~police officer~~	teacher

in a town center *police officer*

a at a swimming pool ____________

b in a garage ____________

c at a theater ____________

d in a hospital ____________

e in a school ____________

3 Complete with words in activity 1.

a I'm looking for an interesting job that pays well. I love animals! I want to be ____________.

b I'm interested in science, and how our bodies work. I can work very hard. I could be ____________.

c I am interested in how things work. I like fixing things, but I don't like cars. I want to work inside. I'm going to be ____________.

d I like swimming, and I'm really good at it. I want to travel and be rich! I want to be ____________.

e I'm interested in design, and I'm good at art. I like looking at buildings and doing practical things. I think I'm going to be ____________.

GRAMMAR 1

should (Affirmative and Negative)

1 Underline the correct words.

You **should** / **shouldn't** sleep more than five hours every night.

a Your friends **should** / **shouldn't** remember your birthday!

b You **should** / **shouldn't** eat a lot of ice cream and cake.

c You **should** / **shouldn't** drink a lot of water.

d Vets **should** / **shouldn't** like animals.

e You **should** / **shouldn't** go swimming after eating.

f Drivers **should** / **shouldn't** text while driving.

g Students **should** / **shouldn't** relax in their free time.

2 Complete the sentences with *should* or *shouldn't* and the verbs in parentheses.

She *should work* harder at school – she wants to be an architect. (work)

a You ____________ chocolate now, it's too late. (eat)

b He ____________ his teeth more often – they're black! (clean)

c We ____________ his laptop without permission. (borrow)

d You ____________ a fire outside in summer – it's dangerous. (build)

e Young children ____________ coffee. (drink)

f I ____________ my homework now before it's too late. (do)

g They ____________ in the rain (run).

3 Use the clues and *should* or *shouldn't* to create green tips.

food waste / increase
We shouldn't increase food waste.

a use / leftovers / to cook / also
____

b throw away / clothes / condition / old / good / in
____

c donate / old / repair / clothes / or
____

d bags / supermarket / buy / plastic / at
____

e our / the / bring / own / to / bags /supermarket
____

f drive / vehicles / private
____

g transportation / instead / take / public
____

4 Match the problems and recommendations to write advice sentences with *should* or *shouldn't*.

a I can't get to sleep after a long time in bed.

b I do lots of exercise and don't lose weight.

c I get too nervous before tests.

d I waste all my money on computer games.

e I'm having trouble making friends at my new school.

☐ join a book club or a sports team

☐ eat too much fat and sugar

☐ spend less time at the computer

[a] drink some chamomile tea

☐ study only the night before

a *You should drink some chamomile tea.*

b ____________

c ____________

d ____________

e ____________

5 Use the verbs in the box and *should* or *shouldn't* to write internet safety tips.

block choose download
give out log out respond

a You ______________ to offensive messages, even if they're from people you know.

b You ______________ attachments from someone you don't know.

c You ______________ suspicious people from your social media accounts.

d You ______________ your password to anyone except your parents.

e You ______________ from your accounts every time you finish checking them.

f You ______________ a long password to protect your accounts and devices.

6 Complete the text with *should* or *shouldn't* and the correct form of the verbs in parentheses.

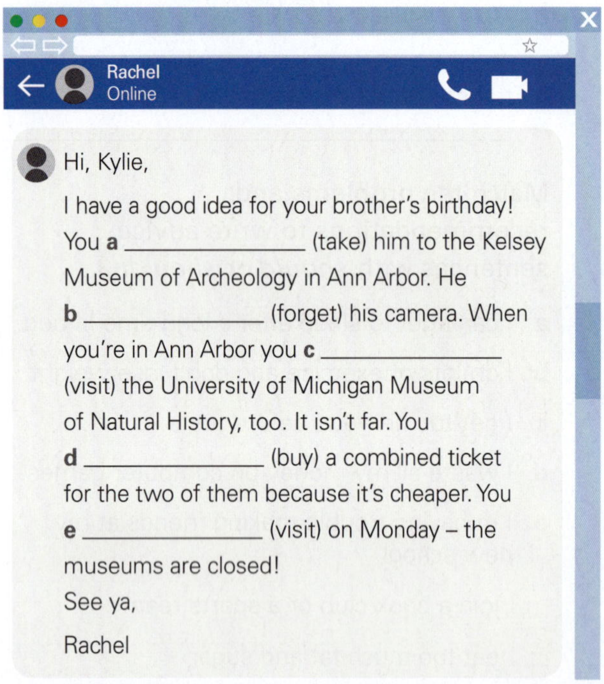

7 Write some recommendations on how to deal with guide dogs.

a You ______________ make way for guide dogs and their owners.

b You ______________ touch or pet the guide dog while it is on duty.

c You ______________ respect the directions given by its owner at all times.

d You ______________ the guide dog without its owner's authorization.

e You ______________ the dog while it has its harness on.

f You ______________ a guide dog organization.

8 Look at Jamila's notes and write sentences with *should* or *shouldn't*.

She should eat pasta.

a ______________________________

b ______________________________

c ______________________________

d ______________________________

e ______________________________

VOCABULARY 2

Health Problems

1 Look at the pictures and complete the words.

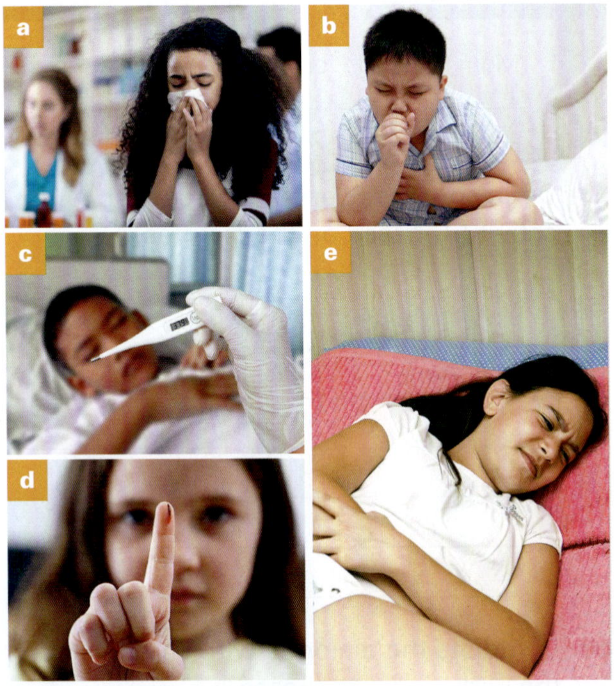

a She has a c*old*______.

b He has a c______.

c He has a t______.

d She has a c______.

e She feels s______.

2 Match a word in box A with a word in box B and write the health problems. Do you write them as one or two words?

A ~~broken~~ ear head insect sore stomach

B ache (x3) ~~arm~~ bite throat

broken arm

a ______

b ______

c ______

d ______

e ______

3 Look at the pictures and complete the sentences with the words in the box. Then match the sentences a-f to the responses 1-6.

broken arm cut headache insect bite sore throat stomachache

a I have a nasty ______ on my hand.

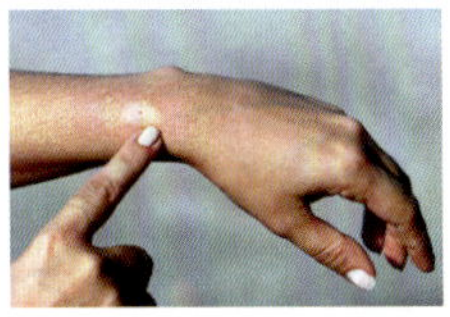

☐

b I have a ______ on my finger.

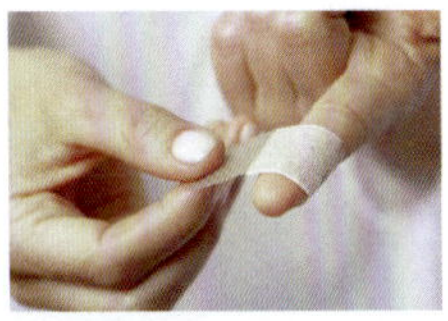

☐

c This ______ is terrible.

☐

d My ______ is getting worse.

☐

e I think I have a ______!

☐

f I have a ______ and I feel sick.

☐

1 Do you want some cough drops?

2 Come on, let's go to the hospital.

3 I think I have some special cream somewhere.

4 Put on a bandage; there are some in the bathroom.

5 Do you need an aspirin?

6 Drink some water, then lie down.

GRAMMAR 2

should (Questions and Short Answers)

1 Order the words to make questions.

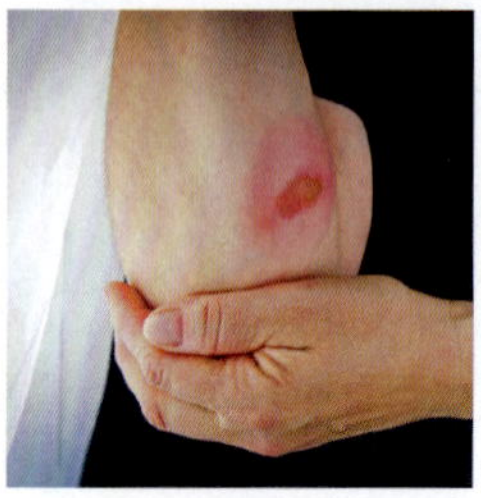

I / bandage / a / cut / Should / put / on / this ?
Should I put a bandage on this cut?
____

a with / us / umbrella / take / Should / we / an ?
____
____
____
____

b some / give / they / Should / pizza / dog / to / the ?
____
____
____
____

c map / a / buy / they / Should ?
____
____
____

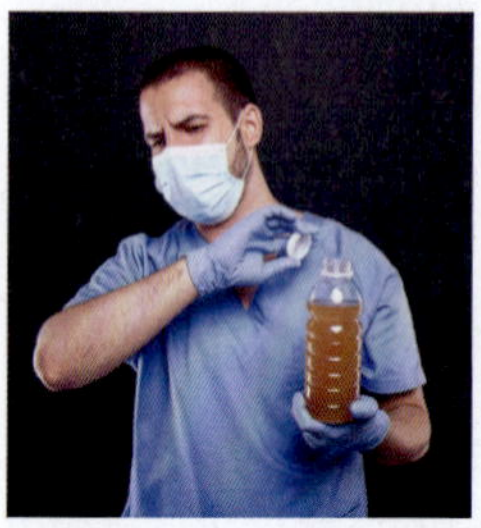

d Should / water / I / drink / the / bottle / from / this ?
____
____
____
____

e about / him / tell / the / Should / we / party ?
____
____
____
____

f Mom / Should / for / I / money / ask / some ?
____
____

2 Write short answers for the questions in activity 1, based on the pictures.

*Yes, you should.*______________________.

a ______________________
b ______________________
c ______________________
d ______________________
e ______________________
f ______________________

3 Complete the dialogue with *should* and the verbs in parentheses.

Ollie I have a test tomorrow and I can't remember anything. What **a** ____________ (I / do)?

Teacher Well, first, **b** ____________ (you / relax). **c** ____________ (you / not get) stressed – it's bad for your memory. And **d** ____________ (you / drink) water because water is good for your brain.

Ollie **e** ____________ (I / study) late at night?

Teacher No, **f** ____________! **g** ____________ (you / sleep). But the most important thing is **h** ____________ (you / not study) the night before the test. Your brain needs to rest!

GRAMMAR CHECK

1 Read the dialogue and circle the correct answers.

Liam: My mom thinks I **a** ______ study architecture when I'm older. I love architecture, but the problem is I can't draw.

Archie: You should **b** ______ some classes, then.

Liam: I'm busy with my math and science classes at the moment. I think I **c** ______ focus on these subjects first.

Archie: If you don't have time to learn to draw, **d** ______ study architecture. I think you **e** ______ think of a different profession! How about being an athlete? You're great at tennis.

Liam: No, I want to be an architect. It isn't going to be easy, but I can do it. When I'm older, I'm going to look for classes in design. They use computers – that's better for me than drawing.

Archie: You **f** ______ at school. Mr. Simms knows about courses and professions.

Liam: You **g** ______ worry so much, Archie. We're 13! Relax! Come on. Let's go and play tennis.

	1	2	3
a	shouldn't	should (circled)	should I
b	to take	take	taking
c	should	should to	shouldn't
d	should you	you aren't	you shouldn't
e	're going	should	shouldn't
f	ask	shouldn't ask	should ask
g	're going to	should	shouldn't

2 🔊 88 Listen and check your answers.

LISTENING

1 🔊 89 Listen to three telephone conversations. Circle the service each caller needs.

Caller 1: police fire ambulance
Caller 2: police fire ambulance
Caller 3: police fire ambulance

2 🔊 89 Listen again and complete the chart with information about each caller.

	Caller 1
What is the problem?	______
Where is the caller?	______
What should the caller do?	______

	Caller 2
What is the problem?	______
Where is the caller?	______
What should the caller do?	______

	Caller 3
What is the problem?	______
Where is the caller?	______
What should the caller do?	______

EXTENSION

Circle the correct words to complete the text.

Médecins Sans Frontières (Doctors Without Borders, in English) is an international NGO (non-governmental organization) that supports war-ravaged countries with medical care. Founded in 1971 by a group of French doctors and journalists, MSF **a has helped / have helped** several nations by providing them with medicine, donations and the work of medical professionals.

Like many NGOs, MSF also needs to be supported in order to bring some comfort to people in need. What **b should you / you should** do to help them? First of all, you **c should to read / should read** as much information as possible on the MSF website, <https://www.doctorswithoutborders.org/>. You'll find detailed instructions about the various ways to contribute.

Money donation: the **d easiest / easier** way to support MSF is by donating money, since you can do it from anywhere in the world. One of the most important rules is that you **e shouldn't to / shouldn't** donate in any currency other than US dollars.

Royalty donation: an author, an actor or a musician can help by donating the royalties from their work. They **f should / shouldn't** contact the Fundraising Events team by telephone or email to get started.

If you **g can't / should** donate anything, but still think you **h should / shouldn't** help, you can publicize their work by sharing this information in your social media. Let's make a difference in these people's lives.

VOCABULARY PLUS

Places of Work

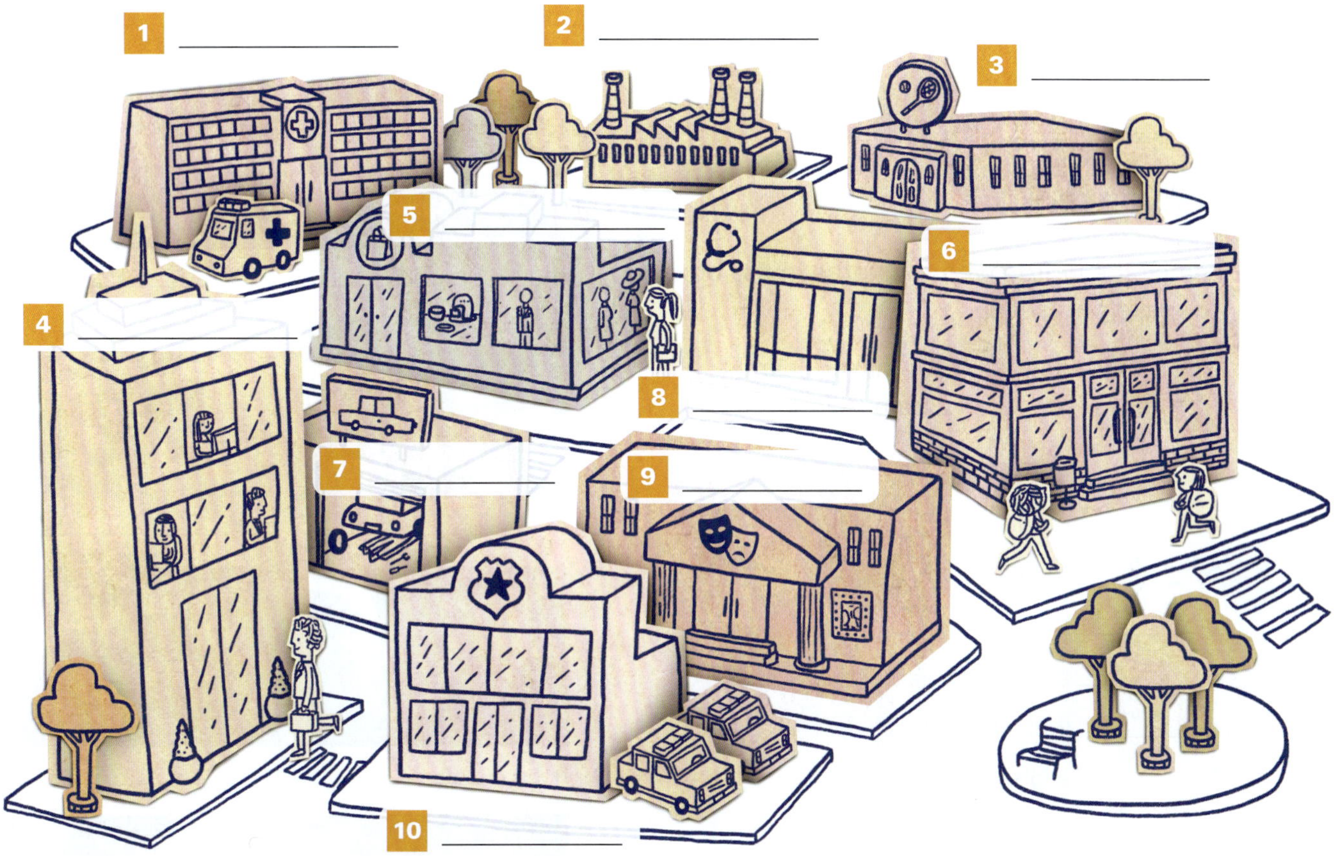

1 🔊 90 Look up the meaning of these words. Then listen and repeat.

department store doctor's office factory garage high school hospital office police station sports club theater

2 Label the picture with the words in activity 1.

3 Match the jobs a-e with the places of work 1-5.

a actor	1 high school
b police officer	2 garage
c surgeon	3 theater
d teacher	4 hospital
e mechanic	5 police station

4 Underline the correct word.

When I'm older I'm going to be a history teacher in a **high school / police station**.

a When my dog was ill, I took him to the vet's **garage / office**.

b My uncle sells computers in a very large **department store / theater**.

c My sister loves cars. She goes to our cousin's **garage / surgery** on Saturdays.

d The **office / factory** in our town makes paper.

5 Answer the questions for you. Write full sentences.

a Is there a theater in your town? Where is it?

____

b How many high schools are there in your town?

____

c How often do you go to the sports club? What do you do there?

____

5 Ambitions

VOCABULARY 1

Life Events

1 Match the words with the verbs in the box to make phrases.

be buy get (x2) go have learn leave (x2) start train work

leave school at 18

a ______ children

b ______ to drive

c ______ born

d ______ to be a vet

e ______ with children

f ______ a job

g ______ school at six

h ______ a house

i ______ married

j ______ to college

k ______ home

2 Label the pictures with the phrases in activity 1.

learn to drive

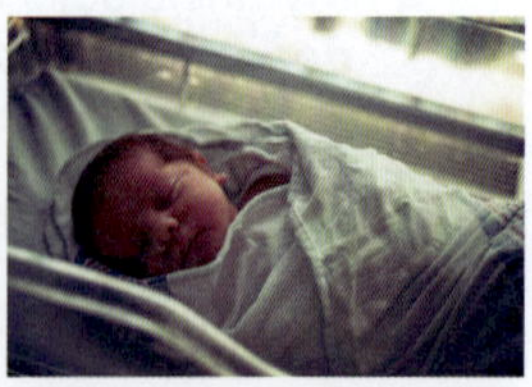

a ______

b ______

c ______

d ______

e ______

f ______

g ______

h ______

i ______

j ______

k ______

3 Complete the sentences using the words in activity 1.

a My sister wants to ______ on a beach in Hawaii. It's gonna be an awesome party!

b My best friend says she wants to ______ five ______! I'd like two: a boy and a girl.

c Rosie plans to ______ when she's older. She loves animals!

d My brother's nearly sixteen; he can ______ in dad's car.

e The oldest person in the world ______ over a hundred years ago.

f I want to ______ when I leave school. I'd like to study math!

GRAMMAR 1

will / *won't*

1 Order the words to write sentences and add *will* or *'ll*.

as / brother / police / work / a / my / officer
My brother will work as a police officer.

a me / lend / Dad / money / and / for / a / present / Mom
____

b a / you / new / need / flash drive
____

c after / go / bed / the / I / news / to
____

d college / we / before / travel
____

e Matt / lot / have / children / a / of
____

2 Write the sentences in activity 1 in the negative form.

My brother won't work as a police officer.

a ______________________
b ______________________
c ______________________
d ______________________
e ______________________

3 Look at the pictures and complete the predictions with *will* / *won't* and the verbs in parentheses.

Joanna *will study* science at college. (study)

a Amy ____________ married to a short, blond man. (get)

b Pippa ____________ to drive a truck. (learn)

c Alfie ____________ a famous actor. (become)

d Mark ____________ Japan. (visit)

e Michelle ____________ a fast car. (buy)

4 Complete the dialogue with *'ll*, *will* or *won't* and the verbs in the box.

be die get get married give go have not want not work train

Iain: Did you see *Family Secrets* last night?
Chloe: Yes, it was exciting! I think Joey **a** ____________ in the next episode. He's very ill.
Iain: No, I don't agree! I think he **b** ____________ better! The doctor **c** ____________ him some amazing medicine. She **d** ____________ to Brazil and buy it there.
Chloe: Yes! And Brad **e** ____________ to Patsy. They **f** ____________ a big wedding.
Iain: Yes, and Brad's mother **g** ____________ really angry. She **h** ____________ Brad and Patsy to be together.
Chloe: And what about Clint, Joey's brother?
Iain: Well, I think he **i** ____________ as a lifeguard any more after the accident. He **j** ____________ to be a nurse at the hospital.
Chloe: Then Clint and the doctor will fall in love.
Iain: Exactly!

5 Complete the sentences for you.

a When I'm 17, I ____________.
b Next week, I ____________.
c My favorite team ____________.
d When I'm older, I won't ____________.

6 Order the words to make questions.

she / Will / tomorrow / class / in / be ?
Will she be in class tomorrow?

a later / you / call / Will / me ? ______

b know / I / the / answer / Will ? ______

c be / difficult / Will / the / test ? ______

d married / Will / next / they / get / year ? ______

e homework / be / Will / today / there ? ______

7 Match questions a-e in activity 6 with the short answers.

[c] Yes, it will.
[ ] Yes, I will.
[ ] No, there won't.
[ ] Yes, they will.
[ ] No, you won't.

8 Write questions with *will*.

I / pass / the exam?
Will I pass the exam?

a he / get / the / job? ______

b you / learn / to drive / a truck? ______

c the new mouse / cost / a lot of money? ______

d vacation / be / boring? ______

e we / buy / a house / by the sea? ______

9 Look at the pictures of what will happen in the future and write short answers for the questions in activity 8.

Yes, I will.

a ______

b ______

c ______

d ______

e ______

10 Write questions with *you* for the answers using *will* and the words in the box.

How What Where Who

a ______
We'll go to Costa Rica next summer.

b ______
Kelly will come with us.

c ______
We'll go there by plane.

d ______
I'll buy some shoes.

11 Answer the questions in activity 10 for you.

a ______
b ______
c ______
d ______

VOCABULARY 2

Musical Instruments

1 Find eleven musical instruments in the wordsnake.

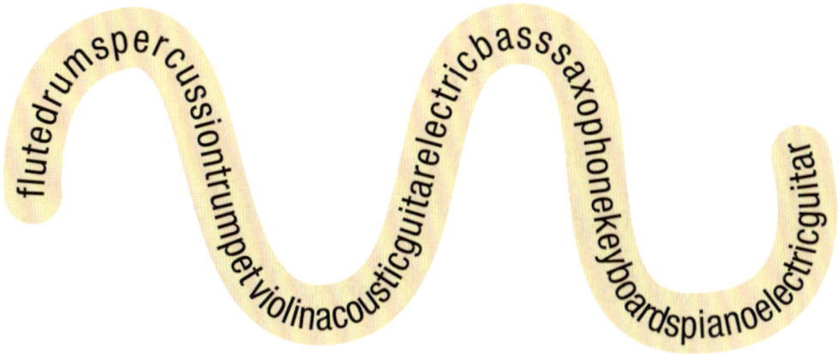

2 Look at the picture and label the instruments with the words in activity 1.

a *percussion*
b ______
c ______
d ______
e ______
f ______
g ______
h ______
i ______
j ______
k ______

3 Read the clues and write the words.

a You usually sit to play this instrument. It has four legs. It doesn't need electricity. ______

b You sit to play this instrument. You hit it with sticks or with your hands, and it's very loud! ______

c You usually hold this with your left hand and you rest it on your shoulder. ______

d You play this instrument with your mouth. Your hands don't go in front of you. It's usually silver. ______

e A lot of rock bands use this 4-string instrument. You need speakers to hear it. You play it with your fingers. ______

f This instrument can sound like a lot of different instruments. You play it with your hands. ______

4 Complete the sentences for you.

a In a pop band, my favorite instrument is the ______.

b In an orchestra, my favorite instrument is the ______.

c I don't like the ______.

d I have a friend who can play the ______.

GRAMMAR 2

First Conditional

1 Underline the correct words.

We **celebrate** / **'ll celebrate** if dad gets the job.

a If my sister **has** / **will have** children, I'll be an aunt!

b I **buy** / **'ll buy** a house near the beach if I earn a lot of money.

c If you **buy** / **'ll buy** a laptop, you won't need new speakers.

d If the rain **doesn't** / **won't** stop, we won't go camping.

e I won't go out tonight if there **'s** / **will be** something good on TV.

f If you **won't** / **don't** do your homework now, you'll have to do it later.

2 Complete the sentences with the first conditional form of the verbs in parentheses.

If you wear those clothes, you *will feel* cold. (feel)

a If you play that song again, he ________ happy. (not be)

b I ________ you if you go to the hospital. (visit)

c If you don't hurry, you ________ time for lunch. (not have)

d If I ________ his T-shirt, I'll buy it. (see)

e She won't go to college if she ________. (not study)

3 Write sentences with the first conditional.

a go to the city / visit the museum

____

b get a job / earn extra money

____

c fail her exams / not go to college

____

d go to college / study art

____

e have enough money / see a movie

____

f become a taxi driver / drive a pink taxi

____

4 Match the beginnings to the endings.

a If you pass your exams,

b If I go out in the rain,

c Will it be warmer

d If we change school,

e Will you tell them

[ ] will we have a uniform?

[ ] if we build a fire?

[ ] if you see them?

[*a*] will your parents be happy?

[ ] will I catch a cold?

5 Complete the questions with the first conditional form of the verbs in parentheses.

If you *come* (come) home early, *will* you *make* (make) lunch?

a ________ you ________ (send) me a postcard if you ________ (have) time?

b If I ________ (tell) you a secret, ________ you ________ (tell) everybody?

c ________ Grandma ________ (learn) to drive if Dad ________ (help) her?

d If they ________ (visit) us, ________ they ________ (bring) the dog?

6 Complete the dialogue with the first conditional form of the verbs in the box. Complete the short answers.

do get go not be not have not leave want

Ben **a** ________ you ________ to college if you **b** ________ school at 18?

Lola Yes, **c** ________. I want to study to be a vet. What **d** ________ you ________ if you can?

Ben I'll get a job. If you **e** ________ enough money as a student, **f** ________ you ________ a weekend job?

Lola No, **g** ________. If I **h** ________ to be a vet, there **i** ________ time for a job!

GRAMMAR CHECK

1 Read the dialogue and circle the correct answers.

Anna: I think I **a** ________ to that concert tonight. **b** ________ fun. Do you want to come?

Maddy: If we **c** ________ a lot of homework, we won't have time.

Anna: I'll do my homework after school. I don't have a lot. It **d** ________ four hours!

Maddy: Well, if my dad **e** ________ it's alright, I'll come. Who's playing?

Anna: Some friends of Ben's. He says if we go, we **f** ________ it.

Maddy: OK. I **g** ________ my dad. If I do my homework early, it **h** ________ be a problem.

Anna: Awesome! Oh, one more thing. If **i** ________ expensive, **j** ________ me some money?

	1	2	3
a	go	going	('ll go)
b	It is	It'll be	It be
c	has	have	will have
d	don't take	to take	won't take
e	will say	says	say
f	'll enjoy	enjoys	enjoy
g	ask	'll ask	am asking
h	won't	isn't	don't
i	it's	is	its
j	will you lend	you will lend	do you lend

2 91 Listen and check your answers.

LISTENING

1 92 Listen to the dialogue and answer the questions.

a What do the people on the show do?

____

b Who does Aisha like?

____

c Who does Callum like?

____

2 92 Listen again and underline the correct words.

a Last year, the winner of the show was a **violin / saxophone** player.

b Callum heard about the show **at school / on the internet**.

c Aisha's favorite singer wears the **most expensive / most creative** clothes.

d Aisha's favorite singer is **older / younger** than Callum's favorite singer.

e Callum's favorite singer plays the **guitar / piano**.

f If Callum's favorite wins, she'll buy **a house / a restaurant**.

g Aisha's favorite singer wants to win to **help her family / be famous**.

EXTENSION

Underline the correct words to complete the text.

If you **a like / will like** classic novels, you **b enjoy / 'll enjoy** Jane Austen. Austen is one of the most famous writers in English literature, and she **c was / were** born in 1775. She only **d was / went** to school for one year, and she didn't **e go / went** to university, but her father and brothers were her teachers at home and she read **f a lot of / much** books. Her ambition was to work as a writer. She practiced a lot, and when she was 35 years old, she **g write / wrote** her first novel, *Sense and Sensibility*. This is one of her **h best / most good** novels. When Jane was writing, women of her social class spent their time visiting friends and family, or at dances. Typically, the **i more important / most important** ambition for men and women was to get married. Jane wrote about these people but she was ironic and laughed at society. Her stories and characters **j is / are** still popular today and probably will **k be / to be** for a long time. You **l should / will** read one of her novels.

VOCABULARY PLUS

Other Life Events

1 🔊 93 Translate the words into your language. Then listen and repeat.

anniversary birth death divorce
engagement funeral retirement wedding

2 Label the picture with the words in activity 1. Which life event is not in the pictures?

____

3 Complete the table with the words from activity 1.

0-18 years old	18-60 years old	60+ years old
birth		

4 Complete these sentences with a word from activity 1.

Do you know what sort of flowers the bride is having at her *wedding*?

a My parents got married in May 2000. It's their wedding __________ tomorrow.

b My uncle's going to stop working next week. He's having a __________ party.

c Our family is having a party next week to celebrate my older brother's __________.

d When my aunt died, I went to her __________.

e Jack and Kerry got married in 1996. Three years later, they got a __________.

f Tahani and Kurt invited their closest friends to celebrate the __________ of their first child.

6 On Screen

VOCABULARY 1

Movies

1 **Complete the words with the vowels.**

d __*i*__ r __*e*__ ct __*o*__ r

a st ____ nt w ____ m ____ n

b m ____ v ____ ____ st ____ r

c scr ____ ____ n

d sp ____ c ____ ____ l ____ ff ____ cts

2 **Find five movie words in the wordsnake and match them with the definitions.**

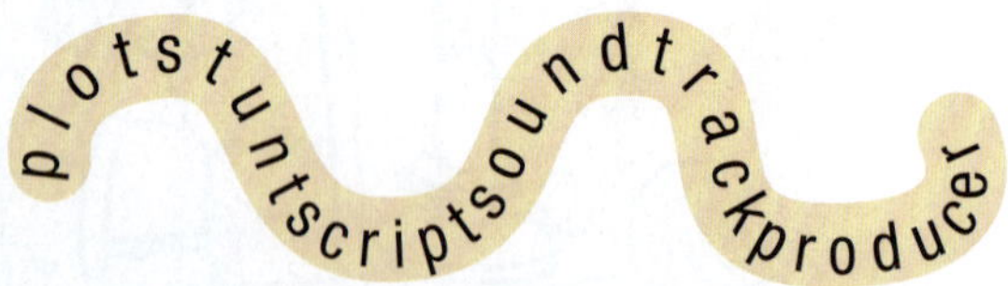

a the words of a movie

____

b a dangerous action in a movie

____

c the music of a movie

____

d the story of a movie

____

e this person organizes the money for a movie

____

3 **Complete the phrases with the verbs in the box.**

film release star win

a ____________ a scene

b ____________ a movie

c ____________ in a movie

d ____________ an award

4 **What are they talking about? Match the words in the box with the sentences.**

movie star ~~plot~~ screen soundtrack special effects stunt man

It's a really good story, with a twist at the end.

____*plot*____

a I loved the song when they were standing at the front of the ship. It was very romantic.

____

b I think the biggest one in the world is 73 meters wide and 18 meters tall.

____

c It's amazing when the gorilla picks her up and carries her up that tall building. How did they do that?

____

d She's amazingly rich and famous. She got $15 million dollars for her part in that movie.

____

e The director made him jump out of the helicopter and ski down the mountain instead of the star.

____

5 **Complete the sentences with the words in the box.**

award ~~director~~ release scene star

Patty Jenkins is a well-known ____*director*____. *Wonder Woman* was directed by her.

a They filmed the desert ____________ in Morocco.

b An Oscar is another word for an Academy ____________.

c Daniel Radcliffe and Emma Watson ____________ in the *Harry Potter* movies.

d When are they going to ____________ the new Marvel movie?

GRAMMAR 1

Future Tense: *will*

1 Order the words to make sentences.

change / probably / movie / life / This / will / your
This movie will probably change your life.

a and terrifying / brilliant / find / it / will / You / definitely
____

b a / be / bored / for / minute / won't / definitely / You
____

c probably / come out / streaming / movie / for / months / on / six / The / won't
____

d after / become / teen actor / definitely / famous / movie / The / this / will
____

e castle / ever / forget / in / Nobody / the scene /the / will
____

2 Complete the sentences with *will* and the verbs in the box.

be have love ~~make~~ pay wear

In the next decade, movies *will make* much more use of computers to create special effects.

a You __________ this movie. It's amazing.

b It's a great movie, but it __________ you cry.

c People __________ more for movie tickets in the future.

d In the future, there __________ special air conditioning in movie theaters to release different smells.

e One day, people __________ headphones at the movie theater, like on planes.

f They __________ special controls on their seats to change the soundtrack and make their seats move.

3 Match the sentence beginnings with the endings. Write sentences using *won't* and the verbs in parentheses.

a [5] We (be) late for the movie, I

b [ ] You (enjoy) that movie because you

c [ ] He's an excellent stunt man, so

d [ ] We (understand) the movie because it's

e [ ] There'll be advertisements first, so

f [ ] Don't worry – the bad guys (win) because

1 all in Japanese.

2 he (hurt) himself.

3 they never do!

4 don't like romantic movies.

5 promise you.

6 the movie (start) at eight.

a *We won't be late for the movie, I promise you.*

b ______________________________

c ______________________________

d ______________________________

e ______________________________

f ______________________________

4 Write questions with *will*. Then answer the questions with your opinions using *will* or *won't*.

In the year 2200 …

the world / be much hotter?

Will the world be much hotter?

Yes, it will be much hotter. / No, it won't be much hotter.

a people / take vacations on Mars?

______

______

b there / be more deserts in Europe?

______

______

c the sea / cover half of the continent?

______

______

d we / travel everywhere by bicycle?

______

______

Future Tense: *be going to*

5 Complete the sentences with the correct form of *be going to* and the verbs in parentheses.

'Have you seen that new Argentinian movie yet?'

'No, but I *'m going to see* (see) it soon. It sounds excellent.'

a I ______ (train) to be a cameraman when I leave school.

b Why are you holding that camera? ______ (you / make) a movie of us?

c Angie and Colin want to go to the States next summer. They ______ (buy) a car when they get there, and they ______ (travel) from the East Coast to the West.

d I don't like this actor, so I ______ (not see) her new movie.

e 'I'm going to a party tonight.' 'What ______ (you / wear)?'

f This movie is awful! It ______ (not win) any awards.

6 You have decided to change things in your life next year. What things are you going to change? Write four sentences.

I'm going to get up early every day. I'm not going to eat too much candy.

a ______

b ______

c ______

d ______

VOCABULARY 2

Suffixes *-ion* and *-ment*

1 Make nouns ending in *-ion* or *-ment* from these verbs.

verbs	nouns
advertise	*advertisement*
a decorate	________
b enjoy	________
c equip	________
d possess	________
e excite	________
f suggest	________

2 Make verbs from these nouns.

nouns	verbs
education	*educate*
a argument	________
b competition	________
c information	________
d development	________
e connection	________
f prediction	________

3 Match two nouns from activity 1 and two verbs from activity 2 with the pictures.

a ________

b ________

c ________

d ________

4 Match the nouns in the box with the sentences.

advertisement ~~argument~~ development
education information prediction
suggestion

'The Government should ban cars in the center of Montreal.' 'No. That's a ridiculous idea. Some people live in the center and they need a car if they have to bring heavy shopping home.' *argument*

a Buy Meow! It's a new kind of cat food and cats LOVE it! ________

b By the year 2080, there will be a vacation hotel on Mars. ________

c Why don't we make some sandwiches and go for a picnic by the river? ________

d When I leave school, I'd like to go to college. I want to get a degree in law. ________

e Ten years ago, there wasn't any water in that African village. Now, they have it and the people are much healthier. ________

f Trains from Platform 2 are for London only. ________

5 Complete the sentences with the nouns in the box.

competition connection decoration
enjoyment ~~equipment~~ excitement
possession

Can I borrow your camping *equipment* next week, please? I have a sleeping bag, but I don't have anything else.

a I couldn't hear him when he called because the ________ was very bad.

b I love this silver necklace. It is my favorite ________.

c This room needs some ________ for the party – maybe flowers, candles and balloons.

d Your photo of the sunset is amazing. You should send it to the photo ________ in this magazine.

e My aunt gets a lot of ________ from her garden. She's always happy when she is working in it.

f There was a lot of ________ at school today because a movie crew was filming in some of the classes.

GRAMMAR 2

Review: Present Progressive for Future Arrangements

1 Look at Andy's diary and complete the questions and answers using the present progressive.

Saturday

morning: Meet Rob at 11 to practice our new song.
afternoon: Play tennis with Adam from 2 to 4.
evening: Take Kate to the movies - pick her up at 6.

Sunday

morning: Go for a run in the park with Adam.
afternoon: Finish science project.
evening: Meet Kate at Moonshine at 7 for a meal.

Who *is Andy meeting* on Saturday morning?
He's *meeting* Rob.

a What time ______ tennis with Adam?
They ______ from two to four.

b Who ______ to the movies on Saturday evening?
He ______ Kate.

c What ______ and Adam ______ on Sunday morning?
They ______ for a run.

d What ______ on Sunday afternoon?
He ______ his science project.

e Where ______ Andy and Kate ______ at seven on Sunday?
They ______ at Moonshine.

2 Complete the sentences with the present progressive form of the verbs in parentheses.

Today at 9 Melissa *is throwing* a party to celebrate the movie release. (throw)

a I ______ lunch with my friends near the movie theater today. (have)

b ______ Peter ______ to the movies at 2 or at 3 on Saturday? (go)

c The cast ______ the main scene tonight. (rehearse)

d My sister ______ all of the series next month. (watch)

e The trailers ______ in a few moments. Hurry up! (start)

f The director ______ a new stunt woman in 15 days. (interview)

3 What definite plans do you have for this weekend? Write five sentences about your plans using the present progressive.

On Saturday I'm meeting my friends for a meal at the Oasis.

a ______

b ______

c ______

d ______

e ______

GRAMMAR CHECK

1 Read the text and circle the correct answers.

When I leave school, **a** ______ probably go to college. I **b** ______ to study modern languages, I think. Then if I **c** ______ a good degree, **d** ______ to get a job with a movie or TV company for a few years. After that, when I've saved some money, I **e** ______ apply to a film school. If **f** ______ possible, **g** ______ go to film school in Los Angeles. I love the States. **h** ______ the whole of next month in California with my aunt Melanie. My friend, Oliver, **i** ______ with me. I can't wait. We **j** ______ a lot of fun there!

	1	2	3
a	I	I'm	(I'll)
b	'm going	going	go
c	will get	get	got
d	I try	I tried	I'll try
e	go to	'm going to	'll go
f	it was	it will be	it's
g	I'll	I	I'm going
h	I'll spend	I spend	I'm spending
i	comes	is coming	will come
j	're going to have	're having	'll having

2 94 Listen and check your answers.

LISTENING

1 95 Listen and circle T for *true* or F for *false*.

a Auguste and Louis Lumière were brothers. **T / F**

b At their first public movie show, the audience didn't have to pay. **T / F**

c The cinematographe was a camera and a projector. **T / F**

d People say *Baby's Breakfast* was the world's first comedy movie. **T / F**

e *The Arrival of a Train at a Station* was a very realistic movie. **T / F**

f The Lumières only filmed real-life situations. **T / F**

g The Lumières never left France. **T / F**

h Louis Lumière said the cinema was never going to become popular. **T / F**

2 95 Listen again and answer the questions.

a In what year was the first public movie shown?

____

b How long was it?

____

c How much did the cinematographe weigh?

____

d How many movies were there in the show?

____

e What did the first movie show?

____

f What was the first comedy movie called?

____

g Which cities did they tour with their movies?

____

h How many Lumière movies were there by 1900?

____

EXTENSION

Circle the correct words to complete the text.

a I've spent / I was spending the last two years watching old movies whenever I get the chance. I love **b watch / watching** them. **c I've done / I did** this **d since / from** I was 13, when I was in bed for a week with a broken leg. During the winter, I **e often stay / am often staying** in all day on Sundays to watch old classics. Last Sunday, I **f watched / have watched** half of *Gone with the Wind*. It was **g too / very** long to watch it all, so **h I'm going / I will** to watch the rest of it next Sunday. My friend Renata **i is coming / will come** to stay next weekend so she'll probably **j watching / watch** it with me. If we **k have / will have** time, **l we watch / we'll watch** *Casablanca* afterwards. **m I've already seen / I already saw** it twice, but I think it's the **n best / better** movie of all time. When I finish school and university, I'm going to get a job as a movie reviewer. **o I'll spend / I'm spending** every day at the movie theater and **p I'll get / I'm getting** paid for it. How **q much / more** fun will that be? Not **r lot / many** people in the world get paid to watch movies, do they?

VOCABULARY PLUS

The Movie Theater

1 ______________________

2 ______________________

3 ______________________

4 ______________________

5 ______________________

6 ______________________

7 ______________________

8 ______________________

9 *autograph*

8 ______________________

1 🔊 96 Label the pictures with the words in the box. Then listen and repeat.

~~autograph~~ box office Hollywood blockbuster movie premiere multiplex movie theater popcorn seat soft drink ticket trailer

2 Complete the definitions with the correct words.

A *Hollywood blockbuster* is an American movie that is extremely popular.

a A ______________________ is a movie theater that has a lot of different screens.

b A ______________________ is an extract from a movie that will be released soon.

c The ______________________ is the place where you buy your movie ticket.

d A ______________________ is the first time a movie is shown in a country.

e ______________________ is a popular snack that people eat at the movies.

3 Circle the correct words.

I love watching the **box offices** / **(trailers)** before the main movie starts.

a 'Would you like a **soft drink** / **seat**?' 'Yes, please. A Coke.'

b 'Two **tickets** / **trailers** for *Avatar*, please.' 'That's $11.00, please.'

c We don't like sitting in the **movie premieres** / **seats** directly below the screen.

d The movie premiere was fantastic. I'm sure it'll be a **soft drink** / **Hollywood blockbuster**.

e I asked a movie star for his **popcorn** / **autograph** and he signed my T-shirt!

7 The World We Live in

VOCABULARY 1

Materials and Containers

1 Find 14 materials and containers in the word search.

L	P	C	A	R	T	O	N	B	I	A
M	P	A	P	O	R	Y	W	O	O	L
S	L	R	P	L	N	U	H	X	E	U
J	A	D	L	E	S	A	S	E	E	M
A	S	B	T	O	R	B	E	T	W	I
R	T	O	W	M	N	O	L	E	H	N
F	I	A	R	S	E	T	C	M	O	U
H	C	R	C	O	T	T	O	N	P	M
I	D	D	A	O	G	L	A	S	S	Z
B	A	G	N	R	M	E	N	L	C	S

2 Match the columns to make compound nouns. Then complete the sentences.

a cardboard ☐ T-shirt
b wool ☐a box
c plastic ☐ can
d cotton ☐ bag
e metal ☐ coat

1 My cat likes sleeping in a *cardboard box*.
2 It's cold today, so he's wearing a ________.
3 If you go to the market, you'll need a ________.
4 For PE, I always wear a cool ________.
5 Soft drinks are often in ________.

3 Complete the paragraph with the words in the box.

aluminum	bottles	cartons
cotton	glass	jars	paper

Hi! I'm Mateo. In my family, we always try to recycle. It's good for the planet! We wash plastic **a** ________ and use them again for water, and we use **b** ________ in the kitchen for rice, beans and sugar. We put all our **c** ________ cans and tins in the recycling bins outside the supermarket. Milk and juice **d** ________ can't be recycled in my town, so we buy these things in **e** ________ bottles. My mother sometimes gives old clothes to other people, and she sometimes cuts up **f** ________ clothes and uses them in the kitchen. We ask for **g** ________ bags in the supermarket, not plastic. Or even better, we take our own bags. How does your family recycle?

4 Complete the sentences for you. Use words from activity 1.

a In my family we recycle ________.
b We don't really need to use ________.
c It'll be difficult to stop using ________.
d When I was younger, I sometimes played with ________.

GRAMMAR 1

Present Perfect (Affirmative and Negative)

1 Write the past participles. Which two are regular?

verb	past participle
open	*opened*
a be	________
b build	________
c buy	________
d fall	________
e have	________
f take	________
g stop	________
h try	________

Opened, ________ and ________ are regular.

2 Underline the correct words.

I **has / <u>have</u>** stopped using plastic bags.

a We **has / have** reduced our garbage at home.

b I **has / have** used this plastic bag about ten times.

c My brother **has / have** recycled his old school T-shirt.

d My parents **has / have** watched three hours of Netflix today.

e The dog **has / have** eaten my homework!

3 Complete the sentences with the present perfect affirmative form of the verbs in parentheses.

We *'ve had* our lunch. (have)

a I ________ to find a recycling bin for cans. (try)

b She ________ the ice cream in the sun. (leave)

c They ________ a store with organic cotton clothes. (open)

d He ________ very famous. (become)

e We ________ old CDs in the garden. (use)

f You ________ all the cake! (eat)

4 Look at the pictures and write sentences about them with the present perfect form of the verbs in the box.

break	build	buy
cut	eat	fall

a ________________________
____

b ________________________
____

c ________________________
____

d ________________________
____

e ________________________
____

f ________________________
____

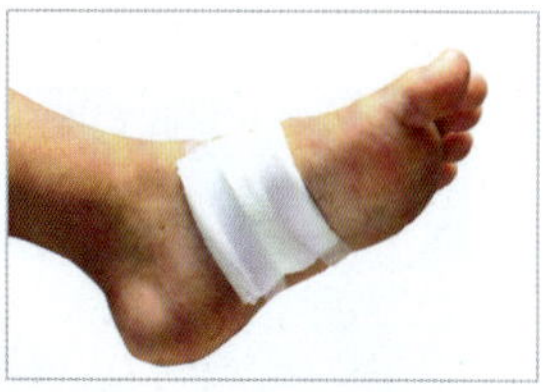

5 Complete the sentences for you.

a The best place I've visited was ________.

b I've met ________.

c I've never ________.

d My friend has ________ today.

6 Complete the sentences with *haven't* or *hasn't*.

The film *hasn't* started. Quick, sit down.

a I __________ heard their new song.

b She __________ cleaned her teeth!

c We __________ seen him today.

d My brother __________ passed his math test.

e They __________ reduced their screen time.

f My cat __________ eaten its dinner.

7 Rewrite the sentences using the information in parentheses.

It's been hot in the last few days. (cold)
It hasn't been hot in the last few days.
It's been cold.

a My teacher has tried sushi. (shark)

____

____

b She's taken your camera. (cell phone)

____

____

c I've seen Chadwick Boseman. (Benedict Cumberbatch)

____

____

d We've visited New York. (London)

____

____

e They've traveled by boat. (by plane)

____

____

f He's adopted an elephant. (dolphin)

____

____

8 Complete the dialogue with the present perfect form of the verbs in parentheses.

Jordan: I **a** __________ (not see) Tom in the last few days. He **b** __________ (not come) to guitar class at all this week.

Elliot: We **c** __________ (have) exams at school so he **d** __________ (be) very busy.

Jordan: Oh, OK. We had exams too, but we **e** __________ (finish) them all now. I **f** __________ (pass) all my subjects except one.

Elliot: Which one?

Jordan: Math.

Elliot: Tom **g** __________ (not pass) math either. He knows it because he couldn't answer a lot of questions. And I don't know if **h** __________ (pass) it. I **i** __________ (study) a lot, so I think it'll be OK.

Jordan: Good luck!

9 Complete the sentences for you.

a I've never been to __________.

b My best friend hasn't this __________ week.

c My parents haven't __________ before.

d I haven't __________ today.

VOCABULARY 2

Endangered Animals

1 Order the letters and write the words.

k a n e s *snake*

a h n o r e o s i c r __________

b p l e d o r a __________

c d a n a p __________

d l o r a p r a b e __________

e t r e g i __________

f p l o d i h n __________

g p a e l e t h n __________

h r u t t l e __________

i g o r n a a t u n __________

2 Look at the pictures and label the animals with the words from activity 1.

a __________

b __________

c __________

d __________

e __________

f __________

g __________

h __________

i __________

j __________

3 Write the animals from activity 1 in the correct group.

animals that live on land
snake,
animals that live in water
animals that live on land and in water

4 Read the clues and write the words.

a I live in China. I am in danger of extinction. I eat bamboo. I am black and white. What am I? __________

b I live in water and on land. I lay eggs. I have a shell. What am I? __________

c I'm a mammal. I'm a good hunter. I'm from the same family as a cat. I have stripes. What am I? __________

d I have four legs but I can't jump. I have big ears but my Indian cousins have smaller ears. I have a shower with my nose. What am I? __________

e I live in the forest. My hands are similar to human hands. I'm very intelligent and I live in Southeast Asia. What am I? __________

f I live in the Arctic but not in the Antarctic. I eat meat and fish. I'm very big. What am I? __________

5 Complete the sentences for you.

a My favorite endangered animal is the __________.

b I don't like the __________.

c I like the __________ better than the __________.

d In a safari park, I visit the __________ first.

GRAMMAR 2

Present Perfect (Questions and Short Answers)

1 Complete the questions with *have* or *has*. Then match the questions with the short answers.

a ___Has___ Ms. Zimmer arrived?

b ________ I seen an orangutan?

c ________ we eaten all the cookies?

d ________ you put recycling bins in your kitchen?

e ________ he reused those jars?

f ________ they drunk my juice?

☐ Yes, they have.
☐ a Yes, she has.
☐ No, we haven't.
☐ No, he hasn't.
☐ Yes, you have.
☐ No, I haven't.

2 Order the words to make questions. Then complete the short answers.

my / seen / you / have / notebook ?
Have you seen my notebook?
No, ___I haven't___.

a homework / rewritten / have / you / your ?
____
Yes, ______________.

b cans and cartons / he / has / his / recycled ?
____
Yes, ______________.

c he / told / has / my sister ?
____
No, ______________.

d some / earned / I / extra allowance / have ?
____
No, ______________.

e have / out / they / taken / the garbage ?
____
Yes, ______________.

f have / the cake / eaten / you ?
____
Yes, ______________.

3 Complete the questions with the present perfect form of the verbs in parentheses. Complete the short answers.

Louis **a** ________________ (you / finish) your homework, Kyle?
Kyle No, **b** ________________.
Louis But I want to play basketball with you. **c** ________________ (you / start) it yet?
Kyle Yes, I **d** ________________. But I'm looking for my pencil case. **e** ________________ (you / see) it?
Louis Yes, I **f** ________________. It's in the kitchen. I'll get it for you.
Kyle Thanks.
Louis **g** ________________ (your teacher / give) you a lot of homework?
Kyle Yes, he **h** ________________.
Louis Ooh. It looks difficult. **i** ________________ (you / do) number four yet?
Kyle No, I **j** ________________. **k** ________________ (you / finish) asking questions?
Louis Why?
Kyle Because I'm trying to do my homework!
Louis Erp… sorry, hahaha!

4 Complete the questions using the phrases in the box or your own ideas. Write answers for you.

eat shark	ride a camel	see a famous person	travel to another country

a Have you ever ________________?

b Have your parents ever ________________?

c Has your friend ever ________________?

d Has your teacher ever ________________?

GRAMMAR CHECK

1 Read the dialogue and circle the correct answers.

Josh How have **a** ___ your habits? Have you **b** ___ recycling?
Ben Yes, **c** ___. We've **d** ___ plastic boxes for meat and fish, so we **e** ___ plastic bags recently.
Josh Has your town **f** ___ recycling bins on your street?
Ben Yes, they have. And they've given us a new bin for food waste this week.
Josh Have you used the new bin?
Ben No, **g** ___, but we want to.
Josh What else **h** ___?
Ben To reduce energy use? We've **i** ___ our lights.
Josh That's great. Have you written about your changes in your blog?
Ben No. I haven't, but my sister **j** ___. I don't have a computer – they use electricity!

a	you change	(you changed)	changed you
b	start	starting	started
c	we have	we have started	we started
d	buy	buying	bought
e	haven't needed	not need	not needed
f	put	to put	putting
g	you haven't	we haven't	we didn't
h	you've done	did you	have you done
i	changing	changed	change
j	did	was	has

2 97 Listen and check your answers.

LISTENING

1 98 Listen to a radio show and underline the animals the speakers mention.

chimpanzees crocodiles lions monkeys rhinoceroses snakes tigers turtles

2 98 Listen again and write T for *true* or F for *false*.

a ☐ London Zoo opened in 1820.
b ☐ London Zoo had the first children's zoo.
c ☐ London Zoo has more than 750 different kinds of animals.
d ☐ There aren't any elephants or rhinoceroses.
e ☐ The monkey house is big.
f ☐ Chris hasn't seen a real crocodile.
g ☐ The only quagga in the world is in London Zoo.

EXTENSION

Underline the correct words to complete the text.

There **a is / are** a lot of different art forms, but there's one that combines sculpture and recycling: scrap-metal sculpture. It's a type of art that **b is becoming / becomes** more popular as people think more about recycling. **c You've / Have you** seen the movie *Wall-E*? **d Much / A lot of** scrap metal sculptures look like the robot. In fact, making these sculptures is great fun and if you **e like / 'll like** science-fiction, you **f love / 'll love** this art because you can invent aliens and robots, and you can make **g bigger / more big** sculptures **h than / that** with normal materials.

You probably **i didn't / haven't** visited the biggest scrap-metal sculpture in the world, because it's in rural Wisconsin, in the north of the USA, but the most famous sculpture in the world is probably Pablo Picasso's work. He **j did use / used** a recycled bicycle and made an animal. American artist John Chamberlain **k make / makes** the most colorful sculptures because he paints **l they / them**, and he is the most famous scrap-metal artist alive today. Why not try scrap-metal sculpture? You'll have a lot of fun, you'll use your imagination, and you'll help the environment.

VOCABULARY PLUS

The Natural World

1 🔊 99 Translate the words from the box into your language. Then listen and repeat.

cliff coast desert hill mountain range
rain forest pond stream valley waterfall

2 Label the picture with words from activity 1.

3 Find seven words in the word search.

K	S	T	R	E	A	M	C	K	V
W	A	T	E	R	F	A	L	L	A
M	K	G	R	D	W	H	I	A	L
D	E	S	E	R	T	K	F	L	L
C	O	A	S	T	A	V	F	F	E
P	O	N	D	D	M	M	Y	S	Y

4 Choose the correct word to complete the sentences.

We went to the *waterfalls* of Iguazu.

1 waterfalls **2** streams **3** deserts

a The temperature in the Sahara ____________ is often 58°C.

1 stream **2** desert **3** valley

b The ____________ is 2 meters deep.

1 pond **2** hill **3** coast

c The Alps are the highest ____________ in Europe.

1 hill **2** cliff **3** mountain range

d People shouldn't chop down trees in the ____________.

1 rain forest **2** stream **3** desert

e We live on the ____________. I can see the beach from my bedroom window.

1 hill **2** coast **3** valley

8 Altruism

VOCABULARY 1

Fundraising Ideas

1 Complete the fundraising ideas with the words in the box.

collect   do   ~~have~~   make
organize   sell (x3)   wash

have a rummage sale

a ______ raffle tickets

b ______ a sponsored swim

c ______ a charity CD

d ______ badges

e ______ money

f ______ cars

g ______ a concert

h ______ candy

2 Match fundraising ideas from activity 1 with the pictures.

a *sell raffle tickets*

b ______

c ______

d ______

e ______

3 Read the sentences and write fundraising ideas from activity 1.

Do you have any old toys or clothes or books? Could you give them to us if you don't need them?
organize a rummage sale

a The musicians are here. The audience is arriving. We're starting in five minutes.

______

b It will take about half an hour. It will be lovely and clean when I finish.

______

c It's for children in need. Put it in the box, please. Thank you very much.

______

d She's trying to do 1 kilometer. I'm paying her $1 for every 100 meters. So, if she finishes, I have to give her $10.

______

e They say SAVE THE RAIN FOREST and they cost 20 cents. Can I put it on your jacket for you?

______

f Tickets are $1 each and you have a chance to win one of these prizes: a weekend for two in Paris, a TV, or a meal for two at The Garden Restaurant.

______

g We're singing and our teacher is recording us.

______

h We have chocolates, chewing gum and fruit pastilles. Everything costs 50 cents.

______

GRAMMAR 1

Present Perfect: *ever, never, yet, already, just*

1 Rewrite the sentences with the words in parentheses.

I've lost my coin purse. (just)
I've just lost my coin purse.

a She has written to me. (never)
____

b You've made a mistake. (just)
____

c Has she been fired? (ever)
____

d It's started to rain. (already)
____

e She has not found it. (yet)
____

f Have you told a lie? (ever)
____

g We have had lunch. (already)
____

h Have you eaten the candy? (yet)
____

i They have visited the Great Wall of China. (never)
____

2 Complete the sentences with the present perfect form of the verbs and the words in parentheses.

Dianne ______*has just run*______ (run / just) 20 kilometers to raise money for charity.

a Dave ______________ (write / already) 30 emails today.

b I ______________ all the raffle tickets ______________ (not sell / yet). I have only $100 for hospitals in the countryside.

c I ______________ (see / just) a movie showing the terrible conditions in the refugee camps.

d They______________ (do / never) work for charities.

e You______________ (make / already) lots of money with your rummage sale.

3 Complete the answers to the questions with the present perfect form of the verbs in parentheses. Use *never* or *yet*.

Did he enjoy the sponsored walk?
I don't know. He _*hasn't told*_ (tell) me _*yet*_.

a What's the charity CD like?
I don't know. ______________ (hear) it ______.

b What did she think of the movie?
She ______________ (see) it.

c Why are they so hungry?
They ______________ (eat) anything ______.

d Are your new shoes comfortable?
I ______________ (wear) them ______.

e When are we having the rummage sale?
I'm not sure because I______________ (speak) to Ellie about it.

4 Match the statements with the questions. Then complete the questions with the present perfect form of the verbs in parentheses. Use *yet* or *ever*.

a I want to do some charity work [2]

b It's Ryan's birthday tomorrow. [ ]

c Katy can't see the board. [ ]

d Let's go to the park. [ ]

e My mother wants to travel, but she doesn't know where. [ ]

f The barbecue is this afternoon. [ ]

1 ______________ (you / buy) the meat and fish ______?

2 *Have you ever done* (you / do) a sponsored swim?

3 ______________ (she / be) abroad?

4 ______________ (it / stop) raining ______?

5 ______________ (she / find) her glasses ______?

6 ______________ (anyone / make) him a cake ______?

5 Complete the quiz questions with *ever* and the present perfect form of the verbs in parentheses. Then answer the questions for you, using *already*, *never* or *yet*.

There are lots of fun and creative ways to raise money for charity or to do something for your community. Which ones have you tried?

Have you ever cleaned up (clean up) a beach?
Yes, I have already cleaned up a beach. / No, I haven't cleaned up a beach yet. / No, I've never cleaned up a beach.

A ______________ (wear) a red nose for a day?
____
____

B ______________ (sing) in front of the whole school?
____
____

C ______________ (have) a pajama party?
____
____

D ______________ (paint) people's faces?
____
____

E ______________ (dance) for twelve hours without stopping?
____
____

F ______________ (organize) a big picnic?
____
____

G ______________ (play) a musical instrument in the street?
____
____

H ______________ (sell) things at a rummage sale?
____
____

6 Write true sentences with *never* about you, your family and your friends.

Write about:

- a sport, game or activity

play	do

My father has never played golf.

a ______________

b ______________

- food

eat	try

c ______________

d ______________

- clothes and fashion

wear	buy

e ______________

f ______________

- places

visit	see

g ______________

h ______________

VOCABULARY 2

make and *do*

1 Complete the phrases with *make* or *do*.

make someone happy

a ______ a decision

b ______ charity work

c ______ a mistake

d ______ exercise

e ______ someone a favor

f ______ friends

g ______ homework

h ______ someone laugh

i ______ nothing

j ______ money

k ______ your best

2 Match phrases from activity 1 with the pictures.

Happy birthday. This is for you.

That's fantastic! It's just what I wanted.

make someone happy

18 + 6 = 25.

No, that's wrong.

a ____________

I'm doing this map for my geography project first, then I'm learning my French vocabulary.

b ____________

I'm going for a run now. I run every day after school.

c ____________

Yes, they're an amazing team. They probably will win, so you have to work very hard.

d ____________

You don't need to get a taxi. I'll drive you to the station.

e ____________

3 Complete the sentences with phrases from activity 1. Use the correct form of *make* or *do*.

I love *doing nothing* on Sunday evening before a busy week at school.

a Come on, hurry up. We need your answer. Please ____________.

b I love those comedy shows on Channel 2. They're so funny. ____________ always make me ____________.

c She's at a new school and she hasn't ____________ with anyone in her class yet.

d Top soccer players ____________ a lot of ____________. They can earn millions of dollars a year.

e She's a doctor, but, at the moment, she's ____________ in a hospital abroad.

f I've ____________ in the exercise, so I need to correct it.

GRAMMAR 2

Present Perfect: *for* and *since*

1 Circle the correct words.

I've known him (**for**) / **since** two years.

a She's been here **for** / **since** four o'clock.

b Gloria hasn't played tennis **for** / **since** March.

c I haven't seen Georgia **for** / **since** years.

d I've lived in Barcelona **for** / **since** I was born.

e I've been at home **for** / **since** a week.

f We've been friends **for** / **since** we were children.

2 Order the words to make sentences.

here / Monday / has / Jane / since / been

Jane has been here since Monday.

a 2010 / has / in a bookstore / My sister / since / worked

____

b since / haven't / the fire / been / They / at school

____

c him / for / known / ages / I've

____

d three / had / years / Anna / a motorcycle / for / has

____

e eaten / since / She / with Harry / that awful meal / hasn't

____

3 Write questions with *How long ....* Then answer using *for* or *since*.

you / live in Granada ? (two years)

How long have you lived in Granada?

I've lived in Granada for two years.

a she / work for that charity ? (2008)

____

____

b that restaurant / be open ? (two weeks)

____

____

c you / have that laptop ? (March)

____

____

d they / know each other ? (they were two)

____

____

e Luis / wear glasses ? (two years)

____

____

4 Complete the email with the present perfect form of the verbs in parentheses. Circle *for* or *since*.

To: Anita
From: Daniel
Subject: Hi! :-)

I'm sorry I *haven't written* (not write) to you (**for**) / **since** a long time. I **a** ___________ (be) very busy **for / since** the beginning of term. I **b** ___________ (join) the basketball team and we **c** ___________ (have) three matches so far. I **d** ___________ (not play) tennis **for / since** last summer because I **e** ___________ (not have) time. I **f** ___________ (not see) Rob **for / since** a very long time. I think he **g** ___________ (go) to live in Brighton. **h** ___________ (you / hear) from him? I **i** ___________ (make) some really nice new friends at the drama club. We **j** ___________ (write) a play together and we're acting in it next term. You must come and see it.

Bye for now,

Daniel

5 Write sentences about you, your family and your friends. Use the present perfect with *for* or *since*.

I have been at this school for four years.

We have lived in our apartment since 2007.

a ___________ been ___________.

b ___________ lived ___________.

c ___________ had ___________.

d ___________ known ___________.

e ___________ studied ___________.

GRAMMAR CHECK

1 Read the text and circle the correct answers.

Since last March, we **a** ___ nearly $700 for Médecins Sans Frontières. We are very pleased. And now we **b** ___ started to raise money for Oxfam, too. So far, Carol **c** ___ organized a rummage sale. We **d** ___ had the sale yet, but some of us have **e** ___ a sponsored swim. We have **f** ___ a charity CD, so maybe we can try that this year. At my school, the teachers and students have done charity work **g** ___ 2010. And we've sponsored a school **h** ___ three years. With our support, they have **i** ___ desks and a board for a new classroom. **j** ___ you ever done anything interesting to raise money?

	1	2	3
a	raising	have raised (circled)	were raising
b	have	did	were
c	did	was	has
d	haven't	didn't	couldn't
e	already did	already doing	already done
f	made never	ever made	never made
g	before	since	in
h	before	since	for
i	bought	buy	buying
j	Did	Have	Were

2 100 Listen and check your answers.

LISTENING

1 101 Listen to two volunteers talking about their work for Clean Beaches. Circle the correct answers.

a The volunteers are cleaning **parks / beaches / roads**.

b Maria Adams is a **teacher / student / secretary** at the community school.

c They're finding **more garbage / less garbage / the same amount of garbage** this year.

d Andy is a **student / teacher / office worker** at the school.

e He arrived at **one o'clock / three thirty / nine thirty**.

f He is volunteering because **he gets free lunch / the school makes him / he cares about the environment**.

2 101 Listen again and answer the questions.

a How many kilometers have they cleaned up so far?

____

b When did the Clean Beaches campaign start?

____

c How much less garbage are they finding this year?

____

d What does Maria say about beaches in the state?

____

e How many items were they picking up per kilometer last year?

____

f How many items are they picking up per kilometer this year?

____

g What has Andy picked up today?

____

h How long has he been there?

____

i What's the strangest thing he has found?

____

____

j What are the fun activities at the end of the day?

____

____

EXTENSION

Circle the correct words to complete the text.

Our school has collected money for different charities **a since / for** five years now. We all really enjoy **b organizing / to organize** different fundraising activities. Last year, we **c made / have made** $3,000 for the Red Cross with a big 'Charity Day.' We **d were selling / sold** cakes, books and raffle tickets, and washed cars. There **e were / was** also a pet show. It was the **f funniest / funnier** event of the day. While Peter Shepherd in Year 9 **g was showing / showed** his parrot to the judges, it started to say really bad words and the principal **h has got / got** very annoyed. He said the parrot was not polite **i enough for / enough to** win! This year we **j are organizing / organize** a concert, a disco, karaoke and a fashion show. We haven't had a disco **k since / for** 2008. And we've **l never did / never done** a fashion show before, although a fashion show isn't as **m interested / interesting** as a pet show. **n Have / Did** you ever done karaoke? I **o haven't / didn't** because I'm too frightened **p for singing / to sing** in public!

VOCABULARY PLUS

Money

1 ____________

2 ____________

3 ____________

4 ____________

5 ____________

6 ____________

7 ____________

8 ____________

9 ____________

10 ____________

1 102 Label the pictures with the words in the box. Then listen and repeat.

ATM (automated teller machine)
bills check coin purse coins
pay by credit card pay in cash
PIN tip wallet

2 Circle the correct words.

I've never had a $50 **coin / bill**.

a 'Waiter! Can we have the **check / tip**, please?' 'Certainly.'

b Someone stole my dad's **ATM / wallet** yesterday.

c I don't have enough bills. I'll pay **by credit card / in cash**.

d You shouldn't show anyone your **coin purse / PIN**.

e You can't get **coins / bills** from an ATM.

3 Read the definitions and write the correct words.

Men usually keep their money in this. *wallet*

a Women usually keep their money in this. ____________

b You can get money from here 24 hours a day. ____________

c You leave this if you're happy with the service in a restaurant. ____________

d If you pay with bills and coins, you do this. ____________

e A piece of paper that shows you how much to pay in a restaurant. ____________

4 Answer the questions for you. Write in full sentences. Use words from activity 1.

a Where do you keep your money?
____

b How do you usually pay in a store?
____

Wordlist

PHONETIC CHART

VOWELS AND DIPHTHONGS 103

/ɪ/ p**i**g	/e/ br**ea**d	/u/ l**o**se	/aɪ/ **I**
/i/ sh**e**	/ɜr/ c**ur**ly	/ə/ act**o**r	/ɔɪ/ t**oy**
/æ/ c**a**t	/ɔ/ b**a**ll	/ʌ/ s**u**nny	/aʊ/ m**ou**ntain
/ɑ/ **a**rm	/ʊ/ g**oo**d	/eɪ/ US**A**	/oʊ/ b**oa**t

CONSONANTS 104

/p/ **p**otato	/tʃ/ **ch**air	/s/ **S**pain	/n/ **n**ewsstand
/b/ **b**lue	/dʒ/ fri**dge**	/z/ ea**s**y	/ŋ/ spri**ng**
/t/ **t**axi	/f/ **f**inish	/ʃ/ **sh**ower	/l/ **l**ake
/d/ **d**rama	/v/ **v**erb	/ʒ/ televi**s**ion	/r/ **r**ead
/k/ **c**arrot	/θ/ ba**th**room	/h/ **h**i	/j/ **y**esterday
/g/ **g**randpa	/ð/ **th**ere	/m/ **m**outh	/w/ **w**ater

A 105

acoustic guitar (n) /əˈkustɪk gɪˈtɑr/
across (prep) /əˈkrɔs/
action-adventure (n) /ˈækʃ(ə)n ədˈventʃər/
actor (n) /ˈæktər/
advertise (v) /ˈædvərˌtaɪz/
advertisement (n) /ædˈvɜrtɪsmənt/
along (prep) /əˈlɔŋ/
already (adv) /ɔlˈredi/
also (adv) /ˈɔlsoʊ/
aluminum (n) /əˈlumɪnəm/
amp (n) /æmp/
anniversary (n) /ˌænɪˈvɜrs(ə)ri/
annoy (v) /əˈnɔɪ/
annoyed (adj) /əˈnɔɪd/
annoying (adj) /əˈnɔɪɪŋ/
answer (v) /ˈænsər/
apartheid (n) /əˈpɑrtˌhaɪt/
appear (v) /əˈpɪr/
architect (n) /ˈɑrkɪˌtekt/
argue (v) /ˈɑrˌgju/
argument (n) /ˈɑrgjəmənt/
around (prep) /əˈraʊnd/
artist (n) /ˈɑrtɪst/
ask (v) /æsk/
ate (v) /eɪt/
athlete (n) /ˈæθˌlit/
ATM (automated teller machine) (n) /ˌeɪ ti ˈem/
autograph (n) /ˈɔtəˌgræf/
autumn (n) /ˈɔtəm/
avalanche (n) /ˈævəˌlæntʃ/
award (n) /əˈwɔrd/
away from (prep) /əˈweɪ frɑm/

B 106

bag (n) /bæg/
be (v) /bi/
be born (v) /bi bɔrn/
be going to /bi ˈgoʊɪŋ tu/
because (conj) /bɪˈkɔz/
began (v) /bɪˈgæn/
begin (v) /bɪˈgɪn/
bill (n) /bɪl/
biomedicine (n) /ˈbaɪoʊˌmedɪsɪn/
birth (n) /bɜrθ/
birthday celebration (n) /ˈbɜrθˌdeɪ ˌseləˈbreɪʃ(ə)n/
blind (adj) /blaɪnd/
blizzard (n) /ˈblɪzərd/
boots (n) /buts/
bore (v) /bɔr/
bored (adj) /bɔrd/
boring (adj) /ˈbɔrɪŋ/
bottle (n) /ˈbɑt(ə)l/
box (n) /bɑks/
box office (n) /bɑks ˈɔfɪs/
break (v) /breɪk/
bric-a-brac sale (n) /ˈbrɪkəˌbræk seɪl/
broken arm /ˈbroʊkən ɑrm/
bulletproof vest (n) /ˈbʊlɪtˌpruf vest/
buy a house /baɪ ə haʊs/
by the end of the year /baɪ ði end əv ði jɪr/

C 107

call (v) /kɔl/
can (n) /kæn/
cardboard (n) /ˈkɑrdˌbɔrd/
carton (n) /ˈkɑrt(ə)n/
cell phone (n) /sel foʊn/
charge (v) /tʃɑrdʒ/

charge a cell phone /tʃɑrdʒ ə sel foʊn/
chat (v) /tʃæt/
check (n) /tʃek/
chimpanzee (n) /ˌtʃɪmpæn'zi/
clean-tech (n) /klin tek/
cliff (n) /klɪf/
cloudy (adj) /'klaʊdi/
coast (n) /koʊst/
coat (n) /koʊt/
coin (n) /kɔɪn/
coin purse (n) /kɔɪn pɜrs/
cold (n) /koʊld/
collect money /kə'lekt 'mʌni/
come (v) /kʌm/
compete (v) /kəm'pit/
competition (n) /ˌkɑmpə'tɪʃ(ə)n/
compost (v) /'kɑmˌpoʊst/
computer (n) /kəm'pjutər/
connect (v) /kə'nekt/
connection (n) /kə'nekʃ(ə)n/
construction worker (n) /kən'strʌkʃ(ə)n 'wɜrkər/
contaminated water (n) /kən'tæmɪˌneɪtəd 'wɔtər/
cotton (n) /'kɑt(ə)n/
cough (n) /kɑf/
cow (n) /kaʊ/
crash (v) /kræʃ/
crocodile (n) /'krɑkəˌdaɪl/
cut (v) /kʌt/
cycle (v) /'saɪk(ə)l/
cyclone (n) /'saɪˌkloʊn/

D 108

death (n) /deθ/
decorate (v) /'dekəˌreɪt/
decoration (n) /ˌdekə'reɪʃ(ə)n/
department store (n) /dɪ'pɑrtmənt stɔr/
develop (v) /dɪ'veləp/
development (n) /dɪ'veləpmənt/
die (v) /daɪ/
digital camera (n) /'dɪdʒɪt(ə)l 'kæm(ə)rə/
digital media (n) /'dɪdʒɪt(ə)l 'midiə/
director (n) /dɪ'rektər/
disease (n) /dɪ'ziz/
disposable glove (n) /dɪ'spoʊzəb(ə)l glʌv/
divorce (n) /dɪ'vɔrs/
do a sponsored swim /du ə 'spɑnsərd swɪm/
do charity work /du 'tʃerəti wɜrk/
do exercise /du 'eksərˌsaɪz/
do homework /du 'hoʊmˌwɜrk/
do nothing /du 'nʌθɪŋ/
do someone a favor /du 'sʌmwʌn ə 'feɪvər/
do your best /du jʊr best/
doctor (n) /'dɑktər/
doctor's office (n) /'dɑktərz 'ɔfɪs/
dolphin (n) /'dɑlfɪn/
dot-com company (n) /ˌdɑt'kɑm 'kʌmpəni/
down (prep) /daʊn/
download a song /'daʊnˌloʊd ə sɔŋ/
download a video clip /'daʊnˌloʊd ə 'vɪdioʊ klɪp/
dress (n) /dres/
drive (v) /draɪv/
drown (v) /draʊn/
drums (n) /drʌmz/
dry (adj) /draɪ/

E 109

earache (n) /'ɪrˌeɪk/
earmuffs (n) /'ɪrˌmʌfs/
earring (n) /'ɪrɪŋ/
educate (v) /'edʒəˌkeɪt/
education (n) /ˌedʒə'keɪʃ(ə)n/
electric bass (n) /ɪ'lektrɪk beɪs/
electric guitar (n) /ɪ'lektrɪk gɪ'tɑr/
electrician (n) /ɪˌlek'trɪʃ(ə)n/
elephant (n) /'eləfənt/
engagement (n) /ɪn'geɪdʒmənt/
engineer (n) /ˌendʒɪ'nɪr/
enjoy (v) /ɪn'dʒɔɪ/
enjoyment (n) /ɪn'dʒɔɪmənt/
equip (v) /ɪ'kwɪp/
e-reader (n) /'iridə(r)/
escape (v) /ɪ'skeɪp/
ever (adv) /'evər/
excite (v) /ɪk'saɪt/
excited (adj) /ɪk'saɪtəd/
excitement (n) /ɪk'saɪtmənt/
exciting (adj) /ɪk'saɪtɪŋ/

F 110

face mask (n) /feɪs mæsk/
factory (n) /'fækt(ə)ri/
feel (v) /fil/
fell (v) /fel/
film a scene /fɪlm ə sin/
financial service (n) /fɪ'nænʃ(ə)l 'sɜrvɪs/
fireman (n) /'faɪrmən/
flash drive (n) /flæʃ draɪv/
flew (v) /flu/
flip-flop (n) /flɪp flɑp/
flute (n) /flut/
for (prep/conj) /fɔr/
found (v) /faʊnd/
friendship (n) /'fren(d)ʃɪp/
frighten (v) /'fraɪt(ə)n/
frightened (adj) /'fraɪt(ə)nd/
frightening (adj) /'fraɪt(ə)nɪŋ/
fundraising (n) /'fʌndˌreɪzɪŋ/

G 111

games (n) /geɪms/
games console (n) /geɪms 'kɑnˌsoʊl/
garage (n) /gə'rɑʒ/
garage sale (n) /gə'rɑʒ seɪl/
get (v) /get/
get a job /get ə dʒɑb/

get married /get 'merid/
give (v) /gɪv/
glass (n) /glæs/
glove (n) /glʌv/
go (v) /goʊ/
go online /goʊ 'ɑnˌlaɪn/
go to /goʊ tu '/
go to college /goʊ tu 'kɑlɪdʒ/
go up /goʊ ʌp/
Good Deeds Day (n) /gʊd dids deɪ/
Goodwill Ambassador (n) /gʊd'wɪl æm'bæsədər/
got (v) /gɑt/
got stuck /gɑt stʌk/
grow (v) /groʊ/

H 112

hailstorm (n) /'heɪlˌstɔrm/
happen (v) /'hæpən/
have a rummage sale /hæv ə 'rʌmɪdʒ seɪl/
have children /hæv 'tʃɪldrən/
headache (n) /'hedˌeɪk/
hear (v) /hɪr/
heat wave (n) /hit weɪv/
helmet (n) /'helmət/
hide (v) /haɪd/
high drama (n) /haɪ 'drɑmə/
high school (n) /haɪ skul/
high visibility jacket (n) /ˌhaɪ vɪzə'bɪləti 'dʒækət/
hold (v) /hoʊld/
Hollywood blockbuster (n) /'hɑliˌwʊd 'blɑkˌbʌstər/
hospital (n) /'hɑspɪt(ə)l/
hot (adj) /hɑt/
how long /haʊ lɔŋ/

I 113

inform (v) /ɪn'fɔrm/
information (n) /ˌɪnfər'meɪʃ(ə)n/
insect bite (n) /'ɪnˌsekt baɪt/
inspector (n) /ɪn'spektər/
interest (n) /'ɪntrəst/
interested (adj) /'ɪntrəstɪd/
interesting (adj) /'ɪntrəstɪŋ/
internet browser (n) /'ɪntərˌnet 'braʊzər/
into (prep) /'ɪntu/
introduce (v) /ˌɪntrə'dus/
invite (v) /ɪn'vaɪt/

J 114

jacket (n) /'dʒækət/
Jamaica (n) /ʤə'meɪkə/
jar (n) /dʒɑr/
jeans (n) /dʒinz/
journalist (n) /'dʒɜrn(ə)lɪst/
just (adv) /dʒʌst/

K 115

keyboards (n) /'kiˌbɔrds/

L 116

lawyer (n) /'lɔjər/
learn to drive /lɜrn tu draɪv/
leave home /liv hoʊm/
leave school /liv skul/
leopard (n) /'lepərd/
lie (v) /laɪ/
lion (n) /'laɪən/
listen (v) /'lɪs(ə)n/
live (v) /lɪv/
look (v) /lʊk/
lost (v) /lɔst/
love (v) /lʌv/

M 117

mailman (n) /'meɪlˌmæn/
make (v) /meɪk/
make a charity CD /meɪk ə 'tʃerəti ˌsi 'di/
make a decision /meɪk ə dɪ'sɪʒ(ə)n/
make a mistake /meɪk ə mɪ'steɪk/
make a phone call /meɪk ə foʊn kɔl/
make friends /meɪk frendz/
make money /meɪk 'mʌni/
make someone happy /meɪk 'sʌmwʌn 'hæpi/
make someone laugh /meɪk 'sʌmwʌn læf/
manage (v) /'mænɪdʒ/
Maori (n) /'maʊri/
market opportunity (n) /'mɑrkət ˌɑpər'tunəti/
meanwhile (adv) /'minˌwaɪl/
mechanic (n) /mə'kænɪk/
medical field (n) /'medɪk(ə)l fild/
metal (n) /'met(ə)l/
mild (adj) /maɪld/
monkey (n) /'mʌŋki/
mountain range (n) /'maʊnt(ə)n reɪndʒ/
movie premiere (n) /'muvi prɪ'mir/
movie star (n) /'muvi stɑr/
movie-maker (n) /'muvi 'meɪkər/
movie-making (n) /'muvi 'meɪkɪŋ/
multiplex movie theater (n) /'mʌltɪˌpleks 'muvi 'θiətər/
must (v) /mʌst/

N 118

notice (v) /'noʊtɪs/
nurse (n) /nɜrs/

O 119

ocean (n) /'oʊʃ(ə)n/
office (n) /'ɔfɪs/
online (adj) /'ɑnˌlaɪn/
open (v) /'oʊpən/
orangutan (n) /ɔ'ræŋəˌtæn/
organize a concert /'ɔrgəˌnaɪz ə 'kɑnsərt/
out of (prep) /aʊt əv/
over (prep) /'oʊvər/
overall (n) /'oʊvərˌɔl/

P 🔊 120

panda (n) /ˈpændə/
paper (n) /ˈpeɪpər/
pass (v) /pæs/
pay by credit card /peɪ baɪ ˈkredɪt kɑrd/
pay in cash /peɪ ɪn kæʃ/
percussion (n) /pərˈkʌʃ(ə)n/
phone (n) /foʊn/
phone call (n) /foʊn kɔl/
phone charger (n) /foʊn ˈtʃɑrdʒər/
piano (n) /piˈænoʊ/
PIN (n) /pɪn/
play a video game /pleɪ ə ˈvɪdioʊ geɪm/
plot (n) /plɑt/
plug (v) /plʌg/
plug in a flash drive /plʌg ɪn ə flæʃ draɪv/
polar bear (n) /ˈpoʊlər ber/
police officer (n) /pəˈlis ˈɔfɪsər/
police station (n) /pəˈlis ˈsteɪʃ(ə)n/
policewoman (n) /pəˈlisˌwʊmən/
politician (n) /ˌpɑləˈtɪʃ(ə)n/
pond (n) /pɑnd/
poor sanitation (n) /pʊr ˌsænɪˈteɪʃ(ə)n/
popcorn (n) /ˈpɑpˌkɔrn/
portable hard drive (n) /ˈpɔrtəb(ə)l hɑrd draɪv/
possess (v) /pəˈzes/
possession (n) /pəˈzeʃ(ə)n/
post a comment /poʊst ə ˈkɑˌment/
predict (v) /prɪˈdɪkt/
prediction (n) /prɪˈdɪkʃ(ə)n/
prepare (v) /prɪˈper/
print a document /prɪnt ə ˈdɑkjəmənt/
producer (n) /prəˈdusər/
put (v) /pʊt/

Q 🔊 121

queue (n) /kju/

R 🔊 122

rain boot (n) /reɪn but/
rainy (adj) /ˈreɪni/
rainforest (n) /reɪnˈfɔrəst/
read an e-book /rid æn i-bʊk/
researcher (n) /rɪˈsɜrtʃər/
recognize (v) /ˈrekəgˌnaɪz/
recycle (v) /riˈsaɪk(ə)l/
reduce (v) rɪˈdus/
refer (v) /rɪˈfɜr/
release a movie /rɪˈlis ə ˈmuvi/
retirement (n) /rɪˈtaɪrmənt/
reuse (v) /ˌriˈjuz/
rhinoceros (n) /raɪˈnɑsərəs/
Royal Bengal Tiger (n) /ˈrɔɪəl ˈbeŋgəl ˈtaɪgər/

S 🔊 123

safety glasses (n) /ˈseɪfti ˈglɑsəz/
sandal (n) /ˈsænd(ə)l/
saxophone (n) /ˈsæksəˌfoʊn/
scan a picture /skæn ə ˈpɪktʃər/
scarf (n) /skɑrf/
science fiction (n) /ˈsaɪəns ˈfɪkʃ(ə)n/
scientist (n) /ˈsaɪəntɪst/
script (n) /skrɪpt/
seat (n) /sit/
see (v) /si/
sell badges /sel bædʒz/
sell candy /sel ˈkændi/
sell raffle tickets /sel ˈræf(ə)l ˈtɪkɪts/
send an email /send æn ˈiˌmeɪl/
shark attack (n) /ʃɑrk əˈtæk/
shirt (n) /ʃɜrt/
shorts (n) /ʃɔrts/
should (v) /ʃʊd/
show (v) /ʃoʊ/
sick (adj) /sɪk/
since (adv/conj/prep) /sɪns/
Singapore (n) /ˈsɪŋəˌpɔr/
skirt (n) /skɜrt/
slipper (n) /ˈslɪpər/
smart TV (n) /smɑrt ˌti ˈvi/
smile (v) /smaɪl/
snake (n) /sneɪk/
sneakers (n) /ˈsnikərz/
snowy (adj) /ˈsnoʊi/
so (adv/conj) /soʊ/
soft drink (n) /sɔft drɪŋk/
soon (adv) /sun/
sore throat (n) /sɔr θroʊt/
soundtrack (n) /ˈsaʊn(d)ˌtræk/
South Africa (n) /saʊθ ˈæfrɪkə/
special effects (n) /ˈspeʃ(ə)l ɪˈfekts/
sports club (n) /spɔrts klʌb/
spring (n) /sprɪŋ/
star in a movie /stɑr ɪn ə ˈmuvi/
start school /stɑrt skul/
stay (v) /steɪ/
stomachache (n) /ˈstʌməkeɪk/
stop (v) /stɑp/
store (v) /stɔr/
store data (n) /stɔr ˈdætə/
stormy (adj) /ˈstɔrmi/
stream (n) /strim/
study (v) /ˈstʌdi/
study abroad (n) /ˈstʌdi əˈbrɔd/
stunt (n) /stʌnt/
stunt man (n) /stʌnt mæn/
stunt woman (n) /stʌnt ˈwʊmən/
suddenly (adv) /ˈsʌd(ə)nli/
suggest (v) /səgˈdʒest/
suggestion (n) /səgˈdʒestʃ(ə)n/
summer (n) /ˈsʌmər/
sun hat (n) /sʌn hæt/
sunny (adj) /ˈsʌni/
surf (v) /sɜrf/
surf the web /sɜrf ðə web/

surgeon (n) /ˈsɜrdʒən/
surprise (v) /sərˈpraɪz/
surprised (adj) /sərˈpraɪzd/
surprising (adj) /sərˈpraɪzɪŋ/
survive (v) /sərˈvaɪv/
swam (v) /swæm/
swap meet (n) /swɑp mit/
sweater (n) /ˈswetər/
swim (v) /swɪm/

T 124

take (v) /teɪk/
take a digital picture /teɪk ə ˈdɪdʒɪt(ə)l ˈpɪktʃər/
talk (v) /tɔk/
teacher (n) /ˈtitʃər/
technician (n) /tekˈnɪʃ(ə)n/
technology sector (n) /tekˈnɑlədʒi ˈsektər/
tell (v) /tel/
temperature (n) /ˈtemp(ə)rəˌtʃʊr/
theater (n) /ˈθiətər/
then (adj/adv) /ðen/
think (v) /θɪŋk/
thunderstorm (n) /ˈθʌndərˌstɔrm/
ticket (n) /ˈtɪkɪt/
tie (n) /taɪ/
tiger (n) /ˈtaɪgər/
tip (n) /tɪp/
tire (v) /ˈtaɪr/
tired (adj) /ˈtaɪrd/
tiring (adj) /ˈtaɪrɪŋ/
tomorrow (adv) /təˈmɔroʊ/
too (adv) /tu/
took (v) /tʊk/
towards (prep) /tɔrdz/
train to be a /treɪn tu bi ə/
Trinidad and Tobago (n) /ˈtrɪnɪˌdæd ænd təˈbeɪgoʊ/
trumpet (n) /ˈtrʌmpət/
try (v) /traɪ/
T-shirt (n) /ti-ʃɜrt/
turtle (n) /ˈtɜrt(ə)l/

U 125

umbrella (n) /ʌmˈbrelə/
under (prep) /ˈʌndər/
up (prep) /ʌp/
upload (v) /ˈʌpˌloʊd/
upload a series /ˈʌpˌloʊd ə ˈsɪriz/
upload a video clip /ˈʌpˌloʊd ə ˈvɪdioʊ klɪp/
URL (n) /ˌju ɑr ˈel/
use (v) /juz/
use Instagram /juz ˈɪnstəgræm/

V 126

valley (n) /ˈvæli/
vet (n) /vet/
video clip (n) /ˈvɪdioʊ klɪp/
video game (n) /ˈvɪdioʊ geɪm/
violin (n) /ˌvaɪəˈlɪn/
visor (n) /ˈvaɪzər/

W 127

wait (v) /weɪt/
want (v) /wɑnt/
warm (adj) /wɔrm/
was (v) /wɑz/
wash cars /wɑʃ kɑrz/
water molecule (n) /ˈwɔtər ˈmɑləˌkjul/
water service (n) /ˈwɔtər ˈsɜrvɪs/
waterproof (n) /ˈwɔtərˌpruf/
waterproof jacket (n) /ˈwɔtərˌpruf ˈdʒækət/
wave (n) /weɪv/
wear (v) /wer/
web page (n) /ˈweb peɪdʒ/
website (n) /ˈwebˌsaɪt/
wedding (n) /ˈwedɪŋ/
were (v) /wɜr/
wet (adj) /wet/
while (conj) /waɪl/
wildfire (n) /ˈwaɪldˌfaɪr/
will (v) /wɪl/
win an award /wɪn æn əˈwɔrd/
windy (adj) /ˈwɪndi/
winter (n) /ˈwɪntər/
wool (n) /wʊl/
work (v) /wɜrk/
work with children /wɜrk wɪð ˈtʃɪldrən/
World Water Day (n) /wɜrld ˈwɔtər deɪ/
World Wide Web (n) /wɜrld waɪd web/
worried (adj) /ˈwʌrid/
worry (v) /ˈwʌri/
worrying (adj) /ˈwʌriɪŋ/
write (v) /raɪt/
write a blog /raɪt ə blɔg/

Y 128

yard sale (n) /jɑrd seɪl/
yet (adv) /jet/

Based on *Motivate!*
© Macmillan Publishers Limited 2013
Written by Emma Heyderman, Fiona Mauchline, Patrick Howarth, Patricia Reilly and Olivia Johnston
Grammar, *Speaking*, *Culture* and *Life Skills* pages adapted by Gisele Marçon Bastos Périgo

Director of Languages Brazil: Patricia Souza De Luccia
Publishing Manager and Field Researcher: Patricia Muradas
Content Creation Coordinator: Cristina do Vale
Art Editor: Jean Aranha
Content Editors: Ana Beatriz da Costa Moreira, Tatiana Martins Santana
Assistant Editors: Daniela Gonçala da Costa, Roberto Homem de Mello
Digital Editor: Ana Paula Girardi
Editorial Assistants: Nádia Muniz, Roberta Somera, Sheila Folgueral
Graphic Production: Thais Mendes P. Galvão, Tatiane Romano
Academic Consultants: Alex Tamulis (Coordinator), Bruno Lancellotti, Pablo Matos, Rodrigo Marques, Sérgio Lins, Virgínia Galvão
Proofreaders: Paulo Winterstein, Márcia Leme, Danielle Costa
Design Concept: Martha Tadaieski
Page Make-Up: Figurattiva Editorial
Photo Research: Marcia Sato
Illustrations: Bruna Assis
Image Processing: Jean Aranha, Denis Araujo
Cover Concept: Jean Aranha
Audio: Argila Music

We would like to dedicate this book to teachers all over Brazil. We would also like to thank our clients and teachers who have helped us make this book better with their many rich contributions and feedback straight from the classroom along our long-lasting partnership!

Acknowledgments:
Adriana Dias, Adriana Leonzo, Aida Rocha de Almeida, Alessandra Andrade Nepomuceno Cirino, Alessandra Gavilan, Alessandra Marques, Alice Stela Ornelas Machado, Aline Bellarmino, Andrea Muner Paulavicius, Angela Burile Carvalho, Angela Melendez Conigliaro, Angela Segatti, Bianca Dewes, Bruno Andrade, Camila Ramalho, Cintia Galendi, Clice Pereira Salles, Clovis Viana Tavares, Cristiane Ramires, Daniela Murasaki, Danielle Pereira, Debora de Conti, Debora Thome, Eduardo Rodrigues Polidorio, Elaine Perrone, Erik Moreira, Euler França do Nascimento Júnior, Evila Rita Pinheiro Damaceno, Felipe Diesel, Fernanda Harrisberger, Fernanda Inácio, Fernanda Lucia Rocha de Sá Freire, Fernanda Maciel Machado Horta, Flavia Viana, Geraldo Vieira Júnior, Giovanna Meneguetti, Gisele Regina Dias da Silva, Glenda Rabitsch, Graciela Irene Turco, Grasiela Marques, Gustavo Rodarte Boechat, Isabella Villas-Boas, Itana Lins, Jacqueline Alves de Souza Carvalho, Juan Pablo Uribe, Juliana Gebra, Juliana Macedo Fiuza, Kelly Barboza da Silva, Kelly Cardoso, Lais Lara Maia Araújo, Leonardo Gomes de Souza, Ligia Araki, Luciana Melarato, Luciana Carnev, Malyina Kazuo, Marcela Cintra, Marcela Maria Vieira Thomazzi, Marcia Akemi, Maria Noeme de Magalhães Oliveira Monteiro, Mariani Barbosa, Michele Geledan, Milena Matos Carmona, Nair Domingues Guimarães, Patricia Salvo, Paula Bitondi, Paulo Rogério, Priscilla Rodrigues Lauro, Regina Lucia Fernandes, Renata Condi de Souza, Renata Perche, Renata Picasso Amarante, Renata Soares Cozzi Bahia, Roberta Silva, Roberta Tassinari Saraiva, Rodrigo Leão, Rôsangela Maria Silva, Samara Formagio, Sandra Magalhães, Sandra Regina Esteves Cardoso de Mello, Santo Tomaz Aquino, Sillas Paulino da Silva, Silvana Reis, Solange Ortencio, Solange Ulhoa Goulart Lucena, Soraya Bernardes da Silva, Ulysses Camargo Corrêa Diegues, Vagner Serafim, Vera Lacava.

The authors, adaptor and publishers would like to thank the following for permission to reproduce the photographic material:
p. 8: Rawpixel/iStockphoto/Getty Images, Nicolas McComber/iStockphoto/Getty Images, Verdateo/iStockphoto/Getty Images; p. 10: Ralwel/iStockphoto/Getty Images; p. 12: Prykhodov/iStockphoto/Getty Images, Adventtr/iStockphoto/Getty Images, Hocus-focus/iStockphoto/Getty Images, Adventtr/iStockphoto/Getty Images, Inspire Finder/iStockphoto/Getty Images, Scanrail/iStockphoto/Getty Images, Artisteer/iStockphoto/Getty Images, Michael Burrell/iStockphoto/Getty Images, MileA/iStockphoto/Getty Images, Lpettet/iStockphoto/Getty Images; p. 13: Sladic/iStockphoto/Getty Images; p. 14: Wsfurlan/iStockphoto/Getty Images, Goir/iStockphoto/Getty Images; p. 15: Stockcam/iStockphoto/Getty Images; p. 16: Asiseeit/iStockphoto/Getty Images, Ozgurdonmaz/iStockphoto/Getty Images, Blackzheep/iStockphoto/Getty Images, Krystiannawrocki/iStockphoto/Getty Images; p. 17: Nikada/iStockphoto/Getty Images, Imtmphoto/iStockphoto/Getty Images; p. 18: Anyaivanova/iStockphoto/Getty Images, Rob Mattingley/iStockphoto/Getty Images, Andrew Howe/iStockphoto/Getty Images, People Images/iStockphoto/Getty Images, Wdstock/iStockphoto/Getty Images, kali9/iStockphoto/Getty Images; p. 19: SWNS Picture Desk; p. 20: Pop jop/iStockphoto/Getty Images; p. 21: Onurdongel/iStockphoto/Getty Images, Hocus focus/iStockphoto/Getty Images, Pawel_p/iStockphoto/Getty Images, Monkey Business Images/iStockphoto/Getty Images, JGalione/iStockphoto/Getty Images, JazzIRT/iStockphoto/Getty Images, Ross Helen/iStockphoto/Getty Images, Lenta/iStockphoto/Getty Images, Slphotography/iStockphoto/Getty Images, Tatomm/iStockphoto/Getty Images, Fizkes/iStockphoto/Getty Images, Rawpixel/iStockphoto/Getty Images, Mario Guti/iStockphoto/Getty Images, Scyther5/iStockphoto/Getty Images, Monkey Business Images/iStockphoto/Getty Images, Pbophotographer/iStockphoto/Getty Images, Andrey Popov/iStockphoto/Getty Images, Jacoblund/iStockphoto/Getty Images, 4x6/iStockphoto/Getty Images, Gremlin/iStockphoto/Getty Images, Digtial Storm/iStockphoto/Getty Images, Aijohn784/iStockphoto/Getty Images, Yin Yang/iStockphoto/Getty Images, Steve Debenport/iStockphoto/Getty Images, Milanvirijevic/iStockphoto/Getty Images, Nomad/iStockphoto/Getty Images, Gregor Bister/iStockphoto/Getty Images, GSMsolutions; p. 24: Alatom/iStockphoto/Getty Images; p. 26: GlobalP/iStockphoto/Getty Images; p. 27: Paolo_Toffanin/iStockphoto/Getty Images, Vnarong/iStockphoto/Getty Images; p. 28: Freemixer/iStockphoto/Getty Images; p. 29: Below Surface/iStockphoto/Getty Images; p. 30: Fevre Dream/iStockphoto/Getty Images, Tramino/iStockphoto/Getty Images, Saturated/iStockphoto/Getty Images, Sturti/iStockphoto/Getty Images; p. 31: Master2/iStockphoto/Getty Images, Jeremy Richards/iStockphoto/Getty Images, Gannet77/iStockphoto/Getty Images, 0shi/iStockphoto/Getty Images, Sarosh Lodhi/iStockphoto/Getty Images; p. 35: Diego Cervo/iStockphoto/Getty Images, Btrenkel/iStockphoto/Getty Images, Web Substance/iStockphoto/Getty Images, Romolo Tavani/iStockphoto/Getty Images, G Stockstudio/iStockphoto/Getty Images, Yin Yang/iStockphoto/Getty Images, Chalabala/iStockphoto/Getty Images, People Images/iStockphoto/Getty Images, Andresr/iStockphoto/Getty Images, Wunder Visuals/iStockphoto/Getty Images, Valentin Russanov/iStockphoto/Getty Images, Extreme Photographer/iStockphoto/Getty Images, Merlas/iStockphoto/Getty Images, Martin Dimitrov/iStockphoto/Getty Images, Ferrantraite/iStockphoto/Getty Images, Cglade/iStockphoto/Getty Images; p. 38: Bjones27/iStockphoto/Getty Images, Evren Kalinbacak/iStockphoto/Getty Images, Jummie/iStockphoto/Getty Images, Sodar99/iStockphoto/Getty Images, Tim Burgess/iStockphoto/Getty Images, Seb Ra/iStockphoto/Getty Images, Jukov/iStockphoto/Getty Images, Allison Ginadaio/iStockphoto/Getty Images, Patcharin Simalhek/iStockphoto/Getty Images, Dragon Images/iStockphoto/Getty Images, BraunS/iStockphoto/Getty Images, Mladen Kostic/iStockphoto/Getty Images, Katarzyna Bialasiewicz/iStockphoto/Getty Images, Alex Brylov/iStockphoto/Getty Images, Martin dm/iStockphoto/Getty Images, Adventtr/iStockphoto/Getty Images, Gilaxia/iStockphoto/Getty Images, pro6x7/iStockphoto/Getty Images, nd3000/iStockphoto/Getty Images, Tarik Kizilkaya/iStockphoto/Getty Images; p. 42: Wundervisuals/iStockphoto/Getty Images; p. 44: Shapecharge/iStockphoto/Getty Images dolgachov/iStockphoto/Getty Images, GlobalStock/iStockphoto/Getty Images, LightField Studios/iStockphoto/Getty Images, Sarah Kate Dorman/iStockphoto/Getty Images, Mohammed Elshamy/Anadolu Agency/Getty Images; p. 46: bugsmom/iStockphoto/Getty Images; p. 48: FatCamera/iStockphoto/Getty Images, Tarasov_vl/iStockphoto/Getty Images, Thiago Santos/iStockphoto/Getty Images; p. 49: Pawel Gaul/iStockphoto/Getty Images, BraunS/iStockphoto/Getty Images, Vince Talotta/Toronto Star/Getty Images; p. 50: Rike/iStockphoto/Getty Images, Grafner/iStockphoto/Getty Images, Vit-plus/iStockphoto/Getty Images, Smitt/iStockphoto/Getty Images; p. 51: Theo Wargo/Getty Images; p. 52: Akg Images/Fotoarena, Nubephoto/iStockphoto/Getty Images; p. 53: Iryna_L/iStockphoto/Getty Images, Bonetta/iStockphoto/Getty Images, Tarzhanova/iStockphoto/Getty Images, Poplasen/iStockphoto/Getty Images, Venakr/iStockphoto/Getty Images, Bettina Sentner/iStockphoto/Getty Images, Rolleiflextlr/iStockphoto/Getty Images, Domin domin/iStockphoto/Getty Images, Tarzhanova/iStockphoto/Getty Images, TPopova/iStockphoto/Getty Images GoodLifeStudio/iStockphoto/Getty Images, Studiocasper/iStockphoto/Getty Images, Simonbradfield/iStockphoto/Getty Images, AlinaMD/iStockphoto/Getty Images, Denis TangneyJr/iStockphoto/Getty Images, Andrew Mayovskyy/iStockphoto/Getty Images, Jctabb/iStockphoto/Getty Images, AGrigorjeva/iStockphoto/Getty Images, Kavram/iStockphoto/Getty Images, aetb/iStockphoto/Getty Images, Cinoby/iStockphoto/Getty Images, Marian Vejcik/iStockphoto/Getty Images, Willowpix/iStockphoto/Getty Images, Dreef/iStockphoto/Getty Images, AGrigorjeva/iStockphoto/Getty Images, CrazyD/iStockphoto/Getty Images, Jimmy villalta/iStockphoto/Getty Images, Bulgac/iStockphoto/Getty Images, Ctermit/iStockphoto/Getty Images; p. 56: kertlis/iStockphoto/Getty Images; p. 58: Squared pixels/iStockphoto/Getty Images, Wavebreakmedia/iStockphoto/Getty Images, Michael Jung/iStockphoto/Getty Images; p. 59: Fat Camera/iStockphoto/Getty Images, Uncleroo/iStockphoto/Getty Images, Gchutka/iStockphoto/Getty Images, Ruben Sprich/Reuters/Fotoarena; p. 60: Christopher Bernard/iStockphoto/Getty Images; p. 61: MarKord/iStockphoto/Getty Images, Weerapatkia tdumrong/iStockphoto/Getty Images, Pablo Rodriguez1/iStockphoto/Getty Images, Phil Augustavo/iStockphoto/Getty Images, Justhavealook/iStockphoto/Getty Images, SelectStock/iStockphoto/Getty Images, Alamy/Fotoarena; p. 62: Chatchaisura kram/iStockphoto/Getty Images, Olga Belova/iStockphoto/Getty Images, Subtropica/iStockphoto/Getty Images, Filo/iStockphoto/Getty Images; p. 63: Pabst Ell/iStockphoto/Getty Images, Pavalena/iStockphoto/Getty Images; p. 64: Baiajaku/iStockphoto/Getty Images; p. 65: dorioconnell/iStockphoto/Getty Images; p. 66: Monkeybusinessimages/iStockphoto/Getty Images, XiXinXing/iStockphoto/Getty Images; p. 67: Joegolby/iStockphoto/Getty Images, Yacobchuk/iStockphoto/Getty Images, Lovro77/iStockphoto/Getty Images, Evgeniy Shkolenko/iStockphoto/Getty Images, Vale_t/iStockphoto/Getty Images, Sturti/iStockphoto/Getty Images, Wave breakmedia/iStockphoto/Getty Images, Gauthier2902/iStockphoto/Getty Images, Andresr/iStockphoto/Getty Images, Muratkoc/iStockphoto/Getty Images, Steve Debenport/iStockphoto/Getty Images, Jevtic/iStockphoto/Getty Images, p. 69: Gilaxia/iStockphoto/Getty Images, Images by barbara/iStockphoto/Getty Images, M-gucci/iStockphoto/Getty Images, Johnny Greig/iStockphoto/Getty Images, Semata design/iStockphoto/Getty Images, Wavebreakmedia/iStockphoto/Getty Images; p. 70: Shironosov/iStockphoto/Getty Images, Xijian/iStockphoto/Getty Images, Karammiri/iStockphoto/Getty Images, Nys444/iStockphoto/Getty Images, Wavebreakmedia/iStockphoto/Getty Images, Rusm/iStockphoto/Getty Images, Laflor/iStockphoto/Getty Images, Baona/iStockphoto/Getty Images, Ben Gingell/iStockphoto/Getty Images, Casarsa/iStockphoto/Getty Images, Simplytheyu/iStockphoto/Getty Images, Skynesher/iStockphoto/Getty Images, Gchutka/iStockphoto/Getty Images; p. 73: Filadendron/iStockphoto/Getty Images; p. 74: Martin-dm/iStockphoto/Getty Images, Rvlsoft/iStockphoto/Getty Images; p. 75: Tzido/iStockphoto/Getty Images, Mmartboy10/iStockphoto/Getty Images; p. 76: CHBD/iStockphoto/Getty Images; p. 78: Fstop123/iStockphoto/Getty Images, MO Skynesher/iStockphoto/Getty Images, Supersizer/iStockphoto/Getty Images, Verve231/iStockphoto/Getty Images, YinYang/iStockphoto/Getty Images, Monkeybusinessimages/iStockphoto/Getty Images; p. 80: People Images/iStockphoto/Getty Images; p. 81: Brainsil/iStockphoto/Getty Images, Wavebreakmedia/iStockphoto/Getty Images; p. 82: Eli Asenova/iStockphoto/Getty Images, DMEPhotography/iStockphoto/Getty Images, Hailshadow/iStockphoto/Getty Images, Alex Raths/iStockphoto/Getty Images; p. 83: Sturti/iStockphoto/Getty Images, Scyther5/iStockphoto/Getty Images, Ridofranz/iStockphoto/Getty Images; p. 84: Tarasov_vl/iStockphoto/Getty Images, Furtseff/iStockphoto/Getty Images, Tsurukamedesign/iStockphoto/Getty Images, Adventtr/iStockphoto/Getty Images, Homeworks255/iStockphoto/Getty Images, RapidEye/iStockphoto/Getty Images, J-Elgaard/iStockphoto/Getty Images, fatihhoca/iStockphoto/Getty Images, Antpkr/iStockphoto/Getty Images, Adventtr/iStockphoto/Getty Images, 58shadows/iStockphoto/Getty Images, Mordolff/iStockphoto/Getty Images; p. 86: Jason Doiy/iStockphoto/Getty Images, Jason Doiy/iStockphoto/Getty Images; p. 87: Shaunl/iStockphoto/Getty Images, fstop123/iStockphoto/Getty Images, Mikolette/iStockphoto/Getty Images, Pixdeluxe/iStockphoto/Getty Images, fstop123/iStockphoto/Getty Images, Tempura/iStockphoto/Getty Images, RichLegg/iStockphoto/Getty Images, Highwaystarz-Photography/iStockphoto/Getty Images, LuminaStock/iStockphoto/Getty Images, Monkeybusinessimages/iStockphoto/Getty Images, Opolja/iStockphoto/Getty Images, Alek Zotoff/iStockphoto/Getty Images, South_agency/iStockphoto/Getty Images, Puhimec/iStockphoto/Getty Images, Sintendo/iStockphoto/Getty Images, ParkerDeen/iStockphoto/Getty Images, Magnolija/iStockphoto/Getty Images, ArisSu/iStockphoto/Getty Images, AJ_Watt/iStockphoto/Getty Images, PeopleImages/iStockphoto/Getty Images, nd3000/iStockphoto/Getty Images, MinnieMenon/iStockphoto/Getty Images; p. 90: Da-kuk/iStockphoto/Getty Images; p. 92: Jason LaVeris/WireImage/Getty Images, guruXOOX/iStockphoto/Getty Images; p. 93: Media Production/iStockphoto/Getty Images, Firebrandphotography/iStockphoto/Getty Images, master1305/iStockphoto/Getty Images; p. 94: Alengo/iStockphoto/Getty Images; p. 95: Sony Pictures/Everett Collection/Fotoarena; p. 96: Izusek/iStockphoto/Getty Images, German skydiver/iStockphoto/Getty Images, Chaiyapruek 2520/iStockphoto/Getty Images, People Images/iStockphoto/Getty Images, Zianlob/iStockphoto/Getty Images; p. 97: Kristin Callahan/Everett Collection/Fotoarena, Danbreckwoldt/iStockphoto/Getty Images, Bjones27/iStockphoto/Getty Images; p. 99: Alex Potemkin/iStockphoto/Getty Images; p. 100: Walt Disney Studios Motion Pictures/Everett Collection/Fotoarena; p. 101: Selimaksan/iStockphoto/Getty Images, kckate16/iStockphoto/Getty Images, Tmarvin/iStockphoto/Getty Images, Ismagilov/iStockphoto/Getty Images, SARINYAPINNGAM/iStockphoto/Getty Images, Paolo Scarlata/iStockphoto/Getty Images, Danr13/iStockphoto/Getty Images, Maor Winetrob/iStockphoto/Getty Images, Gmutlu/iStockphoto/Getty Images, BertrandB/iStockphoto/Getty Images,

Katarzyna Bialasiewicz/iStockphoto/Getty Images, Visual7/iStockphoto/Getty Images, Littlehenrabi/iStockphoto/Getty Images, Image Source/iStockphoto/Getty Images, 72andsunny, Diy13/iStockphoto/Getty Images, Wavebreakmedia/iStockphoto/Getty Images, Skynesher/iStockphoto/Getty Images, Oatawa/iStockphoto/Getty Images, JGalione/iStockphoto/Getty Images, Feellife/iStockphoto/Getty Images, Weekend Images /iStockphoto/Getty Images, Rawpixel Ltd/iStockphoto/Getty Images, Ignatiev/iStockphoto/Getty Images, Sasiistock/iStockphoto/Getty Images, Macniak/iStockphoto/Getty Images, AndreyPopov/iStockphoto/Getty Images, Nullplus/iStockphoto/Getty Images, Portra/iStockphoto/Getty Images; p. 103: Kiuikson/iStockphoto/Getty Images; p. 104: Album/Fotoarena, SolStock/iStockphoto/Getty Images, Baona/iStockphoto/Getty Images, Skynesher/iStockphoto/Getty Images, Monkey businessimages/iStockphoto/Getty Images, Berndstuhlmann/iStockphoto/Getty Images, Fire brandp Photography/iStockphoto/Getty Images, Luoman/iStockphoto/Getty Images, Alffoto/iStockphoto/Getty Images, Pk photoscom/iStockphoto/Getty Images, Hroe/iStockphoto/Getty Images; p. 105: Chris Steer/iStockphoto/Getty Images, Flubydust/iStockphoto/Getty Images; p. 108: FatCamera/iStockphoto/Getty Images; p. 110: KevinDyer/iStockphoto/Getty Images, Kyoshino/iStockphoto/Getty Images, Newbird/iStockphoto/Getty Images, Image Pixel/iStockphoto/Getty Images, Benimage/iStockphoto/Getty Images, Adisa/iStockphoto/Getty Images, Triocean/iStockphoto/Getty Images, Eivaisla/iStockphoto/Getty Images, Sinankocaslan/iStockphoto/Getty Images, Studiocasper/iStockphoto/Getty Images, 3dsguru/iStockphoto/Getty Images, Alamy/Fotoarena, Mbongorus/iStockphoto/Getty Images, Malerapaso/iStockphoto/Getty Images, Deepblue4you/iStockphoto/Getty Images, Dorioconnell/iStockphoto/Getty Images; p. 111: Shironosov/iStockphoto/Getty Images, FlairImages/iStockphoto/Getty Images, RyanJLane/iStockphoto/Getty Images; p. 112: Elizabeth Goodenough/Everett Collection/Fotoarena; p. 113: FatCamera/iStockphoto/Getty Images; p. 114: Mmac72/iStockphoto/Getty Images, Raylipscombe/iStockphoto/Getty Images, Steve Debenport/iStockphoto/Getty Images; p. 115: Jordi Ramisa/iStockphoto/Getty Images, Hansenn/iStockphoto/Getty Images, Oculo/iStockphoto/Getty Images; p. 116: WLDavies/iStockphoto/Getty Images, Young777/iStockphoto/Getty Images, Cinoby/iStockphoto/Getty Images, Bird Images/iStockphoto/Getty Images, Reptiles4all/iStockphoto/Getty Images, Federicoriz/iStockphoto/Getty Images, Byrdyak/iStockphoto/Getty Images, USO/iStockphoto/Getty Images, Dawnn/iStockphoto/Getty Images, Chuvipro/iStockphoto/Getty Images; p. 118: Media24/Gallo Images/Getty Images, Andrzej Sawa/Sunday Times/Gallo Images/Getty Images; p. 119: Pic Studio/iStockphoto/Getty Images, Joy Tasa/iStockphoto/Getty Images, Hayatikayhan/iStockphoto/Getty Images, Kyoshino/iStockphoto/Getty Images, Nevodka/iStockphoto/Getty Images, Arox/iStockphoto/Getty Images, The Lightwriter/iStockphoto/Getty Images, Studio Casper/iStockphoto/Getty Images, Fcafotodigital/iStockphoto/Getty Images, Nenov/iStockphoto/Getty Images, Ilyarexi/iStockphoto/Getty Images, Malerapaso/iStockphoto/Getty Images, Pederk/iStockphoto/Getty Images, Romiri/iStockphoto/Getty Images, Skynesher/iStockphoto/Getty Images, Buckyza/iStockphoto/Getty Images, Skynesher/iStockphoto/Getty Images, Kate Photographer/iStockphoto/Getty Images, Hung Chung Chih/iStockphoto/Getty Images, Alexey Seafarer/iStockphoto/Getty Images, Prasit Chansarekorn/iStockphoto/Getty Images, Paytai/iStockphoto/Getty Images, Pong6400/iStockphoto/Getty Images, Cinoby/iStockphoto/Getty Images; p. 122: Aleksandar Georgiev/iStockphoto/Getty Images; p. 124: Alamy/Fotoarena, Mandy godbehear/iStockphoto/Getty Images, Angie Photos/iStockphoto/Getty Images, Denisfilm/iStockphoto/Getty Images; p. 125: Felicity Marks/Acervo particular; p. 127: Carmendorin/iStockphoto/Getty Images; p. 128: Anthony Rosenberg/iStockphoto/Getty Images, Sol Stock/iStockphoto/Getty Images, Csfotoimages/iStockphoto/Getty Images, JKristoffersson/iStockphoto/Getty Images, Roma Oslo/iStockphoto/Getty Images, iStockphoto/Getty Images, Album/Fotoarena; p. 130: Elizabeth Goodenough/Everett Collection/Fotoarena; p. 132: RosalreneBetancourt 7/Alamy/Fotoarena; p. 133: Brian A Jackson/iStockphoto/Getty Images, JMichl/iStockphoto/Getty Images, RyanJLane/iStockphoto/Getty Images, Kevin Mazur/WireImage/Getty Images, Andresr/iStockphoto/Getty Images, Juanmonino/iStockphoto/Getty Images, Laurad Young/iStockphoto/Getty Images, Materio/iStockphoto/Getty Images, Egal/iStockphoto/Getty Images, Supersizer/iStockphoto/Getty Images, Wavebreakmedia/iStockphoto/Getty Images, JackF/iStockphoto/Getty Images, FatCamera/iStockphoto/Getty Images, Juanmonino/iStockphoto/Getty Images, Georgijevic/iStockphoto/Getty Images, Kali9/iStockphoto/Getty Images, Steve Debenport/iStockphoto/Getty Images, Lumina Stock/iStockphoto/Getty Images, Djedzura/iStockphoto/Getty Images, DGLimages/iStockphoto/Getty Images, Steve Debenport/iStockphoto/Getty Images; p. 135: M_a_y_a/iStockphoto/Getty Images; p. 136: Drazen/iStockphoto/Getty Images, KeithSza franski/iStockphoto/Getty Images, M-imagephotography/iStockphoto/Getty Images, Cla78/iStockphoto/Getty Images, Gilitukha/iStockphoto/Getty Images, Modern Nomads/iStockphoto/Getty Images, Studio Grand Quest/iStockphoto/Getty Images, Malerapaso/iStockphoto/Getty Images, IPGGutenbergUKLtd/iStockphoto/Getty Images, kali9/iStockphoto/Getty Images, Andrea Izzotti/iStockphoto/Getty Images, People Images/iStockphoto/Getty Images, WLDavies/iStockphoto/Getty Images, Photomove/iStockphoto/Getty Images, Studiocasper/iStockphoto/Getty Images, CHBD/iStockphoto/Getty Images, Geber 86/iStockphoto/Getty Images, Nicolamargaret/iStockphoto/Getty Images; p. 140: Maximillion Studio/iStockphoto/Getty Images, Professor25/iStockphoto/Getty Images, Paffy69/iStockphoto/Getty Images, Monkey business images/iStockphoto/Getty Images; p. 141: © UNITED NATIONS, Yulia Malinovskaya/iStockphoto/Getty Images; p. 144: Meilun/iStockphoto/Getty Images; p. 145: AlfazetChronicles/iStockphoto/Getty Images; p. 146: Bombuscreative/iStockphoto/Getty Images, Ronstik/iStockphoto/Getty Images, Juststock/iStockphoto/Getty Images, Hocus-focus/iStockphoto/Getty Images, People Images/iStockphoto/Getty Images, Mikkel william/iStockphoto/Getty Images; p. 147: Believe In Me/iStockphoto/Getty Images; p. 149: Aquariagirl1970/iStockphoto/Getty Images, Bill Oxford/iStockphoto/Getty Images, Fullvalue/iStockphoto/Getty Images, Sunara/iStockphoto/Getty Images, Gkrphoto/iStockphoto/Getty Images, Artisteer/iStockphoto/Getty Images, Plain View/iStockphoto/Getty Images, Shansekala/iStockphoto/Getty Images; p. 151: Antonio Guillem/iStockphoto/Getty Images, Rawpixel/iStockphoto/Getty Images; p. 152: Mixetto/iStockphoto/Getty Images, Sashatigar/iStockphoto/Getty Images; p. 155: Olaf Speier/iStockphoto/Getty Images; p. 157: Martin Dim/iStockphoto/Getty Images, Dmytro Aksonov/iStockphoto/Getty Images, Yin Yang/iStockphoto/Getty Images, Sturti/iStockphoto/Getty Images, Urosh Petrovic/iStockphoto/Getty Images, FatCamera/iStockphoto/Getty Images, Gibson Pictures/iStockphoto/Getty Images, Amygdala Imagery/iStockphoto/Getty Images, Stock Colors/iStockphoto/Getty Images, Drazen/iStockphoto/Getty Images; p. 159: zomby007/iStockphoto/Getty Images; p. 161: Lysogor/iStockphoto/Getty Images, Kovshutin Denis/iStockphoto/Getty Images, Ig0rZh/iStockphoto/Getty Images, Pgiam/iStockphoto/Getty Images, Eddtoro/iStockphoto/Getty Images, TAGSTOCK1/iStockphoto/Getty Images, NASA Goddard, Cinoby/iStockphoto/Getty Images, Mdesigner125/iStockphoto/Getty Images, Mac99/iStockphoto/Getty Images; p. 162: Tarzhanova/iStockphoto/Getty Images, Sankai/iStockphoto/Getty Images, Heinteh/iStockphoto/Getty Images, Mawielobob/iStockphoto/Getty Images, Tarzhanova/iStockphoto/Getty Images, Mawielobob/iStockphoto/Getty Images, Media Production/iStockphoto/Getty Images, Tarzhanova/iStockphoto/Getty Images, Domin_domin/iStockphoto/Getty Images, Siraphol/iStockphoto/Getty Images, Flyfloor/iStockphoto/Getty Images, Rolleiflextlr/iStockphoto/Getty Images; p. 163: Vesna Andjic/iStockphoto/Getty Images; p. 165: Pawel Gaul/iStockphoto/Getty Images, Rapid Eye/iStockphoto/Getty Images, Sadeugra/iStockphoto/Getty Images, Marccophoto/iStockphoto/Getty Images, Tcsaba/iStockphoto/Getty Images, Marian Vejcik/iStockphoto/Getty Images, Andrey Danilovich/iStockphoto/Getty Images, Robertiez/iStockphoto/Getty Images, Pixdeluxe/iStockphoto/Getty Images, Jctabb/iStockphoto/Getty Images, Snpolus/iStockphoto/Getty Images, Mammuth/iStockphoto/Getty Images, Da photos/iStockphoto/Getty Images, Harvepino/iStockphoto/Getty Images; p. 168: Adventure Photo/iStockphoto/Getty Images; p. 170: Gradyreese/iStockphoto/Getty Images, Aijohn784/iStockphoto/Getty Images, Steve Debenport/iStockphoto/Getty Images, Monkeybusinessimages/iStockphoto/Getty Images, Martinan/iStockphoto/Getty Images, M_a_y_a/iStockphoto/Getty Images, Fang Xia Nuo/iStockphoto/Getty Images, Gchutka/iStockphoto/Getty Images, Kupicoo/iStockphoto/Getty Images, JackF/iStockphoto/Getty Images, Shinyfamily/iStockphoto/Getty Images, Diego Cervo/iStockphoto/Getty Images; p. 171: Tatiana Dyuvbanova/iStockphoto/Getty Images; p. 172: Bobbymn/iStockphoto/Getty Images, Ruslan Dashinsky/iStockphoto/Getty Images; p. 173: Steve Debenport/iStockphoto/Getty Images, Saiyood/iStockphoto/Getty Images, Image Source/iStockphoto/Getty Images, kwanchai chaiudom/iStockphoto/Getty Images, Eyenigelen/iStockphoto/Getty Images, HAYKIRDI/iStockphoto/Getty Images, Temmuzcan/iStockphoto/Getty Images, kimberrywood/iStockphoto/Getty Images, 9nong/iStockphoto/Getty Images, M Master1305/iStockphoto/Getty Images, LittleBee80/iStockphoto/Getty Images; p. 174: Positive Focus/iStockphoto/Getty Images, Jure/iStockphoto/Getty Images, Anchiy/iStockphoto/Getty Images, Praetorian photo/iStockphoto/Getty Images, Catalin205/iStockphoto/Getty Images, Katarzyna Bialasiewicz/iStockphoto/Getty Images, Azman/iStockphoto/Getty Images, Monkey business images/iStockphoto/Getty Images; p. 175: Monkey business images/iStockphoto/Getty Images, M_a_y_a/iStockphoto/Getty Images; p. 176: Laflor/iStockphoto/Getty Images; p. 178: Kali9/iStockphoto/Getty Images, Shaunl/iStockphoto/Getty Images, Steve Debenport/iStockphoto/Getty Images, Jikaboom/iStockphoto/Getty Images, People Images/iStockphoto/Getty Images, Fstop 123/iStockphoto/Getty Images, Martin dm/iStockphoto/Getty Images, Brian A Jackson/iStockphoto/Getty Images, Fat Camera/iStockphoto/Getty Images, Fatihhoca/iStockphoto/Getty Images, Andresr/iStockphoto/Getty Images, Select Stock/iStockphoto/Getty Images; p. 179: Asiseeit/iStockphoto/Getty Images, Asiseeit/iStockphoto/Getty Images, Plus69/iStockphoto/Getty Images, Night cat/iStockphoto/Getty Images, Phurinee/iStockphoto/Getty Images, gbh007/iStockphoto/Getty Images; p. 180: FrankvandenBergh/iStockphoto/Getty Images; p. 183: Monkey business images/iStockphoto/Getty Images, Vadym Terelyuk/iStockphoto/Getty Images; p. 184: Macmillan, Jane Austen (engraving); p. 187: Liuzishan/iStockphoto/Getty Images; p. 188: 3000ad/iStockphoto/Getty Images; p. 190: Peshkov/iStockphoto/Getty Images, Wavebreakmedia/iStockphoto/Getty Images; p. 191: CNAM, Conservatoire National des Arts et Metiers, Paris / Bridgeman Images/Easypix, Institut Lumière, Lyon France; p. 192: Everett Collection/Fotoarena; p. 193: Nicolas McComber/iStockphoto/Getty Images, Antonio Diaz/iStockphoto/Getty Images, Danr13/iStockphoto/Getty Images, Talaj/iStockphoto/Getty Images, Urilux/iStockphoto/Getty Images, Paolo Scarlata/iStockphoto/Getty Images; p. 194: Juanmonino/iStockphoto/Getty Images; p. 195: Alexalenin/iStockphoto/Getty Images, fongleon356/iStockphoto/Getty Images, XiXinXing/iStockphoto/Getty Images, Okssi68/iStockphoto/Getty Images, Peanut 8481/iStockphoto/Getty Images, Kiatipol/iStockphoto/Getty Images; p. 196: Federicoriz/iStockphoto/Getty Images, Paul Bradbury/iStockphoto/Getty Images; p. 197: Tall/iStockphoto/Getty Images, Byrdyak/iStockphoto/Getty Images, Hung Chung Chih/iStockphoto/Getty Images, Lynn Bystrom/iStockphoto/Getty Images, Thte Palmer/iStockphoto/Getty Images, Burachet/iStockphoto/Getty Images, Emkaplin/iStockphoto/Getty Images, MoMorad/iStockphoto/Getty Images, Imarly/iStockphoto/Getty Images, skynavin/iStockphoto/Getty Images; p. 198: flocu/iStockphoto/Getty Images; p. 199: Rawpixel/iStockphoto/Getty Images, Iona Skinner/iStockphoto/Getty Images; p. 200: IdealPhoto30/iStockphoto/Getty Images, KukiatB/iStockphoto/Getty Images; p. 202: Juan monino/iStockphoto/Getty Images, Paul Bradbury/iStockphoto/Getty Images, Chris Brignell/iStockphoto/Getty Images, Eva-Katalin/iStockphoto/Getty Images, Laura Dyoung/iStockphoto/Getty Images; p. 203: Real444/iStockphoto/Getty Images; p. 204: Xavigm/iStockphoto/Getty Images, Tatyana Tomsickova/iStockphoto/Getty Images, Image Source/iStockphoto/Getty Images, Aluxum/iStockphoto/Getty Images; p. 205: Martin-dm/iStockphoto/Getty Images, Wave break media/iStockphoto/Getty Images, Esperanza33/iStockphoto/Getty Images, Wundervisuals/iStockphoto/Getty Images, Monkey business images/iStockphoto/Getty Images, Leo Patrizi/iStockphoto/Getty Images; p. 207: Rocks3/iStockphoto/Getty Images, Jason Doiy/iStockphoto/Getty Images; p. 209: Gpoint studio/iStockphoto/Getty Images, George Rudy/iStockphoto/Getty Images, Mathier/iStockphoto/Getty Images, Jitalia17/iStockphoto/Getty Images, Zoranm/iStockphoto/Getty Images, Joe Belanger/iStockphoto/Getty Images, Elitsa Deykova/iStockphoto/Getty Images, Spiderstock/iStockphoto/Getty Images.

Dados Internacionais de Catalogação na Publicação (CIP)

Bibliotecária responsável: Aline Graziele Benitez CRB-1/3129

H53i Heyderman, Emma
1.ed. Insta English 2 / Emma Heyderman ... [et al.]. – 1.ed. – São Paulo: Macmillan Education do Brasil, 2019.
216 p.; il.; 21 x 29,7 cm. – (Coleção Insta English, v. 2)

ISBN: 978-85-511021-14 (aluno)
ISBN: 978-85-511021-21 (professor)

1. Inglês – ensino fundamental II. I. Mauchline, Fiona. II. Howarth, Patrick. III. Reilly, Patricia. IV. Johnston, Olivia. V. Myers, Cathy. VI. Título. VII. Série. CDD 371.3

Índice para catálogo sistemático:

1. Inglês: ensino fundamental II

MACMILLAN EDUCATION DO BRASIL
Av. Brigadeiro Faria Lima, 1.309, 3° Andar – Jd. Paulistano – São Paulo – SP – 01452-002
www.macmillan.com.br
Customer Service: [55] (11) 4613-2278
0800 16 88 77
Fax: [55] (11) 4612-6098

FSC www.fsc.org MISTO Papel | Apoiando o manejo florestal responsável FSC® C041155

Impresso no Brasil, Maistype, 11 2024.